His Name Was Mudd

His Name Was

MUDD

The Life of Dr. Samuel A. Mudd,
Who Treated the Fleeing John Wilkes Booth

by

Elden C. Weckesser

WITH A PREFATORY NOTE BY
RICHARD DYER MUDD

McFarland & Company, Inc., Publishers
Jefferson, North Carolina, and London

Frontispiece: **Dr. Samuel A. Mudd (courtesy of the Library of Congress).**

British Library Cataloguing-in-Publication data are available

Library of Congress Cataloguing-in-Publication Data

Weckesser, Elden C.
   His name was Mudd : the life of Dr. Samuel A. Mudd, who treated
the fleeing John Wilkes Booth / by Elden C. Weckesser ; with a
prefatory note by Richard Dyer Mudd.
     p. cm.
   Includes bibliographical references and index.
   ISBN 0-89950-636-4 (lib. bdg. : 50# alk. paper) ∞
   1. Lincoln, Abraham, 1809–1865—Assassination. 2. Mudd, Samuel
Alexander, 1833–1883. 3. Booth, John Wilkes, 1838–1865.
4. Physicians—United States—Biography. I. Title.
E457.5.W43 1991
364.1'31'092—dc20
[B]   91-52751
                                                        CIP

Manufactured in the United States of America

McFarland & Company, Inc., Publishers
 Box 611, Jefferson, North Carolina 28640

Dedicated to Kathryn Alice Tuttle,
my lovely, devoted, and tolerant wife,
and our four daughters,
Jane, Elizabeth, Nancy, and Mary.
Each has the great capability beyond men—
of womanhood and motherhood.

Contents

Acknowledgments

Much credit is extended to all authors who have preceded me in writing about this very trying situation for young Dr. Mudd and his family.

First in this list is Dr. Mudd's youngest daughter, Mary Eleanor (Nettie) Mudd-Monroe, who in 1906 published *The Life of Dr. Samuel Mudd,* which included the letters written by her father during his incarceration at Fort Jefferson on the Dry Tortugas Islands.

Next is Dr. Richard Dyer Mudd of Saginaw, Michigan, grandson of Dr. Samuel, who has seen *The Mudd Family of the United States* through four voluminous editions, and *Dr. Samuel Alexander Mudd and His Descendants* through six editions. He also republished Nettie's book in 1975 and 1983. He has added the descendants of Dr. Samuel to the latter as well as some letters not included in the first edition. All this has been done in support of his lifetime effort to clear the name of his grandfather. Dr. Richard has been most gracious and extremely helpful to me in providing reference material and personal family information, for which I am grateful. My wife Katy and I also wish to thank Mrs. Mudd for her gracious hospitality.

Next in line comes Mrs. Louise Mudd-Arehart, the youngest granddaughter of Dr. Samuel. She is the capable and dedicated president of the Samuel A. Mudd Society, now located in the former home of Dr. Samuel just north of Bryantown, Maryland. Mrs. Arehart has been extremely helpful in supplying printed material and old photographs, as well as supplying local information about the region and family descendants still living in the area. She is largely responsible for the formation of the Dr. Samuel A. Mudd Society and for arranging, through the cooperation of her brother, Joseph Burch Mudd, for the purchase of the buildings and ten acres of land.

The busy, capable, and helpful staff of the Surratt Society in Clinton, Maryland, gave much help with old maps and manuscripts. The help of Laurie Verge and Joan Chaconas is especially appreciated.

The work of all authors listed in the bibliography has been of unlimited assistance and great effort has been made to give proper credit to them.

The National Archives and the Library of Congress have been of tremendous help in giving access to old papers, publications, maps, and photographs. The personnel were extremely helpful in spite of their heavy workload. They could not have been nicer.

The staff at the Freiberger Library of Case Western Reserve University have been of inestimable value in providing and obtaining old historical volumes without which I could not have proceeded. Special thanks are given to Michael Partington, Mrs. Elsie Finley and Ross Poli.

The library staff at Kent State University went beyond their line of duty in providing the 1893 book written by Thomas A. Jones.

Colonel David V. Harbach, commanding officer of Fort Lesley Mc-Nair in Washington, took time personally to show us about the grounds of the fort and to work out the location of the Arsenal Prison in 1865 where the trial was held. The structures are quite different now but building twenty, where the trial was held and outside of which the gallows stood, still serves as officer quarters. Colonel Harbach as well as Sergeant Long gave invaluable information and access to pertinent photographs.

The Cleveland Allen Medical Library staff, especially Dzwinka Komarjanski, gave great help on medical matters. Deborah N. Bahnsen of the Ohio State Medical Society supplied pertinent material in regard to the legal aspects of medical practice.

The Cuyahoga County Library supplied many publications. The extra effort of historian John Bellamy in locating photographs was great. Our own Chagrin Falls branch and the Regional Mayfield Library were extremely helpful, as were the local branches at Bainbridge, Solon, and West Geauga.

Mrs. Sally Barley of the Charles County, Maryland, Historical Society located the list of Bryantown postmasters. The Ohio Historical Society, the Western Reserve Historical Society, and the Chicago Historical Society were also very cooperative.

John Thornton and Tom Weizer made my introduction to the wizardry of electronic computer word processing possible. Without them, this ingenious, demanding marvel would not have been fathomable.

I give my sincere thanks to these people and organizations, and to all others unmentioned who helped me along what at many times was an unmarked path.

A Prefatory Note

Dr. Weckesser can be congratulated for undertaking another biography of my grandfather. His is different. It is written in a down-to-earth style. It is one of the most complete and detailed that I have read. His photos, maps, and other illustrations are excellent and add greatly to the script. Regardless of how many accounts of Dr. Sam Mudd have been produced, this is one that will be found very worthwhile.

—Richard Dyer Mudd
Saginaw, Michigan
August 1990

1
Introduction

This book is about the doctor who gave needed medical attention to the assassin of President Abraham Lincoln in 1865. John Wilkes Booth arrived at the doctor's farm home twenty-eight miles south of Washington six hours after he had fired the fatal shot into Lincoln's head. Booth had injured his back and broken his left leg while jumping ten feet from the president's box to the stage below in making his escape from Ford's Theater. The unplanned emergency care given by the doctor, the morning and day after Lincoln was shot, nearly cost him his life. How taking care of an injured person placed the doctor in that position is of as much interest today as it was over a century ago.

In order to understand the situation, we need to look at the problems the United States was facing at that time. These problems were intense and emotional even though they concerned former countrymen. Plantation life in the South was based largely on slave labor, while manufacturing in the North used little of it. Before and during the War Between the States, the South developed strong feelings regarding states' rights, the right to secede, and slavery. Lincoln's election in the fall of 1861 polarized the South into opposition to both the Union and the president. This opposition took on fanatical zeal in the minds of some. The South feared economic ruin from the abolition of slavery. A long bloody war resulted. Large numbers of young men from both North and South had been killed defending the ideals of the region in which they lived.

Dr. Samuel Alexander Mudd was a slaveholder, as was his father. The use of slaves had been an integral part of tobacco farming in his area for over two hundred years. The young doctor was deeply interested in preserving his way of life. The general attitude of the populace in southern Maryland was predominantly pro–Confederate, even though the state did not secede. It was hard for the residents of Lower Maryland to give up an accepted social custom upon which the economic welfare of the region depended. The federal government in Washington was aware of this pro–Confederate sentiment.

Consequently, by merely giving professional aid and allowing an injured man whom he claimed he did not know or recognize, and his companion, to rest upstairs in his home for ten hours, Mudd was accused of giving aid to and harboring Booth and Herold and thus being an accomplice in Lincoln's assassination. After a protracted trial before a military commission, Mudd was found guilty but was spared from the gallows by one vote.

At 4:00 A.M. in the early morning darkness of Saturday, April 15, 1865, five days after General Lee had surrendered at Appomattox, Virginia, Dr. Samuel Alexander Mudd, age thirty-one, was asleep with his wife Frances in their upstairs bedroom. Their Maryland farm home was four miles north of Bryantown, Maryland, and twenty-eight miles south of Washington, D.C., away from any main road. They were abruptly awakened by loud knocking on their front door. The intensity as well as the unusual hour of its occurrence spelled urgency in that calm countryside—urgency and seriousness indeed not only for the emergency patient at the door but also for the doctor being roused from his sleep. That fact would haunt Mudd repeatedly during the remaining years of his life.

The doctor, who was not feeling well and probably was not fully awake, first asked his wife to see who it was. She declined, so Mudd went downstairs in his night clothes. He asked who was there before opening the door. When he did so he saw a man on a horse that was being held by a second man.

The second man gave his name as Tyson,[1] and said that his friend had severe pain in his back and left leg. He had been thrown when his horse fell as they were on their way to Washington. The injured man, who identified himself as Tyler, asked for medical care.

Mudd helped bring the injured man into the parlor, where he was placed on a sofa. His pain was severe. Conditions were not right for the necessary examination. The injured man was taken to an upstairs guest room and placed on one of the beds in that room. One of the tall boots the rider was wearing was cut from his left leg and ankle to lessen the pain. Examination of the man's swollen foot and lower leg revealed a fracture of the tibia two inches above the ankle. Booth must have been suffering severe pain from this injury while on his horse, let alone during any attempts to bear weight. It is remarkable that he was able to do the things that we know he did after suffering this type of fracture.

Examination of the patient's back revealed pain there also on movement, which Mudd thought was a result of the fall from the horse. Fracture could not be ruled out.

The injured man had whiskers and a mustache and did not wish to talk, keeping a cloak drawn up about his head and face much of the time. He was about 5'10" tall and weighed 150 to 160 pounds. His hands

Upstairs bedroom at Dr. Mudd's home (courtesy of the Samuel A. Mudd Society).

were smooth and white, not those of one who had been doing manual labor.

The doctor made splints from a cardboard box. He bound the splints on either side of the patient's lower leg, including the ankle, with strips of linen that Mrs. Mudd had torn into strips to make bandages. The patient's leg was then elevated to reduce swelling. Following these procedures, the patient, unable to travel by horseback, was allowed to rest in bed.[2] A discussion followed about getting a carriage for travel in the morning. The patient and his companion were then allowed to rest. Mudd's hired hand, Frank Washington, put the travelers' horses in the stable and fed them. Mudd returned to bed.[3]

At around 7:00 A.M., Mudd, Mrs. Mudd, and Tyson had breakfast together. Tyson said he knew people in the area, including one of the storekeepers in Bryantown. Mudd did not know Tyson. Mudd then went to work in the tobacco fields with his men until noon. When he returned at midday, he checked the patient and found him still in moderate pain. He had not eaten the food brought up by Mrs. Mudd's maid. Mudd noticed that he had shaved off his mustache.

Path to Zekiah Swamp.

At the noon meal, Tyson again asked about a carriage. Inquiry was made at Mudd's father's farm but none was available. Tyson then rode along with Mudd toward Bryantown, where the doctor was going to see patients and get mail. When they neared Bryantown, they saw soldiers ahead on the road and Tyson turned back. The doctor continued on his rounds. In Bryantown people were excited. There were soldiers on the streets. There was word that President Lincoln had been shot. The name of the assassin was not definitely known. Some said Boyd and some said Booth.

When Mudd returned home about four o'clock, he met the two strangers behind his home, ready to leave. They paid him twenty-five dollars for his services and asked the way to the home of Parson Wilmer.

Mudd pointed out two routes, one by road and the other through Zekiah Swamp (which was a mile shorter). They chose the route through the swamp, which began behind the doctor's house and went across one of his fields. He watched as they disappeared across his property toward the swamp and contemplated what to do next. The possibility that his patient was Booth must certainly have occurred to him.

He talked it over with his wife that evening and decided that he should go at once to the authorities. It was Saturday evening. Mrs. Mudd was worried about being left alone, she said, and he decided to think it over. He decided to sleep on his problem. The next morning he went to church.

After John Wilkes Booth broke his leg jumping to the stage of Ford's Theater following the shooting of President Lincoln, the pain became progressively worse. It only worsened during his horseback ride southward through Maryland on his escape route to Virginia. Whiskey, which he drank freely at a tavern about midnight, after the first sixteen miles of his ride, helped temporarily but eventually wore off. Finally, with each stride of his horse, the pain from Booth's swollen left leg was becoming unbearable. He sought medical aid from Mudd, whom he had met several months earlier and who practiced on his farm about six or eight miles off the planned route to Port Tobacco. Mudd gave Booth emergency medical care and allowed him to rest in his home until late afternoon that day due to pain he was having in his leg and back. This meeting with the doctor was not prearranged but one of necessity.

Although Mudd's life at the time of his trial was spared by one vote, the ordeal of his trial and incarceration for nearly four years at Fort Jefferson on the Dry Tortugas Islands, drastically changed and shortened his life.

2
Abraham Lincoln

On April 14, 1865, President Abraham Lincoln, sixteenth president of the United States, arose very relieved by the favorable turn of events. Victory was at hand. On this day, the Stars and Stripes were being raised again over Fort Sumter. General Robert Anderson, who had surrendered the fort four years earlier to the very day, was to be on hand for the ceremony.

After four years and five weeks of the tremendous burden of his office, the president must have felt greatly relieved and pleased by this final success. He ate a light breakfast with his family. He listened to his oldest son Robert, just back from a tour of duty at the front with General Grant's staff, tell of his experiences. Lincoln wanted first-hand information from his son about his favorite general, who had taken the initiative and brought the enemy of the Union to the verge of defeat.

Robert told of the siege of Petersburg, the gallantry of Sheridan, and the great coordinating plans of Grant to surround Lee and cut off his retreat. Lincoln said that Grant was the first general who attacked instead of asking for reinforcements. Later someone remarked, "But Mr. President, General Grant drinks whiskey." Lincoln, who did not use alcohol, is said to have replied, "Tell me his brand and I'll send a barrel to each of my other generals."

After breakfast Lincoln went to his office to admit his first caller of the day. At that time, those who wanted to see the president were allowed to sit on seats outside his office after their scheduled meeting was arranged. The president felt obliged to see as many people as he could in addition to his interviews with members of government.

Senator Hale of New Hampshire dropped by for final instructions before leaving to fill his new post as minister to Spain. (His daughter was infatuated with an actor by the name of John Wilkes Booth, and he wanted to remove his family from the Washington scene for a while.) There were office seekers, and there were persons requesting special favors and help with all sorts of problems. The president felt obligated to see them and he saw as many of them as he could.

Mrs. Lincoln had asked him to make arrangements to go to Ford's

President Abraham Lincoln (courtesy of the Library of Congress).

Theater that evening. He sent a message to John Ford, owner of the theater, asking if the president's box was available and said that Grant would accompany the party.

Later in the morning a cabinet meeting was held in Lincoln's office. The president described it as a meeting to "reanimate the States." Vice President Andrew Johnson was not present. He had not been invited. In fact, Lincoln had an appointment to see him after the cabinet meeting. Johnson called at the office toward the end of the long meeting and went for a walk while waiting for the meeting to end. Lincoln then saw him after lunch. This was nearly six weeks after his inauguration as vice president.

Vice President Johnson had disgraced himself in front of the assembled crowd at the inauguration. It was said that he was ill and had used too much ethanol before coming to the event. Lincoln had seen Johnson's drunken behavior and had it brought to his attention by others. He said to a cabinet member who brought up the subject, "Oh well, don't bother about Andy Johnson's drinking. He made a bad slip the other day, but I've known Andy a great many years and he is no drunkard."[1]

Lincoln opened the meeting by stating that he had had a dream the night before. He had had this same dream before each of the recent great events of the war, and thought that it portended yet another great event.[2] He asked General Grant, who had just returned from the front, if there was any news from General Sherman. The surrender of Confederate General Joseph Johnston in the west was expected soon. The general replied in the negative but said that it was expected at any time. The meeting proceeded. Grant spoke of the final success at Appomattox and gave the details of Lee's surrender. He spoke of the final tasks required to finish the bloody conflict. His reception was very warm by all members of the cabinet. He was applauded heartily when he finished.

Secretary Stanton came in late. He had been working much of the night on a plan for reconstruction of the Southern states at Lincoln's request.

The first action taken was to end the draft. That was agreed upon by all. Following this they talked about the final tasks to finish the war and get on to the problems of reconstruction. Lincoln favored a "soft" peace for the South as expressed in his second inaugural address: "With malice toward none; with charity for all; with firmness in the right, as God gives us to see the right, let us strive to finish the work we are in: to bind the Nation's wounds: to care for him who shall have borne the battle, and his widow, and his orphan—to do all which may achieve and cherish a just and lasting peace, among ourselves and with all nations."

Three days earlier, on April 11, he had spoken in a similar vein from the White House. This was two days after Lee's surrender to Grant at Appomattox. The crowd was not pleased with Lincoln's leniency on that occasion. There were many "radical" members of Congress who wanted a harsh peace for the South instead of Lincoln's soft peace.

Assistant Secretary of State Frederick Seward reported for his father on actions to be taken to secure Southern forts and navy yards, take over customs houses, and reestablish postal services.[3]

As for the leaders of the rebellion, Stanton thought they were traitors and should be hanged. Postmaster General William E. Dennison suggested that they be allowed to escape. Lincoln agreed but wanted a close eye kept on them. For the reconstituted governments in the Southern states, the suggestion was to disenfranchise all leaders, political and military, and allow the people to choose from the remainder; to reanimate the states and get their governments in operation before Congress reconvened in December.[4]

At the close of the cabinet meeting Grant told the president that Mrs. Grant wished to take the evening train to visit their children in New Jersey. (Actually, Mrs. Lincoln had treated Mrs. Grant rudely on her trip to Richmond on April 5 and Mrs. Grant did not want a repetition.)

Following the long cabinet meeting, Lincoln had a brief lunch with Mrs. Lincoln and then saw Vice President Johnson in his office. The afternoon newspapers had reported that the Lincolns and Grant would attend the theater that evening. It was to be a gala event at Ford's Theater.

The president saw more citizens in his office that afternoon. The requests for pardons, releases, and discharges were voluminous. Following this he walked over to the War Department to discuss with Stanton the latest news about the surrender of Johnston.

Lincoln was somewhat uneasy about attending the theater that evening. Stanton had asked him not to go. Rumors of assassination were about. The president asked for someone to accompany the party. Major Thomas Eckert was busy on another assignment, so Major Henry Reed Rathbone was assigned. He brought his fiancée, Clara Harris, daughter of Senator Ira Harris of New York, along.

Late in the afternoon the president and Mrs. Lincoln went for a carriage ride in the park. They talked of many things. The loss of their son Willie in 1862 had been a great tragedy for them both. This along with the heavy burdens of the war had dragged them both down. They spoke of what was to follow. Lincoln said they would return to Springfield, Illinois, where he would resume his legal practice. They would take more time for themselves. They returned to the White House in about an hour.

Around eight in the evening, the president and Mrs. Lincoln left the White House for the theater by carriage with a footman and coachman. Two cavalrymen rode behind. They stopped at the home of Senator Harris, where Major Rathbone and Miss Harris were picked up. The party then proceeded to Ford's Theater on 10th Street, arriving at the front entrance about 8:25. The performance had already begun.

Many people were on the street, delighted and excited to see Lincoln with some of the burdens lifted from his shoulders. The party was escorted to the president's box, located above the stage to the audience's right. The box was gaily decorated with a large American flag over its railing and a picture of President Washington in the center. When the president entered his box, the performance stopped and the orchestra struck up, "Hail to the Chief." This was followed by several minutes of intense applause. The cast then continued with their production of "Our American Cousin." Everyone was in a happy mood, and the president was relaxed.

3
John Wilkes Booth

On Friday, April 14, Booth went to Ford's Theater to get his mail. Because Booth was a traveling actor, John T. Ford, the proprietor, gave him that privilege. Ford also had a theater in Baltimore, where he lived. He spent only three days a week in Washington. There he was assisted by two brothers, H. Clay Ford (treasurer) and James R. Ford (business manager).

James R. Ford testified in court that he learned of the visit of the president and Grant to Ford's Theater at 10:30 on the morning of April 14, and that Booth was at the theater soon after that.[1]

Being well-known and trusted at the theater, Booth had the privilege of coming and going as he pleased. H. Clay Ford testified that Booth frequently engaged box 7 for himself—the one used by the president on April 14. In fact, Booth never used any other when he had guests.[2]

After Booth's morning visit to the theater, he evidently was quite busy making final plans for Lincoln's assassination. Contact was made with his accomplices, Payne, Atzerodt, and Herold. Arnold had left town and John Surratt was in Canada. O'Laughlin was in Washington on April 13, but no participation on the night of April 14 was established at the trial. About noon on April 14, Booth rented a bay mare with black legs from James Pumphry for 4:30 that afternoon. He asked for a hitch tie. Pumphry told him he should have her held, that she broke her bridle if tied. Booth said he was going to Grover's Theater to write a letter.[3] This was probably the article for the *National Intelligencer*, the well-known Washington newspaper of the day, which he planned to have published in the next day's edition. The article never appeared. Booth wrote it and put in in an envelope, then supposedly gave it to a fellow actor, John Mathews, to deliver to the paper the next day. Mathews did not follow through. In this article, Booth is supposed to have referred to the capture scheme to which he had devoted his money, time, and energy. The article was signed, "Men who love their country better than gold or life. J. W. Booth, Payne, Atzerodt, Herold."[4] While delivering this article in an envelope to Mathews, it is thought that Booth saw General and Mrs. Grant on their way to the train station.

Booth was also at the Kirkwood House that afternoon, where Vice President Johnson lived and where Atzerodt had engaged a room that he never used. He left his card in the mailbox of Colonel William Browning, secretary to Vice President Johnson. The card had written on it, "Don't wish to disturb you; are you at home?" Browning had seen Booth on stage several times and had met him personally.[5] The intent of this card is not known. It may have been written to create confusion.

According to Wiechmann's testimony, Booth also left a package with Mrs. Surratt at her home just as they were leaving for Surrattsville in the early afternoon.[6] This package was taken to John Lloyd at the Surratt Tavern late that afternoon and contained Booth's field glass according to Lloyd's testimony.[7]

There was an unidentified brief caller at the Surratt house about 9:30 P.M., just after they returned to the city from Surrattsville that evening. Wiechmann thought the caller was probably Booth, although he did not see him. He was in the dining room having supper. The doorbell rang, and Mrs. Surratt answered it. Wiechmann then heard footsteps into the parlor, a brief inaudible conversation, and then footsteps leaving.

According to Atzerodt,[8] there was a meeting of the "conspirators" about 8:00 P.M. at the Herndon House, at which time the final assignments were made. All four may not have been there at the time but that is when Atzerodt said he received his assignment to shoot Vice President Johnson. Booth was to play the main role at the theater alone. He had complete access there and his presence would not arouse suspicion. More important for Booth, this gave him the star role to which his ego aspired and to which he was accustomed. Payne was to gain entrance to the home of Secretary of State Seward, on the ruse of bringing him medicine from Dr. Verdi, and assassinate him. Seward was bed-ridden with head injuries and a broken arm from a carriage accident five days earlier. Herold was to direct Payne there and then go to the Kirkwood House and assist Atzerodt.

When Atzerodt received his final assignment that evening to go to Vice President Johnson's room and shoot him when he opened the door, he objected. He said he had joined up to capture, not to kill.[9] According to his statement, Booth did not relieve him of his assignment and told him it was too late to back out. It was death to those who backed out. This made his already unsteady hand even more unsteady.

Efforts to implicate O'Laughlin in the plot were not successful at the trial, although he was in Washington that night.[10]

About 9:30 P.M. Booth arrived with his bay mare at the back entrance of Ford's Theater and called for Spangler to hold his horse. Spangler was busy, as scenery shifts were coming up on stage, so he asked Joseph Burroughs ("Peanuts") to do it. Booth then entered the theater through the rear door and went to the front entrance, where he was seen by several

THE NEW YORK HERALD.

WHOLE NO. 10,456.　　　　NEW YORK, SATURDAY, APRIL 15, 1865.　　　　PRICE FOUR CENTS.

IMPORTANT.

ASSASSINATION

OF

PRESIDENT LINCOLN

The President Shot at the Theatre Last Evening.

SECRETARY SEWARD

DAGGERED IN HIS BED,

BUT

NOT MORTALLY WOUNDED.

Clarence and Frederick Seward Badly Hurt.

ESCAPE OF THE ASSASSINS.

Intense Excitement in Washington.

Scene at the Deathbed of Mr. Lincoln.

J. Wilkes Booth, the Actor, the Alleged Assassin of the President,

&c.,　　　&c.,　　　&c.

THE OFFICIAL DESPATCH.

War Department,

POSTSCRIPT.

Saturday, April 15—10 A. M.

DEATH

OF THE

PRESIDENT!

Condition of Secretary Seward.

Ten Thousand Dollars Reward Offered for the Arrest of the Assassins.

THE LATEST NEWS.

Secretary Stanton to General Dix.

War Department,
Washington, April 15—1 A. M.

Major General Dix, New York:—

THE REBELS.

JEFF. DAVIS AT DANVILLE.

His Latest Appeal to His Deluded Followers.

He Thanks the Fall of Richmond a Blessing in Disguise, as it Leaves the Rebel Armies Free to Move from Point to Point.

He Vainly Promises to Hold Virginia at All Hazards.

&c.,　　　&c.,　　　&c.

Jeff. Davis' Last Proclamation.

THE PRESS DESPATCHES.

Washington, April 14—10.30 A. M.

J. Wilkes Booth Identified as the Murderer of the President,

&c.,　　　&c.

people. The president's carriage was waiting there. Sergeant Joseph Dye saw several persons whose appearance aroused his suspicion.[11] The first was an elegantly dressed man, probably Booth, who came out of the passage and started conversing with a rough-looking fellow; then another appeared and the three conversed. One of the three had been at the curbstone looking at the carriage. A number of people came out, probably at the end of the second act, and some went into the restaurant bar next door. Soon they came out and went back into the theater. The well-dressed man then went into the bar, stayed long enough to have a drink, and then came back out and entered the theater. Peter Taltavul, the owner of the restaurant adjoining Ford's Theater, testified that Booth, whom he knew well, came to his bar a little after 10:00 P.M. on the night of April 14 and called for some whiskey and water, which was served to him. After this, he left.[12] About eight or ten minutes later Taltavul heard the news that the president was shot.

Dye saw some other things in front of the theater. When the well-dressed man came out of the bar, he whispered something to the rough-looking one, then went into the passage that led to the stage from the street. The third person then looked at the clock in the vestibule and called out the time as the well-dresssed man reappeared at the front entrance. The third man walked away and returned again and called the time. When he did it a third time at 10:10, the well-dressed man returned to the theater. Dye identified the well-dressed man as Booth when shown a photo of him. The rough-looking man had a mustache, as did the third man who called the time. The latter had a neat appearance. It was about fifteen minutes after Booth entered the theater the last time that Dye heard of the assassination.

How Booth got by the guard seated in front of the entrance of box 7 is not known. It was rumored that the guard had left his post to watch the play. Captain Theodore McGowan testified that he was in the audience the night of April 14 and that his seat was adjacent to the entrance door. A man came by and he had to move his chair to let him pass. This man stopped about three feet from where he was sitting, took a pack of visiting cards from his pocket, and chose one. He then thought that this person showed it to the president's messenger who was sitting just below him. Whether the messenger took the card into the box or looked at it and allowed him to pass, McGowan did not know, but in a moment he saw the man go through the lobby door leading to the president's box and close the door. This was just a few minutes before he heard the pistol shot and then saw a man jump onto the stage with a dagger in his hand. The man who jumped ran backstage to the audience's left and disappeared behind the scenes.[13]

Opposite: **Assassination issue, *New York Herald*.**

When Booth entered the president's box, he quietly propped the door shut from the inside with the wooden leg of a music stand that he had hidden there earlier in the day. The dialogue on stage was rather loud at this part of the play so that the task was not particularly difficult. He then crept behind Lincoln, who was sitting in a rocking chair nearest the audience and, at close range, shot him in the back of the left side of the head with a pistol. The president slumped forward, never to regain consciousness. Major Henry Rathbone, who was sitting farther forward in the box with Miss Harris, looked around and saw, through the smoke, a man between the door and the president.[14] The distance from the door to the president was about four feet, which means that Booth was just a couple of feet from the president when he fired. The major sprang toward the man and grabbed him. Booth wrested himself loose and made a violent thrust at Rathbone's chest with a dagger. Rathbone shielded himself with his left arm and received a deep gash on his left upper arm between the elbow and the shoulder, which bled profusely. They continued to grapple as Booth struggled to the railing of the box and leaped to the stage. Due to Rathbone's pursuit, Booth's heel did not clear the American flag draped about the ledge of the box. His spur caught and tore a piece of it away that was carried to the stage with his spur. He landed off balance, injuring his back and breaking his left leg. Rathbone heard him say, "Freedom," just after the shot was fired. In the audience others heard him cry, "Sic semper tyrannus," after he landed on stage.

Rathbone shouted, "Stop that man," as Booth jumped to the stage. Rathbone then looked to see that the president was in the same position with his head slumped forward and his eyes closed. Realizing that the president was mortally wounded, he rushed to the door for medical aid. The door was barred by the leg of the music stand, one end secured in the wall and the other end wedged against the door. Persons were pushing on the door from the outside. The harder they pushed, the tighter the bar became. It was finally dislodged and a young army surgeon was one of the first to reach Lincoln's side.

The pursuit of Booth by a member of the audience and the near capture of the reins of his horse in the alley according to that man's testimony are told later. This man's testimony was later contradicted by that of the chief of police of the city of Washington.[15]

The account of the care of the unconscious president is told elsewhere. The location of the bullet wound at the base of his skull on the left side was soon found. He was completely unconscious, breathing laboriously, and his right eye was becoming hemorrhagic—all ominous signs.

The difference between emergency care today and that of 1865 is dramatically demonstrated by the fact that the chief executive was carried across the street to the bedroom of a flat, where he was laid diagonally on a bed and examined. Efforts to save him were futile and he expired at 7:20 A.M., April 15, 1865. Secretary of War Stanton was manning a temporary center of government in another room of the building until Vice President Andrew Johnson could be sworn in as president of the United States at the Kirkwood House Hotel later that morning.

4
The Plot and the Man

The Plot

As the War Between the States wore on, limited manpower in the South became a critical factor. Many Confederate soldiers were in Northern prisons instead of on the field of battle. Although many Northern men were imprisoned in the South, the greater manpower of the North prevented this from being such a critical factor. Grant, knowing this shortage, issued an order in April 1864 that no more Confederate prisoners would be exchanged.[1]

Booth did not volunteer his services in the Confederate Army as he might have done in view of his zeal for the Confederate cause. He had a plan he thought would do more for the cause and would also make him famous. It was his intent to kidnap Lincoln and transport him to Richmond, where he would be the strongest bartering factor for the exchange of prisoners.

Kidnap and assassination plots against Lincoln had been rumored frequently during the war. It is not clear whether two plots started simultaneously in the summer of 1864. Surratt maintained that there was a second plot afloat with which they had no connection.[2]

The Confederate underground was stepping up its activities and Captain Thomas Nelson Conrad of the Third Virginia Cavalry was observing the personal habits of Lincoln and exploring the feasibility of escape routes from Washington in September 1864.[3] Information was being gathered. There is no evidence that the work of Conrad and Booth was coordinated. Booth remained in charge of his own efforts. One can speculate that top command may have wisely deferred to his efforts.

Booth's hatred of Lincoln was extreme and well documented. There were bitter discussions in his family on this subject in which he disagreed vehemently with his older actor brother, Edwin, his sister Asia, and her husband John Clarke. He disagreed also with his mother but spared her discussion on the subject, promising her he would not join the Confederate Army. He disagreed less with his other actor brother, Junius Brutus, Jr., but he was the only member of the family disloyal to the Union.

16

An unusual thing happened in Meadville, Pennsylvania, which took on significance after the assassination.[4] Booth gave a performance in that city and stayed at the McHenry House. After he departed from his hotel room the next morning, an unusual message was found etched on one of the window panes: *"Abe Lincoln departed life August 13th, 1864, by the effects of poison."* This pane was removed from the window and preserved in a frame with a dark cloth behind it, which made the writing more legible.[5] A comparison with Booth's signature on the hotel register was said to be similar. The window pane was presented to the War Department and may still be in existence. It was a strange occurrence in retrospect, which took on possible significance after the assassination. A failed poisoning attempt may have been made. Wiechmann points out that Herold, who later became prominent as one of Booth's accomplices, was working as a clerk in the drug store of William S. Thompson at 15th Street and Pennsylvania Avenue not far from the White House at that time.[6] Later in 1864 Booth wrote a very long letter addressed "To whom it may concern," which he placed in a sealed envelope with some U.S. bonds and certificates of shares in oil companies. This was left for safe keeping with his brother-in-law, John S. Clarke, and his sister Asia Booth-Clarke, who lived in Philadelphia. He put his own name on the outside of the envelope. It was a record of his deep inward thoughts and feelings at that time and a message to his family primarily and to "whom it may concern." His sister and brother-in-law had no idea of the contents until the envelope was opened after the assassination. A verbatim copy of this letter is given by Wiechmann and Risvold.[7]

In this long letter, Booth tells of his great zeal for the Southern cause. He asks that God judge him, not man. Many grievances against the Union are told. He cannot understand why the Southern states do not have a right to secede, gives his views on slavery, brags about his annual income, and states that he loves his sister and mother although they disagree politically. It is an apology for his plan to kidnap Lincoln and transport him to Richmond. He writes, "I look upon my early admiration of my country's glories as a dream. My love as things stand today is for the South alone. *Nor do I deem it a dishonor in attempting to make for her a prisoner of this man to whom she owes so much misery.*" His ending sentence is: "A Confederate doing duty on his own responsibility."

Booth's first successful overture to other people to join him in his scheme was made to two boyhood friends, Sam Arnold and Michael O'Laughlin, whom he had known at different times while growing up in Baltimore and at prep school. These were people he could trust and people who held views similar to his on the war.

Booth went to Baltimore where the two men lived. He sent messages to each, asking them to come to Barnums Hotel where he was staying. Arnold arrived first.

This meeting occurred in the latter part of August or the first part of September 1864. It was the first meeting of Arnold and O'Laughlin, who would go through agony together and rue the day of this meeting with Booth. O'Laughlin would die of Yellow Fever because of it. Arnold would spend nearly four years of incarceration and humiliation because of it. Booth was meeting with two of his former school acquaintances in whom he had confidence. He could trust them. For his job he had to have people he could trust and rely on. Reliance was not to be a mutual thing, however; Booth could rely on Arnold and O'Laughlin, but they could not rely on Booth. It was very risky business they were undertaking.

The three shared similar views on the war. Arnold and O'Laughlin were impressed with Booth's success and worldly manner as well as his wealth. They were both swept off their feet on the first meeting, and agreed to cooperate with Booth in his plan.

In October Booth went to Canada to confer there with the "Little Richmond" cabinet and ship his theatrical wardrobe through the blockade to the South. He had given up acting for the time being to devote all his energy to the kidnap plot. He checked in at the St. Lawrence Hall in Montreal at 9:30 P.M. on October 18, 1864.[8] This hotel served as the unofficial Confederate clearinghouse for information. Whom he met there is only partially known. He did meet and become acquainted with Patrick C. Martin, a blockade runner with whom he shipped his wardrobe to Halifax on the seventy-three-foot schooner *Marie Victoria,* without clearing customs. The vessel ran aground and was wrecked in a storm at Bic, Quebec, a few weeks later with all hands lost, including Martin.[9]

Martin had arrived in Montreal in 1862 and was involved in the shipping of contraband materials to the South in small vessels. He was master of a ship rather than serving in Confederate service. He originally came from New York but had been a liquor dealer in Baltimore and was acquainted with Lower Maryland. He gave Booth a letter of introduction to Dr. Queen in Charles County, Maryland, six miles south of Bryantown.

In Montreal in October 1864, Booth also met George N. Sanders, a Confederate with whom he had much in common. Sanders believed in conspiracy and assassination for tyrants. They spent time in the same hotel and were seen together during Booth's ten-day stay.[10] According to Wiechmann, Booth was also seen in the company of Jacob Thompson.[11] What arrangements Booth made with Confederates in Montreal can only be conjectured. They probably listened to him with interest, but whether they actually furnished funds for the project is not known.

Booth returned by way of New York and as soon as he could arrange it went to Charles County, Maryland, where he met with Queen and through John Thompson was introduced to Mudd at St. Mary's Church on a Sunday morning.

This first meeting of Booth and Mudd was in the second or third week of November. There occurs a variation in the sequence of events that occurred in Charles County following this first visit in November. This was brought out a number of years later when persons spoke more freely after the danger to their own lives had eased. The variation in sequence referred to is in regard to the number of visits that Booth made to Lower Maryland during his planning stage in November and December 1864. According to the testimony of John C. Thompson, at the trial of the "conspirators" on Friday, May 26, 1865, Booth made a second visit to Queen's home. The pertinent testimony of Thompson follows. The first question given here is by Stone in regard to the original visit of Booth to Queen, on which occasion Booth brought a letter of introduction from Martin in Montreal.

Q. State the purport of the letter, as near as you can remember.
A. As well as I can remember, it was simply a letter of introduction to Dr. Queen, saying that this man Booth wanted to see the county. That is about it, as well as I can remember. I do not know what the contents of the letter were exactly.
Q. Were you, or not, present at the first meeting between Dr. Samuel Mudd, the accused, and this man Booth?
A. I think I was at the church.
Q. State the circumstances.
A. On Sunday morning, this man Booth, Dr. Queen, and myself went to church at Bryantown, and I introduced Booth to Dr. Mudd. [The questioning then went on in regard to Booth's wish to purchase land at some extent and finally the following question was asked.]
Q. Did Booth stay at Dr. Queen's house during that visit?
A. I think he stayed there that night and the next day, as well as I remember.
Q. Did you ever see Booth again?
A. I think some time, if my memory serves me, in December, he came down there a second time to Dr. Queen's house. Really, I did not charge my memory in regard to the man; but I think it was about the middle of December following after his first visit there.
Q. Did he stay all night on his second visit to Dr. Queen's?
A. I think he did, and left early the next morning.
Q. Did you ever see him in the country but on those two visits?
A. Never after that.
Q. You do not know of his having been there but on those two occasions?
A. When he left Dr. Queen's, I did not know whither he went, and am not conversant with any of his movements thereafter.[12,13,14]

According to Wiechmann,[15] the actor was subsequently introduced to Thomas Harbin by Mudd at the Bryantown Village hotel on that visit. Harbin was a Confederate spy. He was a Marylander who was signal officer for the Confederates in Lower Maryland counties. Booth had private conversations with Harbin in regard to the kidnap plot and said that he had come down to invite cooperation and secure partners in the venture. It was on this second visit that Booth stayed overnight with Mudd and bought the one-eyed horse from George Gardiner on the following morning.[16] This second visit of Booth in December 1865 was not brought out in the trial except by the testimony of Thompson, son-in-law of Queen.

The reminiscences of Harbin are referred to by Tidwell, Hall, and Gaddy.[17] After the war Harbin disappeared for a number of years until things settled down. His life was in danger and he left the country until the danger had passed. He then returned to Washington and was a room clerk at the National Hotel in Washington, Booth's "old" hotel. He often reminisced about his very interesting experiences as a Confederate agent since there was no longer a price on his head. He died on November 18, 1885. After his death someone published his reminiscences in an unknown newspaper, which may have been a hotel paper.[18]

On a return visit to Baltimore in January 1865, Booth purchased a horse and buggy that Arnold and O'Laughlin took charge of and brought to Washington the latter part of that month. This rig was left at Naylor's Livery Stable, just south of Pennsylvania Avenue at 14th Street. Things were ready for the kidnapping but the president did not make himself available.

Booth's second overture for his scheme was to a fellow actor, Samuel Knapp Chester, in New York in November 1864.[19] Chester had been a friend for many years and had become an intimate friend during the previous six or seven years. Booth asked Chester to join him in a big speculation that he had on hand. Chester, knowing of Booth's speculation in oil lands in western Pennsylvania, thought at first that Booth was referring to this.

Booth told Chester that he did not intend to act in that part of the country again and that he had taken his wardrobe to Canada and planned to run the blockade. On a second meeting a short time later, Booth again asked Chester to join him in an important venture. Chester said he had no extra funds to invest. Booth told him that funds were not necessary, that he would supply the funds. The particulars of the venture were not given. Booth returned to Washington and mentioned in several letters that they should join together. He was speculating in farms in Lower Maryland and Virginia and was sure to coin money and said Chester should join him. When Chester asked Booth what his speculation was, Booth would put him off and tell him that he would let him know by and by. Finally, on a return visit to New York in December, after some drinks at several bars, Booth told Chester while walking on an empty street about his scheme.

It was a conspiracy to capture the heads of the government, including the president, and take them to Richmond. Chester asked if that was the speculation he wished him to enter, and Booth said yes. Chester told Booth he could not do it. He said he had two or three thousand dollars he could give Booth. They talked for another half-hour and Booth finally said, "You will not betray me, you dare not. The party is sworn together. If you betray, you will be hunted for life." He asked Chester again to join. Chester said no and bid him good night.

Chester further testified at the trial that the affair was to take place at the Ford's Theater and that Booth wanted him to open the back door at a certain signal, an easy part, and that the plot was sure to succeed. All was in readiness and parties on the other side (rebel authorities and others opposed to the U.S. government) were ready to cooperate. Booth wrote again to Chester from Washington and sent him $50.

In February Booth again called on Chester in New York with a renewal of the offer. He said he had tried to enlist John Mathews, a mutually known fellow actor, to join. Mathews refused and appeared frightened. Booth said he was a coward and that he would not care if he had sacrificed him. Chester told Booth he should not speak like that and returned the $50 Booth had sent and told him not to speak to him again about the undertaking. Booth took the money, saying he was a little low on cash, and that someone must go to Richmond and secure funds for the project.

Booth was again in New York on the Friday before the assassination and met Chester at the House of Lords Cafe. They were sitting at a table when Booth brought his fist down on it, saying, "What an excellent chance I had to kill the president, if I had wished, on inauguration day!" He was as near to the president that day as he was to Chester, he said.

After the agreement to work with Booth was made, Arnold proceeded to locate a horse and carriage in Baltimore, which Booth bought on a return trip from Canada as he stopped in Baltimore. He had been in Montreal conferring with Confederate agents and while there had also purchased two carbines, three pairs of revolvers, three knives, and two pairs of handcuffs. These were to cover their retreat in case of pursuit, Booth said. These things were so heavy that he thought his trunk would be suspicious. Consequently he left them with Arnold to be expressed to him in Washington. Arnold did this a few days later.

In early January Arnold and O'Laughlin drove the horse and carriage to Washington and left it at Naylor's Stable, just south of Pennsylvania Avenue.

They put up at Rullmans Hotel, then Mitchells Hotel near Grover's Theater, and then rented a room from Mrs. Van Tine at 420 D Street. They arrived there on February 10 and remained until March 20. Booth visited frequently during this interval.

Booth arranged a meeting of the conspirators at Gautier's Restaurant in mid–March, the only time the whole group was brought together. Booth proposed capturing Lincoln at the theater on this occasion. The president

April 1865

SUN	MON	TUES	WED	THURS	FRI	SAT
						1
2	3 Fall of Richmond	4	5 Lincoln visits Richmond	6	7	8
9 Lee surrender Appomattox	10	11 Lincoln talks from White House	12	13	14 LINCOLN SHOT	15 LINCOLN DIES — Booth Arr. 4 A.M. Mudd Farm Lv. 4 P.M.
16 Arr. Cox T. A. Jones	17 ———————	18 ——Booth & Herold pine forest——	19 ——forest——	20	21 1st Att. to Cross Potomac	22 2nd Att. to Cross Potomac
23 Arr. VA	24 Dr. Mudd Custody	25	26 Herold captured — Booth shot Garrett's tobacco barn			

was not making his usual trips to the Soldier's Home. To attempt capture in a theater with crowds of people present was considered dangerous and impractical by Arnold and doomed to failure. He was outspoken and told Booth so, and an argument developed. Arnold said he would withdraw because that idea would not work. He also said that any attempt to capture the president should be made when there was not a crowd of people around. If it were not done within a week, he would withdraw. He thought the government would get wise to the plan. Booth said that anyone who withdrew would be shot. Arnold replied that two could play that game, and the meeting broke up.[20] The next day Booth apologized for what he had said the night before, according to Arnold.

On March 17, 1865, Booth and Herold met Arnold and O'Laughlin and advised them that Lincoln was to attend a theatrical performance at the Soldier's Home at the edge of the city that afternoon.[21] This was the opportunity they had been waiting for. Booth ordered his "troops" to proceed. They would take the carriage on the road as it left the Soldier's Home. The driver would be overcome and replaced by Payne, who would charge ahead in the carriage over the Bennington Bridge into southern Maryland while the others overcame the occupants.[22] According to Arnold's account, Herold was sent ahead in Booth's carriage to Surrattsville and T. B., a small village a few miles farther south. In the carriage he had the box of weapons that Booth had bought on his last Canadian trip. The party rode to the scene of the proposed capture in pairs so as not to arouse suspicion.[23] Arnold and O'Laughlin rode together after picking up their arms at their rooming house. They rode to where the performance was to take place and stopped at a restaurant at the foot of the hill, which was the rendezvous spot. They were the first there. They rode farther on and returned. In a short while Atzerodt and Payne arrived and after that Booth and Surratt. They all had a drink together. Booth then went to the encampment and made inquiries about the performance, learning that the president was not there after all.[24]

This was a great letdown for all the participants. After waiting nearly a month, they had their courage up and now it was a false alarm. Arnold, O'Laughlin, and Payne rode back to the city together and turned in their horses. Arnold does not mention how Atzerodt returned. Presumably he did the same thing. Booth and Surratt rode to the country to meet Herold.[25] The firearms were then stored at the Surratt Tavern, hiding among the rafters in a back room, a spot previously known only by Surratt.

This spelled the end of the capture plot for all intents and purposes. Arnold and O'Laughlin, feeling that the government was wise to the plot, returned to Baltimore. Atzerodt and Payne continued to lie in wait for the

Opposite: **Calendar of events, April 1865.**

next assignment. Surratt probably was of the same opinion as Arnold and O'Laughlin. He left town on one of his Confederate courier missions to Richmond, never to take part again. He passed through Washington briefly on the night of April 3, 1865, on his way from Richmond to Montreal with some of his Confederate dispatches. This was the last time his mother saw him. He was in upstate New York having breakfast at his hotel in Elmira on April 15, 1865, when the news of the assassination arrived. When he read his name in the morning newspaper as one of the assassins, he decided he had better head for cover. He went across the Canadian border on the earliest train. After arriving in Montreal, he disappeared completely. Actually, as determined later, he was in hiding with a priest in a small parish north of Montreal. No one in Washington knew where he was. A special detachment of detectives was sent to Montreal. They took along John Wiechmann, Surratt's former friend and roommate, who had turned government witness, but it was to no avail. They could not find him. Back in Washington with the clamor for action great, the trial of the available conspirators before a military commission began without Surratt on May 9. He stayed undetected in his hideout for the next five months, during which time his mother was tried before the military commission and hanged. People wondered how he could desert her during her trial. He probably figured it was him or her or possibly both of them. It would have been a brave thing to try to save his mother, who became the first woman ever given the death penalty by the U.S. government.[26]

DeWitt gives a version of the March 16, 1865, capture attempt that is slightly different than that of Arnold. In his version, the group actually pulled up alongside a carriage in which they expected to find the president, only to discover that it was not him.[27]

DeWitt did not have the published version of Arnold's memoirs (they were not published until 1943). DeWitt was in contact with Arnold, however, and included a letter from him.[28]

The above version of the March capture attempt was also given by Surratt in his Rockville Lecture of December 6, 1870.[29] This was probably the source that DeWitt used. Surratt thought that the occupant of the carriage was Salmon P. Chase instead of Lincoln. He said that they did not disturb him—they wanted someone bigger. He also said that this was the last attempt to kidnap the president. He then said that it was necessary for him to go to Richmond on matters of a different kind and that he was in Richmond the Friday evening before its fall. He saw Confederate Secretary of War Benjamin, who gave him dispatches for Canada and $200 in gold (which was the only remuneration he received from the Confederate government). He also said that the abduction scheme was concocted without the knowledge or assistance of the Confederate government in any shape or form. He said that he and Booth often wondered whether they should inform the authorities in Richmond about their plan. They were sadly in need of money but did not let them know. They were worried that if they succeeded in getting Lincoln to Virginia, that the Confederate authorities might surrender them back again to the United States. They were jealous of their undertaking and wanted no outside help. Surratt also stated that he arrived back in Washington on Monday, April 3, and spent that night in a Washington hotel because detectives had been to his mother's house. He left Washington for Canada on an early train on April 4 and did not return until brought there in irons by the government in 1867.[30]

Another capture attempt is described by DeWitt as occurring on January 18, 1865. It was on this occasion that Booth sent the fifty dollars to Chester. Surratt and Atzerodt had a special boat waiting at Port Tobacco. Accomplices did not show up and the president did not come on that occasion either.[31]

The Man

Mudd was five years old when Booth was born in 1838 in Bel Air, Maryland, just north of Baltimore, at the summer country home (Tudor Hall) of his famous but erratic actor father. Booth was the fifth of six children born to Junius Brutus Booth and Ann Holmes. His father named him John Wilkes for an English agitator who had favored independence from England for the American colonies. Booth spent his boyhood summers at Tudor Hall. Winters were spent on Exeter Street in a good section of Baltimore, eighteen miles to the southwest. Booth's first-grade teacher there was, interestingly, Sarah Ann Mudd, a paternal aunt of Dr. Samuel Mudd.[32]

During the summers Booth enjoyed riding a horse at a gallop through the woods and across fields with a lance in his hand, spouting heroic phrases. His father taught his children that no living thing should be hunted or killed on the plantation, but Booth did not heed his advice. He enjoyed target practice on all animals, even dogs on several occasions. He grew up living for himself, by standards created by an overripe imagination.[33] Booth was later a student at Timothys Hall in Cantonsville, Maryland.

Booth was taught by his father to hate tyranny.[34] His father was unconventional according to most standards. He left a wife in London to immigrate to the United States in 1821, and is said not to have entered wedlock in the United States until after the birth of children here.

His father gained great fame as a tragedy actor before his death in 1852 at the age of fifty-six, when Booth was thirteen years old. Two older brothers, Junius Brutus, Jr., and Edwin, were actors, following in their father's footsteps, making the name Booth very well known on the stage in America at that time.

Since Booth was only thirteen years old when his father died, he did not have the advantage of his father's tutelage on stage as did his brothers. His father influenced him in subtle ways but did not actually instruct him. He prospered because of his own inherited acting ability. Due probably to his early life in Maryland and his experiences in the Southern states during his early theatrical experience, Booth developed a fanatical zeal for the Southern cause.

Booth's older brothers, especially Edwin, added much luster to the name Booth by their acting abilities. Both were Union supporters, particularly Edwin, for whom a theater in New York is named. Junius may have been more sympathetic to his younger brother but still supported the Union. Edwin played mostly in Northern cities, as did Junius, and each was very popular there. Junius was playing in Cincinnati on the night of April 14, 1865. He was having breakfast in his hotel dining room the next morning when word came that Lincoln had been assassinated by Booth, the actor. He was cautioned by the waiter to stay out of sight because a crowd of people outside thought he was the assassin. The waiter feared that Junius was in danger.

Edwin lived in New York with his family and gave a home to his mother there in her later years. There was much discussion about the war when John visited, which led to disagreement in the family. John was the only one who embraced the Southern cause.

At age seventeen Booth first tried the stage. After a shaky start in which he forgot his lines, he was successful. He was bombastic and athletic in his parts, but most of his audience liked this. He had a very rapid rise to fame over the next four years. Some thought he overplayed his parts.

He grew up to be very handsome, tall, and graceful, with glossy black hair and mustache. He was bold and fearless. He was noted for his leaps on stage.[35] He was an excellent horseman and swordsman. He had a rare power of attracting people to him.[36] He was very interesting in conversation and very neat in dress. It is said that most men and all women were attracted to him. He enjoyed the attention of women and broke many hearts with his escapades.

He was accepted and welcomed in high social circles but was also on conversational terms with the man on the street. He spoke to and knew all the stage hands at the theater. He even had the confidence of those guarding the president. What went on inside his depraved, egotistical mind he kept to himself, and he demanded secrecy from those few in whom he confided. He chose accomplices over whom he had control and paid no attention to their safety. He was the great personal star in all that he did.

His acting success gave him the wherewithal to enjoy the finer things

John Wilkes Booth (courtesy of the Library of Congress).

of life. At the National Hotel in Washington he sometimes gave poetic readings in the lobby in the evening. He had a craving for the sensational. He said one time that he would topple the Colossus of Rhodes if it were still standing.

In Booth's native Maryland there was much sentiment for the Southern cause. He was brought up with this. His acting career took him to Southern cities, where he was warmly received. The role of soldier seemed inadequate to his dream of glory. He promised his loyal Union mother that he would not join the Confederate forces. Whether he carried out subversive acts during his Confederate travels, we do not know with certainty.

In his acting Booth admired the Shakespearean character Brutus. His father used this as his middle name as did his brother. He later would quote Brutus's "sic semper tyrannus" after shooting Lincoln.

In Booth's zeal for the Southern cause, he became imbued with the idea of helping the Confederate States in a dramatic way. As an actor he relished dramatic roles. He decided to make this one the most dramatic of his career. He would do this and keep his promise to his mother that he would not join the Confederate Army. He considered himself above that. He could be of greater service in another way, he thought, and carry out an outstanding dramatic deed for the Southern cause.

If Booth could kidnap Lincoln, he could capture the most dramatic role of all time and be the hero of the South. It is not recorded when Booth decided to assassinate rather than kidnap Lincoln. From reconstruction of events and the record in his diary, it is probable that Booth did not definitely decide to assassinate Lincoln until the day he carried his plan out. It may have been in the back of his mind but he kept it to himself. In the diary entry written while he was a fugitive in Zekiah Swamp after the assassination, Booth wrote, "For six months we had worked to capture. But our cause being almost lost, something decisive and great must be done."

Arnold and O'Laughlin were recruited in August or September 1864. They were the first to enlist in the capture scheme, although they were not shown to be active on the day of the assassination. The diary entry indicates that the kidnap plan terminated some time in March 1865, after the aborted capture attempt of March 17, 1865. (This is the date of the failed capture attempt according to Arnold.[37] Wiechmann gives the date as March 16.) The president was not found in his carriage on this occasion when it was stopped by the group near the Soldier's Home. Arnold's version states only that the president did not come on that day.

Arnold and Surratt left town after this episode, thinking that the Union government was wise to the scheme. Booth had Spangler sell his horse and buggy after this failure, which also indicates that he had given up on capturing Lincoln.

The fall of Richmond on April 3 was the final blow to the capture scheme. There was no longer a fixed Confederate capital to which the captured president could be taken. At this time the capture scheme became inoperable. The plot to destroy took shape sometime after this. If it was more than an idea in the back of Booth's mind, he kept it to himself until the day of the event.

5
The Fugitives

After Booth escaped out the back door of Ford's Theater, he managed to mount his horse. It must have been painful and awkward with his broken leg. In the process he struck "Peanuts" Burroughs with the handle of his dagger, knocking him to the ground. The horse turned in a circle and Colonel Joseph Stewart, who was in hot pursuit from the audience, according to his own testimony, nearly caught the bridle of Booth's horse. Booth then clattered out the back alley onto F Street from the theater, with sparks flying from the cobblestones.

The exact route taken by Booth to the navy yard bridge is not known. A man on horseback was seen passing the south side of the Capitol at about 10:30 that night, according to Fletcher's testimony.[1] From the F Street alley, the shortest and quickest route would have been east on F Street to the corner, then to the right, south, on 9th Street, to Pennsylvania Avenue, left southeast on Pennsylvania Avenue, jogging south and east past the Capitol to New Jersey Avenue, then southeast on New Jersey to Virginia Avenue, southeast on Virginia Avenue to 11th Street, then south on 11th Street to the navy yard bridge, which at that time crossed the east branch of the Potomac River (now Anacosta).

Booth may have traveled east on F Street all the way to New Jersey Avenue, then southeast on New Jersey Avenue, through the Capitol grounds to Virginia Avenue. That would have been a little farther for a man in flight with a broken leg who needed desperately to get into southern Maryland as quickly as possible.

Chamlee points out that an even closer route could have been across a vacant lot from the alley behind Ford's Theater to E Street, but there is no evidence that Booth did that.[2] Stewart's testimony was "he swept to the left up towards F Street."[3]

Stewart further testified "nor did I see any person after I passed beyond the door, except the person on the horse, whom I believed to be Mr. John Wilkes Booth, until I had run after the horse, which was around the alley and up to the left some little distance. I then turned and came back and saw that nobody had come out of the theater up to that time."

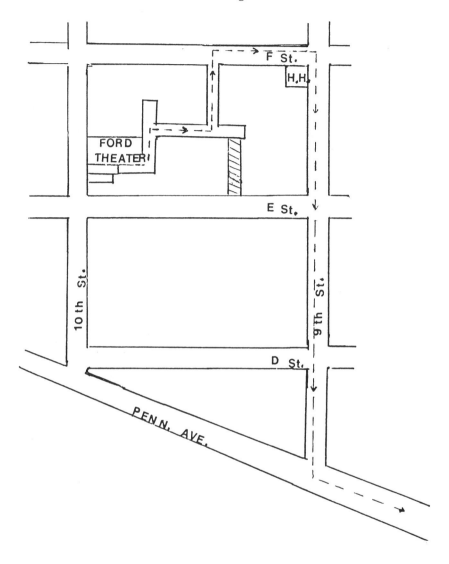

Shortest escape route through Washington, D.C., 1865 (after Pitman, p. 16).

It is doubtful that a rendezvous point had been set up in the city. The conspirators would have been conspicuous as a group. Their best bet was for each of them individually to cross the bridge, and meet outside the city. They then planned to travel as fast as possible through Lower Maryland and across the Potomac into Virginia.

After Payne's assassination attempt on Seward's life at the Seward

home on 15½th Street on the east side of Lafayette Park, he could well have planned to come down 15th Street to Pennsylvania Avenue, which was the shortest route diagonally down to 11th Street and the navy yard bridge. In the confusion that followed his attack, Herold left and did just that. Herold was seen by Fletcher, the hosteler, coming down Pennsylvania Avenue from 15th Street at about twenty-five minutes past ten,[4] a time that would fit with that theory. He could have been looking for Booth or Atzerodt then. Fletcher saw him go up 14th Street and turn east on F Street.

Herold probably headed directly for the navy yard bridge in view of Cobb's testimony about the happenings at the north end of it.[5] Payne failed to do so. He became confused and lost his way. His one-eyed horse was found wandering loose east of the Capitol at about midnight.

Booth could only have wanted to put as much distance between himself and Ford's Theater as he could as quickly as possible. It is most likely that he took the shortest and quickest route to the bridge, especially with his unexpected painful back and broken leg, which were new problems to cope with. His injuries were what slowed him up and prevented his eventual escape. He very likely would have gotten away if it had not been for them.

At the bridge he was challenged by Sergeant Silas Cobb at about half past ten.[6] According to Cobb, Booth gave his correct name and said he was returning to his home in "Charles" near Beantown, that he did not know of the new rule of a 9:00 P.M. curfew. Cobb thought he was a proper person and let him pass. When shown a photo of Booth, he identified him as the person he let pass. He said that he talked to the rider about three or four minutes before he let him go by.[7]

About seven to ten minutes later, a second horseman came along. He had not been riding as hard as the first man. When asked who he was, he gave his name as Smith and said that he was going to his home in White Plains, that he had been in bad company and had been delayed. Cobb allowed him to pass after bringing him up before the guardhouse door, where the light shone on him. At the trial, Herold was asked to stand up for identification. Cobb thought that Herold was about the same size as the second horseman and that he was riding a roan horse. The identification was not positive.[8]

Following this, a third horseman came to the navy yard bridge inquiring about a rider on a roan horse. He did not ask about the first rider. This was surely Fletcher from the Naylor stable. Cobb said he could pass but could not return until morning. With this stipulation, the third man turned back to the city.

Opposite: **The navy yard bridge from the Uniontown end, ca. 1865 (courtesy of the Library of Congress).**

Polk Gardiner, a traveler on the Bryantown road about 11 P.M. on April 14, gave testimony that when on the Good Hope Hill, on what is now Good Hope Road, he met two horsemen, one about a half a mile ahead of the other, both riding very fast. The first asked if a horseman had passed ahead and then asked about the road to Marlboro, whether it turned to the right. Gardiner told him no, that he should go straight. He rode a dark bay horse. When he met the second rider, teamsters were passing and he heard the man ask whether a horseman had passed ahead. During cross-examination, Gardiner said he met the first horseman two and a half to three miles from the city, halfway up the hill, and that he was off the hill completely when he met the second rider. The second man rode a roan or iron grey horse.[9]

Herold evidently overtook Booth down the road after passing Gardiner. Booth and Herold arrived together at the Surratt Tavern about midnight. Here they drank whiskey and picked up field glasses and a rifle from the proprietor, John Lloyd. Because of his injury Booth could not carry his so they took only one of the two Spencer rifles. The other was left with Lloyd, who secreted it back among the rafters of the tavern. Booth drank freely from a bottle of whiskey while on his horse to help ease the pain in his back and leg. On leaving, Booth said to Lloyd that he was certain that they had assassinated Lincoln and Seward.

After the brief stop at Surrattsville, they galloped together southward. The pain relief from the alcohol was only temporary and medical aid became necessary.

To cross the Potomac, they wanted to take a southwest route to Port Tobacco, where a boat had been purchased and secreted by Surratt and Atzerodt. They had the name of Dr. Samuel Cox in the Bel Alton area, but we do not know that Booth had visited him as he had Mudd. This would have been ten to thirteen miles farther. At the rate they were traveling it would have taken them another two or three hours to get there.

The pain in Booth's swollen leg was too great. Booth changed his objective from river crossing to pain relief. Either that or he developed a fear of daylight since his progress was not as rapid as he had anticipated. This was most unfortunate for Mudd. The poor man would have been spared all his troubles if Booth had stayed on his course toward the river. It has been said that we never would have heard of Mudd if Booth had not broken his leg.

It is questionable that Booth had definite plans for this portion of his journey. We know that the plan of action began about 10:30 in the morning, when Booth learned that Lincoln would attend the theater. If we believe the testimony of Atzerodt, the plan for assassination was not announced until 8:00 in the evening at the Herndon House on F Street.

From Surrattsville they went south but deviated their route to the east to Mudd's farm. The exact route they took is uncertain. They may have

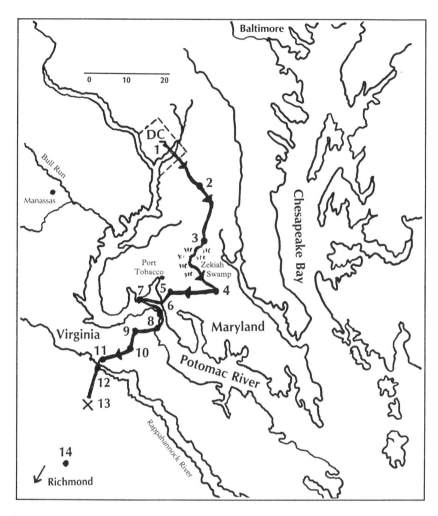

Escape route of Booth and Herold. 1—Ford's Theater. 2—Surratt's Tavern. 3—Farm of Dr. Samuel Mudd. 4—Home of Oswell Swann. 5—The thicket near home of Col. Samuel Cox. 6—"Huckleberry," home of Thomas Jones near Dent's Meadow, which was the departure point. 7—Blossom Point and Nanjemoy Creek. John Hughes. 8—Home of Mrs. Elizabeth Quesenberry on Machodoc Creek. 9—"Cleydael," home of Dr. Richard Stuart. 10—Home of William Lucas. 11—Port Conway. 12—Port Royal. 13—The Garrett place. 14—Bowling Green, Va.

gone through Horsehead according to Hall[10] or down the Beantown Road to St. Peter's Church. Either route would have taken them to Mudd's farm. The two made the fifteen-mile trip from Surrattsville to Mudd's farm in four hours. The loud knock on Mudd's door occurred about four A.M.

Saturday, April 15, was spent at Mudd's farm. In the evening, between four and five o'clock, they left going out the back way into Zekiah Swamp. After leaving Mudd's home, Booth and Herold made their way through Zekiah Swamp southwestward toward Allen's Fresh and the Potomac River. After losing their way, they finally arrived at the home of Oswald Swann on the east side of Zekiah Swamp in the vicinity of Hughesville.[11] Swann was a free black who owned a modest farm.

The fugitives asked Swann to take them to the home of Dr. Samuel Cox. He cooperated and led them southwestward about ten miles to "Rich Hill," Cox's stately home, across Zekiah Swamp, to the west side of it near the present village of Bel Alton. They arrived there about midnight.[12] Booth had his letter of introduction that he had secured in Montreal the previous October from Patrick Martin, a Baltimore merchant and Confederate agent. It was not necessary to show it as Cox was well aware of Booth and what he had done. Booth had previously used his letter as an introduction to Queen.

Cox may or may not have admitted the two fugitives to his house. Cox afterward said that he did not admit them. He took them to a dense pine thicket a mile or so from his home, where they were secreted.

Cox enlisted the aid of his foster brother, Thomas A. Jones, who lived about four miles south of Rich Hill just below Pope's Creek near the bank of the Potomac. Cox sent his adopted son, Samuel Cox, Jr., as a messenger to Jones, asking him to come to his home about an urgent matter.

Jones came to the home of his foster brother in response to the request.[13] Cox took him aside and told him who the men were and asked, "Can you get them across the river into Virginia?" Jones said the patrol traffic on the river was very heavy in the neighborhood and that it would be very risky. He also pointed out that there were many detectives and cavalrymen in the area. He would see what he could do.

Jones was in charge of Confederate mail to and from Richmond and knew the ins and outs of crossing the river. The Union patrols had been increased on the river and soldiers were canvassing the countryside looking for the fugitives. It was going to be a particularly hard job to get them safely out of Virginia. It was particularly hazardous for Jones personally, who had already been in trouble with the federal government. He had spent time in Old Capitol Prison for his river crossings. He was actually out on parole, but told his foster brother he would do all he could. Things had to be done just right. To get caught would be a disaster for all concerned.

Booth and Herold waited in accordance with instructions from Jones for the right time to attempt the crossing, trusting both Jones and Cox, who were risking their lives for them. Jones supplied them with newspapers in addition to food, so that Booth could take pride in his notoriety. He told them that they must do away with their horses to make their seclusion more secure. He did not want their horses to welcome the mounts of the cavalry. On several occasions the cavalry came within earshot but did not detect them. Jones knew that he had the only two remaining boats in the area and a boat was an absolute necessity for crossing the river. During the day Jones had his hired hand, Henry Woodland, fish in the river for shad. This kept the boat occupied in the safest way during the day. At night it was carefully hidden in the thicket surrounding the stream that flowed from Dent's Meadow. This stream was chosen because of its secluded location; the expected departure would be less likely to be detected. Jones or his hired hand fished for shad in the Potomac River by day, not only to prevent the boat from being stolen but also to keep an eye on river traffic. The boat was carefully hidden on shore at night in readiness for the getaway.

During the long wait, Booth made entries in a pocket diary. This diary, although described in the newspapers at the time of Booth's death as among his possessions, strangely was not produced at Mudd's trial. It did not come to light until Surratt's trial in 1867, two years later. The other contents of Booth's pockets—a knife, two pistols, a belt holster, file, pocket compass, spur, pipe, carbine, cartridges, and bills of exchange—were recorded and exhibited at Mudd's trial. Stanton was accused by some people of deliberately withholding the diary from evidence.

When the diary finally was brought into evidence in 1867, pages were missing. This caused quite a stir and the issue was never settled. Some pages had been removed by Booth himself for writing paper during his period of hiding.

In one entry, Booth makes the statement: "Until today nothing was ever thought of sacrificing to our country's wrongs. For six months we have worked to capture." The diary speaks of "we" without being more specific. This certainly refers to himself and the group around him and to the plot to capture Lincoln and hold him for ransom, particularly for the return of Confederate prisoners. This reference possibly could have been helpful in the defense of Mudd, had it been entered as evidence at the court-martial. It is not known if this was an oversight on General Ewing's part or whether he did it intentionally.

They remained in the thicket from Sunday, April 16, until Friday, April 21. Jones made trips to Port Tobacco and other surrounding communities to keep track of what was going on. Cox and Jones were aware of the large rewards posted for the capture of Booth and Herold. Captain Williams, a detective at Port Tobacco in the old Brawner Hotel, was drinking with some men when Jones arrived. The captain said to Jones after he was introduced, "I will give one hundred thousand dollars to any one who will give me information that will lead to the capture of Booth." Jones replied, "That is a large sum of money and ought to get him if money can do it."[14] This was no small temptation. Jones could have paid off the large

SURRAT.　　　　　BOOTH.　　　　　HAROLD.

War Department, Washington, April 20, 1865,

 # $100,000 REWARD!

THE MURDERER

Of our late beloved President, Abraham Lincoln,

IS STILL AT LARGE.

$50,000 REWARD

Will be paid by this Department for his apprehension, in addition to any reward offered by Municipal Authorities or State Executives.

$25,000 REWARD

Will be paid for the apprehension of JOHN H. SURRATT, one of Booth's Accomplices.

$25,000 REWARD

Will be paid for the apprehension of David C. Harold, another of Booth's accomplices.

LIBERAL REWARDS will be paid for any information that shall conduce to the arrest of either of the above-named criminals, or their accomplices.

All persons harboring or secreting the said persons, or either of them, or aiding or assisting their concealment or escape, will be treated as accomplices in the murder of the President and the attempted assassination of the Secretary of State, and shall be subject to trial before a Military Commission and the punishment of DEATH.

Let the stain of innocent blood be removed from the land by the arrest and punishment of the murderers.

All good citizens are exhorted to aid public justice on this occasion. Every man should consider his own conscience charged with this solemn duty, and rest neither night nor day until it be accomplished.

EDWIN M. STANTON, Secretary of War.

DESCRIPTIONS.—BOOTH is Five Feet 7 or 8 inches high, slender build, high forehead, black hair, black eyes, and wears a heavy black moustache.

JOHN H. SURRAT is about 5 feet, 9 inches. Hair rather thin and dark; eyes rather light; no beard. Would weigh 145 or 150 pounds. Complexion rather pale and clear, with color in his cheeks. Wore light clothes of fine quality. Shoulders square; cheek bones rather prominent; chin narrow; ears projecting at the top; forehead rather low and square, but broad. Parts his hair on the right side; neck rather long. His lips are firmly set. A slim man.

DAVID C. HAROLD is five feet six inches high, hair dark, eyes dark, eyebrows rather heavy, full face, nose short, hand short and fleshy, feet small, instep high, round bodied, naturally quick and active, slightly closes his eyes when looking at a person.

NOTICE.—In addition to the above, State and other authorities have offered rewards amounting to almost one hundred thousand dollars, making an aggregate of about TWO HUNDRED THOUSAND DOLLARS.

mortgage on his farm, but he said nothing further and kept a sober face. He would not betray the trust that the fugitives had placed in him. His main reason for going there was to get information about the Union patrols on the river and the whereabouts of the cavalry, and there were a lot of both around at that time.

On the fifth day, Jones rode three miles over to Allen's Fresh, to hear the news there. He stopped at Colton's store, which was the place where things usually happened. Soon a group of cavalry rode up and the men came in for a drink. In a few minutes the leader of the group, John Walton of St. Mary's Co., came in and exclaimed, "Men, I have news that they have been sighted in St. Mary's." With that the men downed their drinks and dashed off toward St. Mary's to check things out. Jones waited in the store for a while so as not to arouse any suspicion, then slowly rose and said he must be on his way. He mounted his old horse and rode slowly out of the village. This was the break he had been waiting for. It was now or never. Out of the village he put his horse into a gallop toward the fugitives. It had been a cool week and had rained a great deal. It was just dusk and mist was rising from the swamp. The night was dark with no moon, a good night for the escape.[15]

By the time Jones reached the thicket it was very dark. By means of the signal whistle he entered the thicket where he found the fugitives anxious to follow his advice. Under his instruction, Booth rode on Jones's horse with Herold at the bridle. It was a risky trip to his place, "Huckleberry," above Pope's Creek a distance of three and a half miles. Part of the journey had to be on a main road past two houses, one of which had dogs that barked. Jones went cautiously ahead by himself and would give an "all clear" whistle when the other two with the horse were to advance. They carried out this procedure repeatedly and got by the two homes without rousing the dogs. Jones heaved a sigh of relief after they passed the houses and were leaving the main road without being recognized.

Jones had the fugitives wait outside his house in the darkness. He brought them food, which they ate while he had his supper with his children and his trusty black hired hand who had been faithfully fishing for shad in the river that day. Jones had a very close relationship with his hired hand, Henry Woodland. If Henry did not see the fugitives, he could reply to interrogation, which was bound to come, with a clear conscience.

Booth wanted to enter the house but Jones told him it was not a wise thing. After they were fed, the party continued the last mile down to the little stream in Dent's Meadow. Woodland told Jones at supper that he had caught shad and that the boat was hidden at the proper place in from the

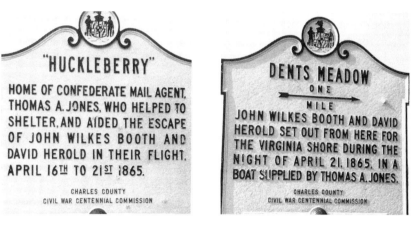

Markers for "Huckleberry" and Dents Meadow.

mouth of the stream. The horse was tied to a fence at the top of the steep river cliff. The last part of the journey was down the steep bluff, eighty to one hundred feet, with poor footing. The two helped the disabled Booth down the cliff and into the boat. Jones described Booth's leg as extremely swollen and painful.

When they got to the water's edge, Herold was placed in the beam of the boat to row and Booth in the stern with a paddle to steer. Jones set them a course on Booth's compass by candlelight, which, not allowing for tide, would take them across the Potomac River to Mathias Point, Virginia.

Their destination was Machodoc Creek and the home of Mrs. Elizabeth Quesenberry. The dark moonless night made the crossing safer from the standpoint of detection but more hazardous for navigation. The benefactor was given eighteen dollars for all his help and the boat.[16]

After his charges pushed off into the darkness that night of April 21, Jones did not seem them again nor did he tell his story until many years later, when the danger of his mission no longer was a hazard to his own safety.[17]

The two fugitives had serious problems in the little boat that dark night. They missed Mathias Point by a few degrees and, due to the sharp turn of the Potomac River to the west in that area, they ended up in Nanjemoy Creek, back in Maryland, on the far side of the river bend. This was after very strenuous effort. Herold, the oarsman, must have been worn out. They may have been carried upstream by an incoming tide. Trying to avoid Union patrols may have been the cause. Booth wrote in his diary about being chased by gunboats. (It is a little difficult to visualize a row boat being chased by a gunboat, but along shore it is possible.) Herold recognized the shoreline of Nanjemoy Creek and they made their way ashore to the farm of John J. Hughes near Nanjemoy Stores, Maryland, directly west of Pope's Creek, Maryland.[18] Here they hid on shore and were brought food but it was a risky hiding place. The countryside was being canvassed for them. On Saturday, April 22, they made their second attempt to cross the Potomac to Mathias Point. Although they had some difficulty finding Machodoc Creek and the home of Mrs. Elizabeth Quesenberry, they finally made it.[19]

The following article appeared in the Washington *National Intelligencer* on April 22, 1865, one week after the visit to Mudd's home:

THE WAR DEPARTMENT

The counties of Prince Georges, Charles and St. Mary's have during the whole war been noted for hostility to the Government and their protection of Rebel Blockade runners, Rebel spies and every species of public enemy; the murderers of the President harbored there before the murder and Booth fled in that direction. If he escapes, it will be owing to Rebel accomplices in that region. The military commander of the Department will surely take measures to bring Rebel sympathizers and accomplices to murder to sense their criminal conduct.

At the home of Mrs. Quesenberry they were met by Thomas Harbin,[20] who enlisted the help of William Bryant to give them transportation to Cleydael, the summer home of Dr. Richard Stuart on higher ground inland. This man had been a strong Confederate but realized that the cause was lost.

Booth and Herold reached Virginia on Sunday, April 23, and arrived at Stuart's home that evening. Here, to their surprise, they did not receive a warm welcome. They were given some food but were refused shelter and medical attention. They had to push on and finally spent the night in the cabin of a free black named Lucas. The next morning they paid Charles Lucas, the son, $20 to take them ten miles by wagon to Port Conway on the Rappahannock River.

The lack of expected hospitality from Stuart was taken as an insult by Booth. He tore a leaf from his diary and wrote the following note to his reluctant benefactor, which he sent, via Lucas, back to Stuart with $2.50. This note turned out to be a life saver for Stuart, who saved it and used it to prove to federal authorities that he had not harbored Booth.[21]

Dear Sir: Forgive me, but I have some pride. I hate to blame you for your want of hospitality; you know your own affairs. I was sick and tired, with a broken leg, in need of medical advice. I would not have turned a dog from my door in such a condition. However, you were kind enough to give me something to eat, for which I not only thank you, but on account of the reluctant manner in which it was bestowed, I feel bound to pay for it. It is not the substance, but the manner in which kindness is extended, that makes one happy in the acceptance thereof. The sauce in meat is ceremony; meeting was bare without it. Be kind enough to accept the enclosed two dollars and a half (though hard to spare) for what we have received.

Yours respectfully,

April 24, 1865   Stranger.

The fugitives arrived by wagon at Port Conway late in the morning of Monday, April 24. This was ten days after the shooting of Lincoln, and it was the same day that Mudd was taken from his home to Old Capitol Prison in the city of Washington.

There was delay at this point in getting across the river to Port Royal on the south bank. The tide was low, the wind was blowing,[22] and the ferry scow was on the far side of the river. The ferryman was fishing and waiting for calmer and deeper water. It was probably during this delay that Booth wrote his note to Stuart.

In a while three Confederate cavalrymen rode up on their horses. They also wanted to cross to Port Royal. They had just been released from Mosby's command, and were on their way to Bowling Green, about ten miles south, for recreation. Their names were Major Mortimer Ruggles, Lieutenant Absalom Bainbridge, and Captain Willie Jett. The latter was courting the young daughter of the proprietor of the Star Hotel in Bowling Green and Ruggles had relatives there.[23] They all waited together to cross to Port Royal.

During this wait, Herold approached the three soldiers, assuming they were heading south, and asked to join up with them. They were at first reluctant to have anything to do with the strangers but finally Herold confided that his companion, posing as a wounded Confederate soldier, had shot Lincoln. This startled the three young men. They finally joined up, however, and poled across the Rappahannock River together on the ferry scow. Because of Booth's incapacity, two of the five men rode double on the cavalry horses. There was difficulty finding a willing recipient who would take in the two "wounded Confederate" brothers named Boyd. They were then taken by horseback three miles farther down the road to the home of Richard H. Garrett. Here Booth was taken in and was allowed to rest. Herold went on to Bowling Green with the soldiers for recreation. He returned the next day and rejoined Booth. Garrett in the meanwhile was getting uneasy about his strange visitors in view of the amount of cavalry traffic on the road and asked them to take to the woods. In the evening they were allowed to return to the Garrett tobacco barn to spend the night.[24]

The Union forces were closing in. Back in Washington General La Fayette C. Baker, chief of the National Detective Service, had been placed in command of the effort to capture the fugitives, who had been free a week since the murder of the president. Word was telegraphed to the Baker

Marker for the Garrett place.

headquarters in Washington that two men had been seen embarking in a small boat south of Port Tobacco. A detachment of twenty-five cavalrymen under Lieutenant Edward P. Doherty and two trusted detectives, Colonel Everton I. Conger and Lieutenant Lewis Byron Baker, were dispatched by ship down the Potomac to Bell Plain, Virginia. This was considered the most likely escape route for the fugitives. The cavalry and the detectives arrived on the Virginia shore Monday night (April 24). They scoured the area, coming to the Rappahannock ferry about noon on Tuesday, about twenty-four hours after the fugitives had passed. The ferryman recognized the pictures of Booth and Herold and also knew the cavalryman named Jett. Jett was known to have a girl friend in Bowling Green. The cavalry then galloped to Bowling Green past Garrett's place, arriving at night. This was the cavalry traffic that alarmed Garrett, causing him to ask Booth to take to the woods. Jett was seized at gunpoint and made to ride back in the middle of the night, acting as guide for the troop. They arrived at the Garrett place about 2:00 A.M. Some of the things that happened next were recounted by Conger, who was in charge of the federal detachment to capture Booth and Herold. This is taken from testimony given before the military commission.

The testimony of Colonel Conger May 17th. For the Prosecution:

This starts with the pursuit of Booth and Herold after they crossed the Rappahannock River and were two or three miles below Port Royal, Virginia in Garrett's place, Tuesday April 25th, the day before the early morning capture and shooting of Booth. Willie S. Jett was one of the Confederate soldiers with whom Booth and Herold crossed the Rappahannock by ferry on Monday April 24th, before going to Garrett's place.

Judge-Advocate. Will you please take up the narrative of the pursuit at the point where you met with Willie Jett and state what occurred until the pursuit closed?

Witness: On the night of the capture, I found Jett in bed in a hotel in Bowling Green. I told him to get up; that I wanted him. He put on his pants and came out to me in the front part of the room. I said, "Where are the two men who came with you across the river?" He came up to me and said, "Can I see you alone?" I replied, "Yes, sir, you can." Lieutenant Baker and Lieutenant Doherty were with me. I asked them to go out of the room. When they were gone, he reached out his hand to me and said, "I know who you want, and I will tell you where they can be found." Said I, "That's what I want to know." He said, "They are on the road to Port Royal, about three miles this side of that, at Garrett's house. I will go there with you and show you where they are now, and you can get them." "You say they are on the road to Port Royal?" He replied, "Yes, sir." I said, "We just came from there." "You have come past them, we must go back."

He dressed, his horse was saddled and we rode back as a cavalry group, the eight or ten miles to Garrett's farm. Just before we got to the house, Jett, riding with me, said, "We are very near now." He and I rode together. I rode forward to find the gate and sent Lieutenant Baker to the back. I went back to the cavalry and we rode rapidly up to the house and the barn and stationed the men around both.

I went to the house and found Lieutenant Baker at the door, telling someone to strike a light and come out. The first individual we saw was an old man, whose name was said to be Garrett. I said to him, "Where are the two men who stopped here at your house?" "They have gone to the woods." I said to one of my men, "Bring a lariat rope and we will string this man up on one of those locust trees." One of his sons came to the door and said, "I will tell you where they are. My father is frightened. They are in the tobacco barn."

We then left the house immediately and went to the barn and stationed the remaining men there. As soon as I got there, I heard somebody walking around inside the dark barn. It was about two A.M. Another Garrett son arrived. Lieutenant Baker said to him, "You know these men, go in and get their arms." He did but came back out very soon alone and said, "This man says, 'Damn you, you have betrayed me and threatened to shoot me.' He reached for his gun." We then told the men inside they must pass out their arms and come out or we would fire the barn in five minutes.

I told one of the Garretts to pile brush against the side of the barn. There was talk in the barn between the two men. After a while Booth said, "There's a man in here who wants to come out." Lieutenant Baker said, "Tell him to hand out his arms." There was conversation and I heard Booth say to the other man, "You damned coward, go on out." Herold came to the door of the barn and said, "Let me out. I have no arms." Lieutenant Baker said, "This man carried a carbine and he must hand it out." Booth said, "The arms are mine and I have them. He has no arms." I said to Lieutenant Baker, "Never mind the arms, if we can get one man out, let's do it." The door was opened and he put out his hands. Lieutenant Baker took hold of him, pulled him out and passed him to the rear.

I went around the corner of the barn, pulled some hay out, twisted up about six inches and set it on fire. I then tossed it back on top of the hay in the barn through a crack in the siding. It blazed up immediately. We could then see Booth. When I first got a glimpse of him, he stood with his back partly toward me. He turned toward the door. He had a carbine in his hands and looked around to see who set the fire and then to see if he could put it out. It was blazing quite high. He turned and started for the door. I ran back toward the barn door and when about half way back, there was a pistol shot.

When I entered the barn Lieutenant Baker was already there. I said, "He shot himself." Lieutenant Baker said, "No, he did not." He was quite earnest about it. We looked at the side of his head and his neck. Blood was coming from a wound on the right side of his neck. We then carried him outside under the locust trees. I went to the barn to see if it could be saved, but it was too late. The barn burned to the ground. When I returned to Booth who looked as though he was dead, he revived slightly and said, "Tell mother I died for my country." He was then carried to the porch of the house and laid on an old straw bed.

After this he revived even more and could talk in a whisper. I took what things were in his pockets and tied them up in a piece of paper. These consisted of a knife, pair of pistols, belt, holster, file, pocket compass, spur, pipe, cartridges, and bills of exchange. The witness identified these.[25]

Strangely, there was no mention of a diary among Booth's effects. One had been reported in the newspapers. This was completely overlooked by the commission and by the defense for some reason. The diary and its contents would have brought up the plot to kidnap Lincoln and would have been helpful in the defense of Mudd. For some reason it was overlooked by Ewing. He and Stone apparently were ignorant of its existence. Stanton, convinced at that time of the involvement of Confederate leaders, may have withheld it.

Later, in Surratt's trial in 1867, this subject came up. The diary had been given to the secretary of war and was not produced as evidence in 1865.

Conger, who was one of the first into the burning tobacco barn along with Baker, a relative of General L. C. Baker, head of the National Detective Service, immediately after the pistol shot was fired thought at first that Booth had shot himself. This was never completely resolved but it is very unlikely that Booth would have shot himself in the neck instead of the head if he did attempt to end his own life. Testimony is conflicting. Some of this conflict possibly occurred due to testimony being slanted because large sums of money had been offered for the capture of Booth. Here, as in other parts of Mudd's trial, there were accusations that some witnesses perjured themselves for personal gain.

There were ill feeling and controversy among possible recipients about rewards and who was entitled to them. The final amounts awarded by Congress were as follows:

General Baker	$ 3,750.00
Colonel Conger	15,000.00
Lieutenant Doherty	5,250.00
Lieutenant Baker	3,000.00
Sergeant Corbett and each of the other cavalrymen	1,653.48 each[26]

The testimony of Willie Jett is also given here because of its relevance.[27]

Willie S. Jett
Prosecution May 17

I was formerly a member of the Ninth Virginia Cavalry. More recently, I was stationed in Caroline County, Virginia as commissary agent of the Confederate States Government. I was on my way from Fauquier County (where I had been with Mosby's command) to Caroline County, Virginia, in company with Lieutenant Ruggles and a young man named Bainbridge. At Port Conway, on the Rappahannock, I saw a wagon down on the wharf, at the ferry, on the Monday week after the assassination of President Lincoln. A young man got out of it, came toward us, and asked us what command we belonged to. We were in Confederate uniform. Lieutenant Ruggles said, "We belong to Mosby's command." He then said, "Can I ask where you are going?" I spoke then, and replied, "That's a secret, where we are going." After this we went back on the wharf and a man with a crutch got out of the wagon. One of us asked him what command he belonged to, and he replied, "To A. P. Hill's Corps." Herold told us their name was Boyd; that his brother was wounded below Petersburg, and asked if we would take him out of the lines. We did not tell him where we were going. Herold asked us to go and take a drink, but we declined. We then rode up to the house there, and having tied our horses, we all sat down. After we had talked a short time, Herold touched me on the shoulder and said he wanted to speak to me; he carried me down to the wharf and said, "I suppose you are raising a command to go South?" and added that he would like to go along with us. At length I said, "I cannot go with any man that I don't know anything about." He seemed very much agitated, and then remarked, "We are the assassinators of the President." I was so confounded that I did not make any reply that I remember. Lieutenant Ruggles was very near, watering his horse. I called to him and he came over and either Herold or myself remarked to Lieutenant Ruggles that they were the assassinators of the President. Booth then came up and Herold introduced him to us. Herold passed himself off to us first as Boyd, and said he wanted to pass under that name. He afterward told us his true name. Booth kept the same name, Boyd. Booth, I remember, had on his hand "J. W. B." We went back to the house and sat down on the steps. Then we went across the river. Booth rode Ruggles' horse. Herold was walking. We then got on the other side of the river, before they got out of the boat. I got on my horse and rode up to Port Royal, went into a house and talked to a lady. I asked her if she could take a wounded Confederate soldier, just as he had represented himself to me. She at first consented and then said she could not. I walked across the street to Mr. Cattlitt's, but he was not home. We then went down the road to Mr. Garrett's, and there we left Booth. Herold and all of us went on up the road, then to within a few miles of Bowling Green. Bainbridge and Herold went to Mrs. Clark's and Ruggles and myself to Bowling Green. The next day Herold came to Bowling Green, spent the day, had dinner, and left in the evening, and that was the last I saw of him, except the night they were caught, when I went down there; I saw him the next morning in the custody of the officers. I recognize the prisoner Herold as the man I saw with Booth.

Cross-examination by Mr. Stone

Herold said he wanted us to help in getting Booth farther South, but we had no facilities; and he seemed a good deal disappointed after we made known our real object, that we were going on a visit. Booth was not present when Herold told me they were the assassinators of the President; when he came up, he said he would not have told, that he did not intend telling. Herold did not appear very self-possessed. His voice trembled and he was a good deal agitated. His language was, "We are the assassinators of the President," and then, pointing back to where Booth was standing, he said, "Yonder is J. Wilkes Booth, the man who killed the President," or he may have said "Lincoln." I have never taken the oath of allegiance, but am perfectly willing to take it.

Captain (formerly Lieutenant) Edward Doherty had command of the Sixteenth New York Cavalry detachment that tracked down Booth and Herold. He also testified how the capture of Herold was carried out and stated that it was he who pulled Herold out of the barn. The following is some of his testimony:

I said to him as I was pulling him out of the barn, "Have you any weapons at all upon you?" He said, "Nothing but this," pulling out of his pocket a piece of map of Virginia. I then put my revolver under my arm and ran my hands down him to see if he had any arms and he had none. Just at this time the shot was fired and the door thrown open, and I dragged Herold back into the barn with me. Booth had fallen on his back. The soldiers and two detectives there carried Booth out. I kept charge of Herold; and when I got him back outside he said, "Let me go. I will not leave." I said, "No sir." Said he to me, "Who was that that was shot in the barn? He told me his name was Boyd." Said I, "It was Booth and you know it." He said again that he did not know it was Booth.

I then took Herold and tied his hands to a tree about two yards from where Booth's body had been carried on the veranda of the house and kept him there until we were ready to return. Booth in the mean time died, and I sewed him up in a blanket. Previous to this I had sent some of the cavalry for a doctor. We got a negro with a wagon who lived a mile away. We put the body on the wagon and all started back with Herold for Belle Plain.

Belle Plain was the port on the Potomac River. From here it was a ship ride up the Potomac River to Washington. On arrival back at the navy yard in Washington, Booth's body was laid on the deck of the monitor *Montauk,* one of the monitors at anchor, where the other prisoners were confined. Herold was delivered below deck. The body of Booth was then examined and identified by Surgeon-General J. K. Barnes. He testified at the trial on May 20 as follows:

> I examined the body of J. Wilkes Booth after his death, when he was returned to this city. He had a scar upon the large muscle of the left side of his neck, three inches below the ear, occasioned by an operation performed by Dr. May of this city for the removal of a tumor some months previous to Booth's death. It looked like the scar of a burn instead of an incision, which Dr. May explained by the fact that the wound was torn open on the stage when nearly well.

Following identification of the body and its pathological examination, it was secretly buried in the dirt floor of a cell in the Old Arsenal Penitentiary.

It is interesting to speculate what would have happened if Booth had been captured alive and would have been brought to trial. The War Department and the enraged nation would have been able to center their attention on him rather than on the relatively innocent people he had cleverly drawn into his depraved scheme.

The wrath of the nation would have been centered on him where it rightfully belonged rather on his acquaintances whom he did not keep posted on the change of his plans. Atzerodt, for example, said in his confession that he did not know of his actual assignment until eight P.M. on the evening of the assassination. He had been recruited by Surratt because he was a boatman from Port Tobacco and was expert in crossing the Potomac to Virginia. He fit into the original scheme of capture, kidnap, and hold for ransom, for the return of Confederate prisoners to the South. He objected in vain when told he was to shoot Vice President Johnson. He did not sign up for that he told Booth. Booth told him it was too late to back out.

Booth was nearly captured at the theater. Rathbone grappled with him but was slashed with a dagger and could not restrain him.

Colonel Joseph B. Stewart, an officer in the Union Army seated in the audience, rushed across stage and nearly caught the bridle of Booth's horse in the alley behind the theater according to his testimony given at the trial. He probably would have accomplished this if a door had not been slammed in his face as he rushed through the unfamiliar back stage passageways. Last of all, could Sergeant Boston Corbett, who shot Booth in Garrett's tobacco barn, have withheld his fire?

Here first is the testimony of Joseph B. Stewart.[28]

Questioning by the Judge-Advocate:

Q. State to the Court whether or not you were at Ford's Theater on the night of the assassination of the President.

A. I was.

Q. State whether or not you saw the assassin leap from the President's box upon the stage.

A. I did.

Q. Did you follow him? State the circumstances of your pursuit.

A. I did follow him. I was sitting in the front seat of the orchestra, on the right hand side. There are two aisles in the orchestra. My seat was the one forming the corner seat on the left hand side of the right hand aisle, which would bring me immediately next to the music stand. The report of the pistol, which was evidently a charged pistol—a sharp report—startled me. I was talking at the moment to my sister, who sat by me, my head leaning to the left. I glanced still farther left and immediately back to the stage; and at the same time an exclamation was made and simultaneously a man leaped from the President's box, alighting on the stage, exclaiming, as he came out, some words which I understood.

He came down with his back slightly to the audience but rising and turning, his face came in full view. At the same instant, I rose up and attempted to leap on the stage directly from where I sat. My foot slipped from the rail. My eye, at the same time, discovered the distance; and, without stopping my motion at all, I turned and made two or three steps on the railing and jumped on the stage to the right of the foot lights from where I sat; keeping my attention all the time, after selecting my course, upon the man who was crossing the stage and who had just jumped from the President's box. I perceived that he disappeared at the same instant around the left hand stage entrance. Being on stage, I crossed it as quick as possible. I had never been on stage and knew nothing about the condition of the building or the means of exit; but I supposed the person was getting out and I followed the direction he took. I exclaimed, "Stop that man!" three times.

The last time and when I passed the length of the stage and turned to the right and when, I suppose, within a distance of from twenty to twenty-five feet from the door, it slammed decidedly—came to, closed. I was going just as fast as I could and got to the door, of course, very quickly. Coming against the door, I touched it first on the side where it did not open. I then caught hold of the door at the proper point, opened it and passed out.

The last time that I exclaimed, "Stop that man!" someone said, "He's getting on a horse"; and at the door, almost as soon as the words reached my ears, I heard the tramping of a horse. On opening the door after the balk at the door which prevented me from opening it at first, I perceived a man mounting a horse.

He was at that instant rather imperfectly mounted. The moon was just beginning to rise and I could see a little elevated better than I could immediately down on the ground. The horse was moving in a quick, agitated motion as a horse will do if prematurely spurred in mounting, with the rein drawn a little to one side; and, for a moment, the horse described a kind of circle from the right to the left. I ran in the direction where the horse was heading and when within eight or ten feet of the head of the horse the rider brought him around again left to right. I crossed in the same direction aiming at the rein and was now on the right flank of the horse. Again he backed to the right hand side of the alley, brought the horse forward and spurred him, the rider crouching down over the pommel of the saddle. The horse went forward then and swept to the left towards F Street.

Stewart, according to his testimony, thought he would have caught the bridle of the horse if he had not been delayed in his pursuit by the slammed door. A small boy called "Peanuts," who had been holding the horse, was knocked to the ground during this scuffle. Ned Spangler, a stage hand at Ford's Theater and a friend of Booth's, had arranged to have "Peanuts" hold Booth's horse at the rear entrance of the theater. There was question also that he may have slammed the door that delayed Stewart. Spangler received a six-year sentence at hard labor and spent time on Dry Tortugas with Mudd.

Booth escaped from the theater but it was close according to Stewart. If his escape had been prevented or altered, Mudd might have been spared his ordeal completely.

Stewart's testimony went unchallenged until the publication of Wiechmann's book in 1975, 110 years after the assassination.[29] A. C. Richards, the chief of police for Washington, was in the audience upstairs in the dress circle at the time Lincoln was shot. When Wiechmann was preparing the manuscript of his book, he wrote to Richards. Richards wrote several letters back to Wiechmann in regard to the manuscript. On June 10, 1898, he wrote the following:

> When I heard the shot and saw someone jump onto the stage I thought possibly some one was shot in the President's box. I rushed down stairs and through the crowd at the orchestra circle and onto the stage. I knew and recognized Stewart already there and no other person then in sight on the stage or among the curtains. I must have been upon the stage within two minutes from the time the shot was heard. Stewart had had no time to make any explorations of the stage when I reached him. Together we searched among the scenery and finally found the door from the stage leading into the alley open. It was quite dark both among the scenery on the stage and in the alley. As we stepped out into the alley, I saw a man (Peanut John I think) standing there and heard the rattling of a horse's feet moving rapidly down the alley but not in sight. The man found there on demand explained that the footsteps of the horse we heard were those of the one he had been holding for a man whom he claimed he did not know and said that the man had had some difficulty in mounting his horse and so on. No such scene as described as part of Stewart's testimony occurred there. The statement is apocryphal and imaginary. The gyrations

Stewart describes as having participated in could not have taken place as there was no horse and rider then there and in sight.[30]

Next is the testimony of Sergeant Thomas P. ("Boston") Corbett.

The Judge-Advocate:

Q. Lieutenant Colonel Conger has detailed to the Court the circumstances connected with the pursuit and capture and killing of Booth, in which, I believe, you were engaged. I will ask you what part you took, not in the pursuit, but in the capture and killing of Booth, taking up the narrative at the point when you arrived at the house.

A. When we rode up to the house, my commanding officer, Lieutenant Doherty, as we were standing in the road, rode up to me and told me that Booth was in that house saying, "I want you to deploy the men right and left around the house, and see that no one escapes." That was done: the men were deployed around the house. After making inquiries at the house it was found that Booth was not in the house, but in the barn.

A guard was then left upon the house, and the main portion of the men thrown around the barn, closely investing it with orders to allow no one to escape, but previously being cautioned to see that our arms were in readiness for use. After being ordered to surrender and told that the barn would be fired in five minutes if he did not do so, Booth made many replies. In the first place, he wanted to know who we took him for. He said that his leg was broken and what did we want with him? He was told that it made no difference.

His name was not mentioned at all in the whole affair; not giving them satisfaction to know whether we knew who they were or not, any further than he was told that they must surrender, and give themselves up as prisoners. He received no satisfaction but was told that he must surrender unconditionally, or else the barn would be fired. The parley lasted much longer than the time first set; probably, I should think a full half-hour. It was time for many words to and fro.

He was positively declaring that he would not surrender. At one time he made the remark, "Well my brave boys, you can prepare a stretcher for me" and at another time, "Well, captain, make quick work of it. Shoot me through the heart!" Or words to that effect. I knew that he was perfectly desperate and did not expect that he would surrender. After a while, we heard the whispering of another person—although he (Booth) had previously declared that there was but one there, himself—who proved to be the prisoner Herold. Although we could not distinguish the words, his object seemed to be to persuade Booth to surrender.

After hearing him a while, he sang out, "Certainly!" Seeming to disdain to do it himself. He said, "Captain, there is a man in here who wants to surrender mighty bad." Then Booth said, "Oh, go out and save yourself, my boy, if you can," and then he said, "I declare before my Maker that this man here is innocent of any crime whatsoever," seeming willing to take all the blame on himself, and trying to clear Herold.

They were then told that if both would not surrender, the surrender of one would be accepted and he was told to hand out his arms. Booth declared the arms all belonged to him and that the other man was unarmed. Herold was finally taken out without arms. Immediately after Herold was taken out, the detective, Mr. Conger, came from that side of the barn where he had been taken out, around to the side where I was and passing me, set fire to the hay through one of the cracks of the boards, at the end of the same side of the barn where I was, a little to my right. I had previously said to Mr. Conger, though, and also to my commanding officer, that the position in which I stood left me in front of a large crack—you might put your hand through it and I knew that Booth could distinguish me and others through these cracks in the barn and could pick us off if he chose to do so. In fact, he made a remark to that effect at one time. Said he, "Captain, I could have picked off three or four of your men already if I wished to do so. Draw your men off fifty yards and I will come out." When the fire was first lit, which was almost immediately after Herold was taken out of the barn, as the flames rose, he was seen. We could then distinguish him, apparently, I think, about the middle of the barn, turning towards the fire, either to put it out or else shoot the one who started it, I did not know which. He was then coming right towards me, a little to my right—a full front breast view.

I could have shot him then much easier than the time I afterwards did. As long as he was making no demonstration to hurt any one, I did not shoot him but kept my eyes on him steadily.

Finding the fire gaining upon him, he turned to the other side of the barn and went towards where the door was. As he got there, I saw him make a movement towards the floor. My mind was upon him attentively to see that he did no harm. When I became impressed that it was time, I shot him. I took steady aim on my arm and shot him through a large crack in the barn. He died about two or three hours after he was shot, about seven o'clock in the morning.[31]

From the above testimony, it is obvious that the situation at Garrett's barn was a dangerous one. The officers had attempted to reason with Booth for more than a half-hour. The barn was on fire and the man was desperate. He refused to surrender. It is likely he may have killed someone as his last diabolical act. The sergeant cannot be criticized for what he did.

It was never proven beyond doubt that the bullet that shattered Booth's neck came from Corbett's pistol. No record of a comparison of the bullet or the caliber of that taken from Booth's neck to those in Corbett's possession is known.

6
Edwin McMasters Stanton

Secretary of War Edwin Stanton set the stage for the harsh treatment of the conspirators in Lincoln's assassination. He seems to have been motivated by a desire to bring the conspirators to instant justice and somehow avenge the great wrong that had been done. He took charge of things immediately after Lincoln was shot. He set up headquarters in the Peterson house across the street from Ford's Theater that night and served there until Vice President Johnson was sworn in Saturday morning at the Kirkwood Hotel. Stanton doubtless would have continued to dominate things longer but Johnson soon became assertive.

Stanton was a brusk, mean, high-strung man. He had been a tireless administrator, serving as the easy-going Lincoln's hatchet man. He had served his country very well during the prosecution of the war. He had a bearish, ungracious manner, especially to those below him. He sometimes made people stand at his desk several minutes before looking up to recognize them. He was patronizing and sometimes obsequious to those above.[1] He was rude to Lincoln during the McCormick reaper trial in Cincinnati in the late 1850s prior to Lincoln's rise to political prominence. The McCormick reaper trial, first convened in Chicago and later transferred to Cincinnati, commanded great attention. Lincoln, one of the leading attorneys in Illinois, was called on to help with the defense of John H. Manny, who was being sued by McCormick for infringement of his reaper patent. The defense attorneys were George Harding, Edward M. Stanton, Peter H. Watson, and Abraham Lincoln.[2]

When Stanton first met Lincoln, he was not impressed with Lincoln's lanky, awkward appearance and the fact that his coat showed perspiration stains beneath the armpits. He and his high-powered associates ignored Lincoln and did not ask him to give his arguments. They even shunned him at lunch and at the hotel. They did not ask him to join their group as was the usual custom for attorneys assigned to the same case. The case was won for Manny and Lincoln received a $2,000 fee, one of his largest. This was the first meeting of Lincoln and Stanton. Later Lincoln and Stanton developed a strong friendship and respect for each other.

53

Stanton began his career as an attorney in Steubenville, Ohio, after graduating from Kenyon College. He entered politics and worked his way to Washington by way of Pittsburgh. He was attorney general in the latter part of the Buchanan administration during the bleak days of January–February 1861. He was a special counsel during Cameron's tenure as secretary of war in the early Lincoln cabinet and was advanced to secretary on January 20, 1862. Lincoln had the ability to make good personal choices when they were needed, and his choice of Stanton at that time falls into that category. The war effort was larger than anything previously undertaken by the War Department, and a person with great energy and organizational ability was needed.

Stanton took charge with vigor. His unbounding energy and tough methods served to get things done when they needed to be done. He was a great impetus to the successful Union war effort, especially during the latter portion of it. His dispatch of 23,000 men to support General Rosecrans at Chattanooga has been described as spectacular. His actions greatly aided the speedy final conclusion of the conflict.[3]

Stanton acted with an iron hand in the emergency created by the sudden death of Lincoln. He thought the plot to overthrow the Union government was directed from Richmond and acted accordingly. The persons named in the charges presented at the trial bear this out. Testimony heard at the trial indicates that the Confederate headquarters in both Montreal and Richmond knew about the plot. How deeply they were involved is questionable. Booth had met with Sanders in Canada so he knew of the plot to capture with certainty.

The accusations against the Southern leaders made at the time of the military trial were most unfortunate for Mudd and the other defendants. This elevated them from their peripheral position to a position of equal status with the Confederate government.

Kidnapping is no small crime. Why was the plot to capture Lincoln not brought up at the military trial? This is a question that has not been answered.

Stanton wanted to punish the perpetrators of the crime as quickly as possible and in so doing left out many who had a part in it.

7
The Mudd Family

According to family legend, three brothers by the name of Mudd came to America among the original group of immigrants who arrived on the *Ark* and the *Dove* in 1634 and settled at what is now St. Mary's, Maryland, the first official English settlement.[1] There is evidence that Thomas Mudd arrived in 1665, thirty-one years later. Richard D. Mudd, in *The Mudd Family in the United States,* claims Thomas Mudd (1647–1697) of Virginia and Maryland as the earliest family immigrant to Maryland.

From here on the story of the Mudds in America is definite and prolific. They took part in the development of Maryland in its early struggles for existence and statehood. They were landowners, farmers, doctors, and lawyers, good solid citizens. They pushed westward into Kentucky when the latter was an extension of Virginia and on to the Pacific Coast. They are said to have become prevalent on the West as well as the East Coast of America. There is still a hardy group in Charles County, Maryland, where some of them continue to own land that has been in Mudd possession for nearly three centuries.[2] Richard Mudd describes them as "generally a home loving people. Their affection has been well organized; they love God; they love themselves and their neighbors. They built homes, churches, civic and social institutions." He goes on to say that generally they are tolerant and individually do not tend to force their opinions on others.[3]

The ancestors of the vast majority of the Mudds in America came from England. Some came from Suffolk, near Ipswich, others from Yorkshire. There was a high concentration of Mudds in Yorkshire, England, in the 1890s near North and East Ridings. Other Mudds originated in Germany and Denmark but these were fewer in number.[4]

Henry Lowe Mudd (1798–1877), the father of Samuel A. Mudd, was the sixth generation of his family born in the New World. He was born in Bryantown, Maryland, during the second year of the presidential term of John Adams, second president of the United States, and lived to be seventy-nine years old. His death occurred eight years after Mudd returned from prison. Sarah Ann Reeves-Mudd, Mudd's mother, died on December

31, 1868, three months before his return. Both parents were greatly shaken by and suffered a great deal from what happened to their son.

Henry Lowe Mudd married Sarah Ann Reeves when he was twenty-nine years old. They had seven children. Samuel was their third. He had one younger two older and brothers. One of the older boys died in childhood, leaving just three boys in the family when war broke out in 1861. During the course of the war, the three sons became of military age. James and Henry were drafted for the Union Army, but their family paid for substitutes for them. Samuel, being a doctor, was exempt from service.[5] When he later married Sarah Frances Dyer, he called her "Frank" to avoid confusion with his sister Frances.

Nettie Mudd describes her great-grandfather as a wealthy planter and owner of more than a hundred slaves. She also speaks of the kindness with which these people were treated. Gatherings of the entire clan were frequently held in the evenings, at which time the slaves would gather for song-fests. Her father frequently played the violin on these occasions, and there were dancing and singing. Mudd had studied music while away at school and was a good violin player.[6]

8
Samuel Alexander Mudd

Samuel Alexander Mudd was born at Oak Hill Farm, the plantation home of his father four miles north of Bryantown, Maryland, on December 20, 1833. He was the third child born to Henry Lowe Mudd and Sarah Ann Reeves.[1]

Mudd's childhood was spent on Oak Hill Farm. The farm was located near a small stream named Sekiah, just a half-mile from what later became Mudd's land. In fact, Mudd's farm was originally part of his father's property. The land sloped upward from the stream, leading to the prominent high area where the house was located among a cluster of oak trees.

When he was seven years old, Mudd went to public school, where he attended for two years. His father then engaged a teacher, Miss Peterson, for Mudd and his sisters and classes were held in the north wing of his home.[2] The second-floor chapel above the classroom reflected the religious nature of the family and the fact that public Catholic worship had been forbidden in past times.

At age fourteen Mudd was sent to St. Johns College in Frederick, Maryland, where he studied for two years. Following this he attended Georgetown College in the District of Columbia, where he finished his undergraduate college education. While there he mastered in languages and music. He became proficient in Greek, Latin, and French, and became an accomplished musician on the violin, piano, and flute.[3]

Mudd developed his interest in medicine at this point. He became an apprentice to his second cousin, Dr. George Mudd, who practiced in Bryantown. He probably was under the tutelage of Dr. George Mudd for several years since this was the accepted method of instruction at that time.

The period of apprenticeship in Ohio at that time was three years, and requirements in Maryland were probably similar.[4] Following this, two years of successful college instruction qualified the candidate for the M.D. degree. It was possible in some states to practice medicine with a certificate only, issued by the preceptor, but this did not convey a medical degree.

Mudd took the medical courses offered at the Baltimore Medical College (now the University of Maryland) and received a medical degree from

Dr. Samuel Alexander Mudd after his release from prison (courtesy of Dr. Richard Dyer Mudd).

that institution in 1856. During his last year at the medical college he practiced in the hospital of that institution. This could have been an internship or fellowship, which constituted advanced training in those days. For this he received a certificate of merit on completion of his assignment. Mudd was well trained medically when he left Baltimore Medical College, proficient in foreign languages and able to play several musical instruments.

Mudd returned home with his new medical degree and set up practice near his second cousin. They probably shared medical calls.

While at St. John's College in Frederick, Maryland, Mudd had become closely attached to a childhood friend, Sarah Frances Dyer, who was attending Visitation Convent in that city. They had kept in touch with each other during college and medical school days and eventually became engaged. Frances was a lovely girl and they were very fond of each other. Mudd called her "Frank."

Wedding bells rang on Thanksgiving Day, November 26, 1857, at the Dyer home, which was not far from Oak Hill. The newlyweds lived in the Dyer household the first two years of their marriage with Jere Dyer, a bachelor brother of Frances. Following this or during this time, with the help of his father, Mudd secured the property known as Rock Hill Farm. This property was located on the Bryantown road, four and one-half miles north of Bryantown and one-half mile north of Oak Hill. The house was originally built about 1830.[5]

This farm was to be the Mudd home during all the subsequent troubled times that followed. The family of nine children were all born here. Four were born before Mudd's incarceration, and five after his return home.

After Mudd's marriage to Frances in 1857, a family was soon on the way. In 1858 a son, Andrew, was born. The year after that a daughter, Lillian, was born, followed by Thomas Dyer Mudd in 1861 (through whom Richard Dyer Mudd of Saginaw, Michigan, became the grandson of Samuel A. Mudd). In January 1864, Samuel Alexander II was born, making him just fifteen months old when tragedy struck.

The 1850s and 1860s, just prior to the War Between the States, were very unsettled times in the United States. Issues of slavery and states' rights caused great dissension throughout the North and South. The economy of the South—the cotton industry and, in Maryland, particularly the tobacco industry—had been built around slave labor. How, with the rising awareness of the injustice of slavery, the practice could be stopped without economic ruin to the Southern states was the problem. Economic considerations are exceedingly strong at any time. They were not insignificant in leading many colonists to favor the break from England seventy-five years earlier.

Secession seemed imminent since one of the tenets of the Bill of Rights indicated that government must have the consent of its people. Maryland teetered on secession. This sentiment was particularly strong in southern Maryland and the city of Baltimore. The state probably would have seceded if it were not for its proximity to Washington, strong political leadership by Lincoln, and, soon, the presence of Union soldiers. Although Maryland did not secede, it became an extreme hotbed of Confederate sympathy and intrigue.

Mudd, age thirty in the fall of 1864, eight years out of medical school, was developing his practice and directing the work on his tobacco farm. He had four young children, a lovely wife, and eleven slaves. His life was before him. He could be a gentleman farmer like his father and his wife's father. But could he?

Let us now turn to a letter written by Mudd on January 13, 1862, which reveals something of his character and convictions at that time and how he reacted to a most exasperating experience.[6]

Mudd wrote this letter to the New York publisher of the *Review*, a publication that dealt with the issues of the day. Mudd had been a subscriber to this journal but had objected to certain things published in it and had cancelled his subscription in 1859. In spite of his cancellation, the journal continued to come in the mail. This occurred even after a second and third attempt to cancel it were made.

In his letter he states that he had been receiving bills from the New York publisher in spite of the fact he had cancelled his subscription in 1859. He says he will again repeat what had transpired and that he had not been a subscriber since 1859. In that year he had cancelled his subscription through his agent, Rev. Father Vizinanzi. When the first volume of 1860 was received, he called Father Vizinanzi, who reassured him that the cancellation had been made. He then considered it a gratuity or an inducement to further subscription until another bill was received from the publisher. He immediately notified the company that he was no longer a subscriber and again ordered cancellation. The journal continued to come and the company was again notified. He had refused to take many of the issues from the post office and offered to have them returned at the publisher's expense. He states that this is the third time that he has been troubled with the account and he hopes that the company will not bother him again unless they can show clearly that he is indebted to them.

"It is hard to kiss the hand that smites. Through you, our country, wonder of the world, has received an irreparable injury." Mudd writes that the publication is given to sectionalism and fears that it is rendering itself unpopular in the North.

> The present Civil War now raging, was not brought about entirely by fear on the part of the South, that their property in slaves was endangered, but more by an unwillingness to yield up rights guaranteed by the Constitution.

The South could not give up States Rights—The North found slavery unprofitable, therefore, abolished it, without any interference by the South—and all we asked is the exercise of the same power and right.... A majority of the people of the North believe slavery to be sinful, thereby they attempt to force down our throats, their religious conviction, which is Anti-Catholic and uncharitable. The North on account of its pride, short-sightedness and philanthropy, has caused the destruction of one of the most glorious nations upon the face of the earth.... One thing seems certain to us all, the Union can never be restored by war.

Mudd goes on to say that the people of the South are differently constituted from those of the North, attributable to education and climate. They are more sensitive, he states, and would sooner run the risk of death than live with an injured reputation. As an example of this, one seldom hears of a duel in the North, where parties are challenged to mortal combat to settle their grievances, but find instead a recourse to law. He also states that those of the South have the virtues of forbearance, endurance, and magnanimity. The letter continues on for several pages. Mudd talks of Yankees and their attitude toward the Bible. Then, addressing the publisher of the *Review*, he writes, "You and Bishop Hughes have put yourselves upon the same footing as the rest of the demagogues and preachers of your Section such as Beecher, Cheeves, Smith, Phillips."

Finally, he writes, "You will please excuse this hasty and roughly scribbled epistle—it was not my intention to rob you of that jewel—honesty of intention. Slavery being a State institution recognized by every administration and confirmed by many acts of Congress, can only be abrogated by State will.... The South has stood a high protective tariff for many years without a murmur (except S. Carolina) to support manufacturing interests in the North. Christ our Saviour found slavery at his coming and made no command against its practice." Mudd ends by writing that he would like to give some practical illustrations of the two systems of labor from a medical, religious, and temporal point of view but that he must conclude by wishing the publisher prosperity in all undertakings when directed for the honor and glory of God.

This long letter, only portions of which are given here, portrays the convictions, attitudes, and opinions of Dr. Mudd and many of those in the South in that era—opinions and attitudes quite different from those held in the North. It was these differences that divided the two sections of the country. It leaves no doubt about Mudd's convictions at that time. Later, in 1864, he took the oath of allegiance to the Union and voted for a Union candidate.

Lincoln issued the Emancipation Proclamation on January 1, 1863, about a year later. After the proclamation, Mudd no longer had a workforce of slaves on his tobacco farm.

Into this setting rode a handsome young actor, nearly five years younger than Mudd, one Sunday morning in November 1864. Through a neighbor and good friend, Dr. Queen, Mudd met Booth at St. Mary's Church at Bryantown on that Sunday morning. He was introduced by J. C. Thompson, Queen's son-in-law. We do not know precisely what conversation they had but they talked together and Mudd showed Booth around the countryside that afternoon, or sometime later, when he came to his place. Booth ended up spending the night at Mudd's home either on this visit or a second one on December 22, according to the testimony of J. C. Thompson given at the military trial on May 26.[7] It was said that Booth was looking for land to purchase in Lower Maryland and for riding horses. The former was only a coverup for the real plan that Booth had in mind. Things were not going well for the Confederacy. The army needed manpower. Booth was making plans to kidnap Lincoln, take him to Richmond, and there hold him for ransom in exchange for Confederate prisoners. Mudd may have been considering selling land at this time and spending more time at his profession in another location. For Booth, contemplated land transactions were only a coverup for his kidnap scheme. He was studying the roads, buying some horses, meeting trustworthy people, and enlisting help.

Mudd did not sell him any land but arranged for him to buy a horse from his neighbor. The horse was blind in one eye, but fast, which pleased Booth.

Later, during Mudd's military trial, the testimony of Wiechmann brought out the fact that Mudd had been with Booth in Washington in December 1864 and that Mudd introduced Booth to Surratt, who was then a Confederate agent. This was a bomb shell when brought out at the trial. Mudd had not mentioned it previously. It was headline news across the country. Mudd had met Booth at least twice before Booth came to his farm the morning of April 15. Later, Thomas H. Harbin, another Confederate agent, would claim that he also was introduced to Booth by Mudd at the Bryantown Hotel in December 1864.

Let us now go back to Mudd and what transpired after he treated Booth on Saturday, April 15. He did not go to the authorities immediately after the suspicious strangers left. He decided to sleep on his problem. It was very complicated. In southern Maryland there was much pro–Confederate feeling, which Mudd did not wish to antagonize.

Next morning he went to Saint Mary's Church below Bryantown, the Catholic Church that he sometimes attended. He talked to his second cousin, Dr. George Mudd, his former mentor and a good Union man. He gave him the full story.

George thought the authorities should be notified. He had talked with Lieutenant Dana, head of the troops in Bryantown, and felt he knew him slightly because of this. Since Mudd had some hesitancy about making the notification himself, George said he would do it for him.[8]

On Monday, April 17, Dr. George Mudd contacted Dana in Bryantown and told him of the two visitors to the home of his cousin on Saturday. He reported for the first time that one of the men had a broken leg and that Mudd had treated it.[9] Up to this time the authorities did not know that one of the fugitives had a broken leg. Mudd worked at home and waited. Nothing happened. In the late afternoon of Tuesday, April 18, Mudd was notified while working in his tobacco fields that authorities were at his home and wished to talk to him. When he returned to his house he met his cousin and four detectives: Lieutenant Alexander Lovett, William Williams, Joshua Lloyd, and Simon Garacan. George explained that they wished to talk to him about the two visitors that he had had on the previous Saturday. These men had come because of Mudd's request through his cousin, as would be pointed out by Mudd's counsel at the trial that followed. They questioned Mudd about the two men and what he did for the injured man. Following this, they left.

Two days passed. On Thursday, April 20, a reward of $100,000 was offered by the War Department by Edwin M. Stanton, Secretary of War, for the apprehension of the murderer of Lincoln. This was published widely in the newspapers and displayed in large poster form in public buildings. Rewards of $25,000 each were also offered for the apprehension of Surratt and Herold. The following paragraph was also included in the announcement, which must have sent chills through Mudd and many others when they read it:

> All persons harboring or secreting said persons, or either of them, or aiding or assisting their concealment or escape, will be treated as accomplices in the murder of the President and the attempted assassination of The Secretary of State, and shall be subject to trial before a Military Commission and the punishment of DEATH. Let the stain of innocent blood be removed from the land by the arrest and punishment of the murderers.
>
> All good citizens are exhorted to aid public justice on this occasion. Every man should consider his own conscience charged with this solemn duty, and rest neither night or day until it is accomplished.

On Friday, April 21, the four detectives led by Lovett returned with two dozen Union cavalrymen. Lovett said later at the trial that he planned to arrest Mudd that day but did not tell him.

Lovett asked Mudd for the razor that the wounded man had used to shave off his mustache and this was produced by Mrs. Mudd. Then Mudd told of the boot that he had cut from the injured man's leg and with the aid of Martha the house girl it was brought from upstairs. She had found it under the bed when cleaning the room.

On examination by Lovett, the name of the maker and "J. Wilkes"' name were found written on the inside. Mudd had not noticed this. When one of the men said that the last name had been effaced, Mrs. Mudd asked to see it and then corrected him saying that it was only a blank line and no name had been there.[10] This was the prize they had been looking for. It was evidence that John Wilkes Booth had been treated by Mudd. Also this man, the fugitive they were pursuing, had a broken leg that Mudd had splinted. Mudd was shown a photo of Booth from the wanted poster and asked if that was the whiskered man he had treated. He did not recognize the man from the photo but said there was some resemblance about the forehead and eyes. When asked if he knew John Wilkes Booth, he told them of meeting him in November 1864 when Booth had inquired about buying land and had bought a horse from his neighbor.

After the discovery of the boot, Mudd was taken to Bryantown to be further interrogated by Colonel H. H. Wells, an officer on General Augur's Headquarters Staff. This was an extensive interview lasting five or six hours and at its conclusion Mudd made a written statement. Following this, late in the evening, Mudd was allowed to return home. He was asked to return for further interrogation next morning. This he did and returned home Saturday evening.[11]

The statement made by Mudd was originally written in his own handwriting for Wells at Bryantown on April 21, 1865. The official version, given in appendix 2, has some small differences from the original handwritten copy. In the handwritten copy Mudd states that his farm is about twenty-five miles from Washington and about eighteen to twenty miles from the nearest point of the Potomac River. He is a practicing physician of eight years and had graduated from "Baltimore" in 1856. He writes that neither of the two men said anything to him to lead him to believe they were associated with the assassination of the president.

He says that he had been shown a photo of Booth and did not think from the photograph that it was him. From other sources of information, however, he thought that it was. (There was confusion about photographs in the early postassassination period. At one time a photo of Edwin Booth was circulated as that of John Wilkes.)

Mudd describes how he cut off the leather riding boot from the patient's left leg before applying the splint. He described how the name "J. Wilkes" was found on its inner surface when the officers came to his home on their second visit. The wounded man gave his name as Tyser or Tyson and the younger man as Henson.

After the patient's leg was splinted, a crude crutch was made out of wood so that the patient could "hobble about."

We cannot be certain that Mudd recognized Booth at the time he treated him. He said he did not, but this was under the stress of attempting to protect himself and his family. It would be strange if he did not recognize Booth. He had spent an afternoon and evening with him five months earlier when Booth was looking for land in Lower Maryland. He had put him up for the night on that visit and the next morning had taken him to his neighbor, where Booth purchased a riding horse blind in one eye.[12]

If Mudd did recognize Booth, did Booth tell him what he had done? Even if he recognized Booth on April 15, he did not know with certainty that Booth had shot Lincoln unless Booth told him so. He had heard the name Boyd given as the assassin later that day in Bryantown. Although many people in Ford's Theater recognized Booth as he jumped to the stage after shooting Lincoln, the War Department did not list him as the assassin until mid-afternoon the next day. The early newspaper accounts on Saturday, April 15, did not list his name. News still traveled slowly in 1865. Messages were being transmitted by telegraph but for some reason, never fully explained, the telegraph lines from Washington were temporarily out of order on Saturday, April 15.

The actual testimony of Lovett and Wells at the military trial is given here because of its relevance.

Testimony of Lieutenant Alexander Lovett:[13]
[The questions are being asked by an Assistant Judge-Advocate. "He" refers to Mudd.]
Q. Did he state to you for what purpose these men had gone into the swamp?
A. He said they were going towards Allen's Fresh. [Allen's Fresh is a small stream southwest from Mudd's farm that leads from Zechiah Swamp into the Potomac River.]
Q. Did he state for what purpose he supposed the lame man had shaved off his mustache?
A. No, sir. He said it looked suspicious. Some of the men along with me made a remark that it looked suspicious and Dr. Mudd also said then that it did look suspicious.
Q. Will you state whether you had a subsequent interview with the prisoner, Dr. Mudd?
A. I had.
Q. How long after the one of which you have spoken?
A. At the time of the first interview, I had my mind made up to arrest him when the proper time should come.
Q. When did the second interview occur?
A. I think, on Friday, the 21st of April. I then went there for the purpose of arresting him.
Q. Will you state to the Court what he then said in regard to these two men?
A. When he found that we were going to search the house, he said something to his wife; and she brought down a boot, and handed me the boot.
Q. What did he say in regard to the boot?
A. He said he had cut it off the man's leg in order to set the leg. I turned down the top of the boot, and saw some writing on the inside, saw the name "John Wilkes" written in it. I called his attention to it; and he said he had not taken notice of that before.

Q. [Exhibiting a boot] Is that the boot?

A. It is.

Q. Did he at that time still insist that they were strangers to him?

A. He still said they were strangers.

Q. Did he at any subsequent time admit to you that he knew Booth?

A. Yes, sir. He subsequently said he was satisfied that it was Booth.

Q. Did he state why he was so satisfied?

A. No, sir.

Q. When was that?

A. That was on Friday, that same day. I made the remark that his wife said she had seen the whiskers disconnected from the face. I suppose he was satisfied then.

Q. I understand you that he said quite distinctly, and insisted on it, that he had not know this man Booth before?

A. Yes, sir.

Q. Did he or not, in any subsequent conversation in regard to this man Booth, admit that he knew him?

A. After I left, we got our horses, and, going on the main road, I told one of the men to show him Booth's photograph. The man held it up to him and he said that it did not look like Booth.

Q. [Exhibiting to the witness Booth's photograph] Is this the same kind of photograph you exhibited?

A. The same. The photograph we showed may have had Booth's name written or printed on it.

Q. Did Dr. Mudd say it was not like him, or was like him?

A. He said it looked like him across the eyes. Shortly after that, he said he had had an introduction to Booth last fall, in November or December....

Q. Did you understand him to say that this brace of revolvers were the only weapons they had? the party?

A. The injured man had a pair of revolvers. I had more conversation with other parties in the house than I did with him (Dr. Mudd), because he seemed so reserved. He did not seem to care much about giving me information.

Q. State what his manner was. Was he frank or evasive?

A. Very evasive. He seemed reserved in everything.

Q. Did he not speak of these men having any other weapons than the brace of pistols of which you have spoken?

A. Not to me.

Q. Did I understand you to say that Dr. Mudd stated that he did not hear the news of the assassination of the President until Sunday, at church?

A. It was on Sunday morning at church, as I understood him.

Q. At the time he spoke of having heard of the assassination of the President on Sunday, did he mention the name of the assassin?

A. No, sir.

By Mr. Ewing:

Q. Did not Dr. Mudd say that he only heard the circumstances of the assassination on Sunday?

A. I understood him to say that he only heard it on Sunday morning.

Q. At what interview was that?

A. That was the first one on Tuesday.

Q. Did he not speak about his having been at church, and heard the details of the assassination on Sunday morning?

A. I do not recollect that he did. There was very little talk about details. We held very little conversation about the matter of the President; in fact I was thinking about what I was attending to at the time.

Q. You did not very closely attend to what he did say in regard to that?

A. Not in regard to that. I know I made the remark at the time to one of the officers, that he must have known it, because the cavalry was close to his house on Saturday and everybody in that neighborhood knew it on Saturday.

Q. Are you certain that Dr. Mudd said anything himself about these men going in the direction of Allen's Fresh?

A. Yes, sir. I am positive of that.

Q. Did he mention it in connection with their going to the Reverend Wilmer's?

A. He said they inquired for Mr. Wilmer's, and he took them to the swamp; and they were going across the swamp towards Mr. Wilmer's.

Q. They inquired for Wilmer's?

A. Yes, sir; I went to Mr. Wilmer's and searched his house, a thing I did not like to do. I was satisfied before I searched it that there was nothing there, because I knew the man by reputation. I was satisfied it was only a blind to throw us that way.

Further testimony of the officers who questioned Mudd on Friday, April 21, and on Sunday, April 23 follows. Wells was questioned by an assistant judge-advocate at the military trial as follows:[14]

Q. I understand you to say that Dr. Mudd stated distinctly that he had not seen Booth since that introduction in November last?

A. Yes, sir. Until the Saturday morning when he arrived at his house.

Q. And that he did not recognize him?

A. No, sir. He said he did not recognize him at first; but on reflection, he knew it was the same person.

Cross-examination by Mr. Ewing:

Q. Did Dr. Mudd seem unwilling to give you this information?

A. Dr. Mudd's manner was so very extraordinary, that I scarcely know how to describe it. I will undertake, if you desire me, to do it as well as I can.

Q. I wish you would.

A. He did seem very much embarrassed.

Q. And alarmed?

A. I should think, not alarmed at the first or second interview; but I think, that, at the third interview, he was, from some statements that I made to him.

Q. At what time on Friday was the first interview?

A. It was not far from mid-day. It might have been a little before or after noon.

Q. That was about noon on the Friday after the assassination?

A. I think the day was Friday. I think it was the 21st.

Q. At that interview, there was no written statement made?

A. Not at the first interview. I should say here that we kept talking for several hours. I deemed it of so much importance, that I kept talking with him for a long time, tried to get the facts; and after I had a general statement of facts, I had it taken down in writing.

Q. You said that, at the last interview, he was very much alarmed from some statements that you made to him. What were the statements you made to him?

A. I said that it seemed to me he was concealing the facts, and that I did not know whether he understood that that was the strongest evidence of his guilt that could be produced at that time, and might endanger his safety.

9
In Custody

On Monday, April 24, nine days after the loud knock on Mudd's door, an officer and three soldiers in uniform came to the Mudd home. The officer told Mudd to pack his things, that he must go to Washington. He did not know it then but he would not be back soon. He would be tried before a military court and avoid being hanged by only one vote, five to four. He would not return for four years and these four years of humiliation, danger, illness, and exasperation would forever change his life as well as shorten it.

His horse was saddled in preparation for departure and as he prepared to leave, Mrs. Mudd, who had been quite stoic, broke down and cried. The commanding officer comforted her by saying, "Do not grieve, I'll see that your husband soon returns to you." Mrs. Mudd wished later that she could remember this man's name because he showed "some heart."[1] Her womanly instincts made her more aware of the situation than her husband, who thought he was going for further questioning. Strong as she was, she cried as he rode out the lane, leaving her and four small children behind. She sensed danger in the uncertain future.

She would fight like a true soldier, with all odds against her, to get him back. She would leave no stone unturned in her fight and would rear the children and hold the farm together with the meager help affordable and available. She would fight harder and do more than Mudd would realize while he was incarcerated in exile. He had been caught by the dragnet set for Booth. Booth would soon be dead, leaving Mudd and others to suffer for his foul deed. The situation can be defined even further. Mudd was caught up in the whole affair because Booth broke his leg while leaping to the stage. If Booth had not injured himself, Mudd would have lived a normal planter's life in Lower Maryland, and we never would have heard of him. But in 1865 he was caught like a fish with its fins tangled in the interstices of a net. The fins that held him there were his natural Southern sympathies displayed during the war, some of his utterances (claimed or real), and his friendships—particularly those with Surratt and Booth.

On his arrival in Washington, Mudd at first was fortunate in being taken to the so-called Carroll Annex of Old Capitol Prison on First Street, just behind the present Capitol. This was a newer portion of the prison but still austere. He was alone in his cell with a simple cot, bench, and table.[2] There was no communication with others and no provision for exercise. Old Capitol had been built just after the British burned the Capitol during the War of 1812. Its name came from the fact that Congress met in this building after the War of 1812 until the new Capitol was finished. It then fell into disuse until the 1860s, when it became a prison for prisoners of war. The Carroll Annex portion was the newer portion of it. It was reserved for more important prisoners and women.

Mudd remained at Carroll Annex during the preparations for the trial. The first of May, when these preparations had been made, he was transferred to the Washington Arsenal Prison near Greenleaf Point in what is now Fort Lesley J. McNair. All eight defendants were housed in the same building in which the trial was held. Mudd was allowed no personal visitors during this time. Even Frances could not visit him. She saw him only once after he left the farm on April 24, and that was on July 6, just after the trial and after he had been sentenced to life imprisonment.

When Mudd was taken to the Carroll Annex in Washington, a company of soldiers was stationed at his farm. This was more to keep track of visitors than to protect Mrs. Mudd and the children. These soldiers were destructive. They burned fences, destroyed wheat and tobacco crops, and pulled boards off the side of the corn crib. The corn fell out and what their horses did not eat was trampled into the ground. Mrs. Mudd was alone and in danger but she stayed and did what needed to be done to hold things together. Mudd wrote home from Washington on April 24, 1865.

> Dearest Frances:
> I am very well. Hope you and the children are enjoying a like blessing. Try and get some one to plant our crop. It is very uncertain what time I shall be released from here. Hire hands at any price they demand. Urge them on all you can and make them work. I am truly in hopes my stay here will be short, when I can return again to your fond embrace and our little children. [He at this time did not yet realize that he was a prisoner.][3]

At Washington Arsenal Prison, a canvas hood was placed over Mudd's head. His eyes and ears were covered with cotton and the hood, which extended to mid-waist, was tied tightly about his neck and waist. He could not see or hear. He was completely incommunicado in the worst possible way. His hands were shackled together. No explanation was given for this treatment, which was being applied to the others also. The others, with the exception of Mrs. Surratt, also had irons applied to their legs.

After about a week of complete hooded isolation, at midnight, Brevet General John F. Hartranft came to Mudd's cell with a lantern. The hood was removed and he was given a sheet of paper to read. The paper listed

Top: Arsenal Prison, Washington, D.C., 1865; *bottom:* Arsenal Prison, 1990.

Payne in irons onboard the *Saugus* after his capture (courtesy of the Library of Congress).

the charges against him and sixteen other people, including Jefferson Davis.

CHARGE AND SPECIFICATION

Against

DAVID E. HEROLD, GEORGE A. ATZERODT, LEWIS PAYNE, MICHAEL O'LAUGHLIN, EDWARD SPANGLER, SAMUEL AR-NOLD, MARY E. SURRATT AND SAMUEL A. MUDD

CHARGE. — For maliciously, unlawfully, and traitoriously, and in aid of the existing armed rebellion against the United States of America, on or before the 6th day of March, A.D. 1865, and divers other days between that day and the 15th day of April, A.D. 1865, combining, and conspiring together with one John H. Surratt, John Wilkes Booth, Jefferson Davis, George N. Sanders, Beverly Tucker, Jacob Thompson, William C. Cleary, Clement C. Clay, George Harper, George Young, and others unknown, to kill and murder, within the Military Department of Washington, and within the fortified and intrenched lines thereof, Abraham Lincoln, late, and at the time of said combining, confederating, and conspiring, President of the United States of America, and Commander-in-Chief of the Army and Navy thereof; Andrew Johnson, Vice President of the United States aforesaid; William H. Seward, Secretary of State of the United States aforesaid; and Ulysses S. Grant, Lieutenant-General of the Army of the United States aforesaid then in command of the Armies of the United States, under the direction of the said Abraham Lincoln; and in pursuance of and in prosecuting said malicious, unlawful, and traitorous conspiracy aforesaid, and in aid of said rebellion, afterward, to-wit, on the 14th day of April, A.D., 1865 within the Military Department of Washington.

SPECIFICATION. — In this: that they, the said David E. Herold, Edward Spangler, Lewis Payne, Michael O'Laughlin, Samuel Arnold, Mary E. Surratt, George A. Atzerodt, and Samuel A. Mudd, together with the said John H. Surratt and John Wilkes Booth, incited and encouraged thereunto by Jefferson Davis, George N. Sanders, Beverly Tucker, Jacob Thompson, William C. Cleary, Clement C. Clay, George Harper, George Young and others unknown, citizens of the United States and who were then engaged in armed rebellion against the United States of America within the limits thereof, did, in aid of said armed rebellion, on or before the 6th or March [etc.] combine, confederate and conspire together at Washington City, within the intrenched fortifications and military lines of the United States, there being, unlawfully, maliciously, and traitorously to kill and murder Abraham Lincoln, then President of the United States and Commander-in-Chief of the Army and Navy thereof . . . [naming the other intended victims as in the charge].[4]

With the very uncomfortable hood over his head for a week and now these accusations, the whole situation was staggering for Mudd. He was accused of conspiring with people that he only vaguely knew and some of whom he had never heard. Things kept getting worse. His case was not to be tried on its own merits. He was going to be tried with others, including Jefferson Davis. His situation had gone from impossible to hopeless. He was a victim and could not change his situation. Any changes or defense must come from the outside.

Mudd's wife, with help from others in the family, had been very active in securing good legal counsel. Three prominent attorneys in Washington turned down the request to represent Mudd. Somehow Frances, with the help of Dr. George Mudd, secured the services of Thomas Ewing, Jr., who had just resigned his commission as brigadier general in the Union Army. He was a man of stature in the North, with a keen legal mind, capable and able. He along with Frederick Stone, an attorney acquaintance from Port Tobacco in Charles County, Maryland, would, it turned out, make a very strong defense for Mudd.

The background for the Ewing agreement to defend Mudd is based on the antipathy between General William T. Sherman and Secretary of War Edwin M. Stanton.[5] Sherman was resentful of the way the secretary of war had reacted to the surrender terms that he had given Confederate General Joseph E. Johnston three weeks earlier. Sherman had given lenient terms to Johnston, which he understood Lincoln had desired. These were openly repudiated by Stanton in a very tactless way. Ewing was the brother-in-law of Sherman and took the assignment as an ally of the defense opposing the war secretary, who had assumed leadership of the prosecution.

10
Monitors, Chains, and Hoods

When the male suspects in the conspiracy plot were apprehended, they were placed in solitary confinement on two ships of war, the *Saugus* and the *Montauk*, both lying at anchor midstream in the Anacosta River just off the navy yard pier. The first prisoner to arrive on board was Payne, taken at Mrs. Surratt's boarding house on the night of Monday, April 17, and identified by Seward's butler as the man who nearly killed several members of the Seward household.

Another early suspect to be taken into custody was Arnold at Old Fort Comfort, Virginia, near Fortress Monroe. He had left the group after the

Crew of the *Saugus* (courtesy of the Library of Congress).

Booth and eight "conspirators" (courtesy of the Library of Congress).

failed attempt to capture Lincoln on March 16 or 17. Thinking the government had wind of the plot and wanting nothing to do with an attempt at the theater, he had gone to his home in Baltimore and had taken a clerking position with a Mr. Wharton at Old Point Comfort near Fortress Monroe, Virginia. He would have been in the clear except that he foolishly wrote a letter to Booth, which the latter left in his trunk at the National Hotel and which was discovered there after the assassination. This letter linked him with the conspiracy to capture Lincoln and made him a serious suspect. He was also placed on the *Saugus* in irons in solitary confinement.

Spangler, a scene shifter at Ford's Theater, arrived on Wednesday, April 19. He was the most likely suspect at the theater to have helped with Booth's escape.

On Thursday, April 20, Atzerodt arrived from Montgomery County, where he had been talking to the neighbors and working in his cousin's garden.

On Monday, April 24, O'Laughlin was taken into custody near his home in Baltimore and added to the group.

Mudd and Mrs. Surratt were taken to Carroll Annex of Old Capitol Prison and placed in irons. They were at least spared the indignity of the monitors.

The final inmate was Herold, who arrived on Thursday, April 27, the day after his capture at Garrett's barn below Port Royal. He received irons and a hood. With Booth's body lying on the deck of the *Montauk*, the group was at this time complete except for John Surratt, who had disappeared in Canada. Stanton urged and President Johnson supported proceeding at once against those in captivity.

11
The Trial

With the sudden death of Lincoln on the morning of April 15, 1865, the government of the United States and the country as a whole were thrown into turmoil. Andrew Johnson, himself a target of Booth's assassination plot spared only by the failure of one of the assassins, was sworn in as the seventeenth president of the United States.

Johnson had had very little to do with the day-to-day operation of the government. He had not even been in attendance at the cabinet meeting on April 14. He had waited and had seen Lincoln briefly after it was over.

Secretary of War Edwin McMasters Stanton stepped quickly into the vacuum created by the death of Lincoln and took temporary charge of things on the night of the assassination, setting up a temporary head-quarters and giving directions. The extent of the assassination plot was not known at that time. The killers might strike again. Stanton was certain that the plot was a Confederate scheme and acted on that assumption.

The assassination of Lincoln, the commander-in-chief in time of war, was a military crime of greatest magnitude. Secretary of War Stanton, with the approval of President Johnson, took firm action to apprehend the assassins and bring them to justice as quickly as possible. Attorney General Speed gave the opinion that the conspirators should be tried before a military commission even though they were civilians.

In time of war safeguards on the life of the individual are less viable than in peacetime. Military personnel are at greatest risk, but the attitude of national defense carries over to others as well. The military commission has war power and acts under the unusual circumstances of war differently than in peacetime. Justice is measured in terms of wartime values. Military officers listen to charges and evidence and make decisions in regard to guilt and punishment. Rights of the individuals are not the same before the military commission as before a civil court. The rules of evidence are less strict. There is no jury of peers. The defendants cannot take the witness stand in their own defense. The judge-advocates sit with the commission during deliberation.

Mudd's attorneys dwelt heavily on this aspect since the defendants were civilians. They questioned the right of the commission to try civilians when civil courts were open. The commission, which had been named by the president with the approval of the attorney general, denied these motions and proceeded on its wartime mission. This would lead to much controversy over the following months and years.

Following the assassination, a courtroom was set up in the northeast corner of the third floor of Old Arsenal Penitentiary. The walls were painted, floor covering was laid down, and gas was brought in to provide light in case the sessions ran late.

All eight defendants were to be tried simultaneously. The trial would prove to be very confusing and drawn out, with witnesses called indiscriminately for one defendant and then another. Two hundred and fifty-nine witnesses were called, 131 for the prosecution and 128 for the defense. Nineteen of the prosecution witnesses were against Mudd; seventy-three of the defense witnesses were for him.

The proceedings of the trial attracted much attention nationwide. Daily newspapers throughout the country carried accounts of it. People read about it with much interest even though the length of the trial caused many to grow weary as the hot months of summer wore on.

The trial started on May 9. When it finally ended on June 30, 1865, four books were written about the testimony. The best were written by Ben Perley Poore and Benn Pitman.

The first is a sequential account of the testimony day by day as it appeared in the Washington newspapers. It is given in its original question-and-answer form. It is written in three volumes; the third volume is particularly scarce. There is no index. The witness stand was occupied 426 times by 328 witnesses. Witnesses were recalled sixty-eight times. Due to the haste in carrying out the trial, witnesses were called in random order, making continuity of testimony less than easy to follow. Witnesses were mixed together, not taken in sequence for any one defendant. These volumes were published in 1865.

Benn Pitman, a trained court reporter, made the official account of the trial. He was the brother of Sir Isaac Pitman, who devised a system of shorthand. His single volume is indexed and classified; testimony can be readily found. It is given in prose rather than question-and-answer format. This has shortcomings when specific points are to be verified. For brevity, questions are omitted and only answers are given. The fine print is exceedingly hard on the eyes. Pitman has preserved the original wording of the answers as much as possible, yet his account lacks the clarity of direct questioning.

The Charges

Following is the executive order of President Johnson, issued May 1:[1]

Executive Chamber, May 1, 1865
Whereas, the Attorney-General of the United States hath given his opinion:
That the persons implicated in the murder of the late President Abraham Lincoln and the attempted assassination of the Honorable William H. Seward, Secretary of State, and in an alleged conspiracy to assassinate other officers of the Federal Government at Washington City, and their aiders and abettors, are subject to the jurisdiction of, and lawfully triable before, a Military Commission;
It is ordered : 1st. That the Assistant Adjutant-General detail nine competent military officers to serve as a Commission for the trial of said parties, and that the Judge Advocate General proceed to prefer charges against said parties for their alleged offenses, and bring them to trial before said Military Commission; that said trial or trials be conducted by said Judge Advocate General, and as recorder thereof, in person, aided by such Assistant and Special Advocates as he may designate;
2nd. That Brevet Major-General Hartranft be assigned to duty as Special Provost Martial General, for the purpose of said trial, and attendance upon said Commission and the execution of its mandates.
3rd. That the said Commission establish such order or rules of proceeding as may avoid unnecessary delay, and conduce to the ends of public justice.

[Signed] Andrew Johnson

War Department, Adjutant-General's Office
Washington, May 6, 1865

4. A Military Commission is hereby appointed to meet at Washington, D.C. on Monday, the 8th of May 1865, at 9 o'clock A.M., or as soon thereafter as practicable, for the trial of David E. Herold, George A. Atzerodt, Lewis Payne, Michael O'Laughlin, Edward Spangler, Samuel Arnold, Mary E. Surratt, Samuel A. Mudd, and such other prisoners as may be brought before it, implicated in the murder of the late President Abraham Lincoln, and the attempted assassination of the Honorable William H. Seward, Secretary of State, and in an alleged conspiracy to assassinate other officers of the Federal Government at Washington City, and their aiders and abettors.

Detail for the Court
Major-General David Hunter, U.S. Volunteers.
Major-General Lewis Wallace, U.S. Volunteers.
Brevet Major-General August V. Kautz, U.S. Volunteers.
Brigadier-General Albion P. Howe, U.S. Volunteers.
Brigadier-General Robert S. Foster, U.S. Volunteers.
Brevet Brigadier-General James A. Ekin, U.S. Volunteers.
Brigadier-General T. M. Harris, U.S. Volunteers.
Brevet Colonel C. H. Tomkins, U.S. Volunteers.

Brigadier-General Joseph Holt, Judge-Advocate General, U.S. Army.
Lieutenant-Colonel David R. Clendenin, Eighth Illinois Cavalry.
The Honorable John A. Bingham and Brevet Colonel H. L. Burnett,
Assistant or Special Judge-Advocates.
The Commission will sit without regard to hours.
By order of the President of the United States.
[Signed] W. A. Nichols
Assistant Adjutant-General[2]

CHARGES

DAVID E. HEROLD, GEORGE A. ATZERODT, LEWIS PAYNE,
MICHAEL O'LAUGHLIN, EDWARD SPANGLER, SAMUEL AR-
NOLD, MARY E. SURRATT, SAMUEL A. MUDD.
CHARGE.—For maliciously, unlawfully, and traitorously, and in aid of
the existing armed rebellion against the United States of America, on or
before the 6th day of March, A.D. 1865, and on divers other days between
that day and the 15th day of April, A.D. 1865, combining, confederating,
and conspiring together with one John H. Surratt, John Wilkes Booth,
Jefferson Davis, George N. Sanders, Beverly Tucker, Jacob Thompson,
William C. Cleary, Clement C. Clay, George Harper, George Young, and
others unknown, to kill and murder within the Military Department of
Washington, and within the fortified and intrenched lines thereof,
Abraham Lincoln, late and at the time of said combining, confederating
and conspiring, President of the United States of America, and Com-
mander-in-Chief of the Army and Navy thereof; Andrew Johnson now
President of the United States aforesaid; William H. Seward, Secretary of
State of the United States aforesaid; and Ulysses S. Grant, Lieutenant-
General of the Army of the United States.
    And in pursuance of and in prosecuting said malicious, unlawful, and
traitorous conspiracy aforesaid within the fortified and intrenched lines of
said Military Department, together with said John Wilkes Booth and John
H. Surratt, maliciously, unlawfully and traitorously murdering the said
Abraham Lincoln, traitorously assaulting, with intent to kill and murder
William H. Seward, Secretary of State . . . with intent to murder Andrew
Johnson, then Vice President, and Ulysses S. Grant, Lieutenant-General
in command of the Armies of the United States.[3]

The Defendants

Samuel Bland Arnold

Samuel Arnold and Michael O'Laughlin, two of Mudd's staunch allies at
Fort Jefferson, had been the first recruits of Booth for his grand scheme to
kidnap President Abraham Lincoln.

    Booth was stopping at Barnums Hotel in Baltimore and sent word to
his former schoolmates to meet him there. This was in the latter part of
August or the first part of September 1864. Arnold and Booth had been

schoolmates in their teens at St. Timothys Hall, Cantonsville, Maryland, a prep school in the modern sense. The two had not seen each other for thirteen years.

When Arnold came to Booth's hotel, he was warmly greeted and ushered up to his room. He was soon seated at a table in Booth's room, smoking a fine cigar supplied by Booth as they conversed together about school days. A lot of water had gone over the dam since they had last been together. Booth had heard that Arnold had been in the Confederate service and they talked about that and the war.

There was a knock on the door and a young man who entered was introduced as Michael O'Laughlin. This was the first meeting of these two who would go through torture together and rue the day of this meeting with Booth. O'Laughlin would die of Yellow Fever because of it.

O'Laughlin was a former acquaintance of Booth's. They had lived next to each other in Baltimore when they were young and had gone to school together. Booth was meeting with two of his former school acquaintances in whom he had confidence. He could trust them. For his job he had to have people he could trust. Booth was not bashful about his success in life and showed his former schoolmates some entries of his earnings for recent performances. This impressed them. He also told of lucrative oil ventures in western Pennsylvania. Conversation soon drifted back to the war and the nonexchange of prisoners between the North and the South. After wine was served, Booth laid out his plan. With only brief consideration, Arnold and O'Laughlin both joined up.

At Booth's request Arnold picked out a horse that Booth purchased on a return visit in January. Booth also purchased a carriage and harness at this time. This return trip to Baltimore was after a trip to Canada, where he had purchased firearms that he left with Arnold to be shipped to Washington.

Arnold told his family he was in the oil business with Booth so they would not worry.

In January Arnold and O'Laughlin went to Washington, driving the newly purchased horse and carriage. They put up at Rullmans Hotel, then Mitchells Hotel near Grover's Theater, then rented a room from Mrs. Van Tine at 420 D Street. They arrived at Mrs. Van Tine's on February 10, and remained until March 20. Booth visited them here frequently. When Booth gave his last paid performance on stage at Ford's Theater in mid–March, which they both attended, the two gave Mrs. Van Tine a ticket to attend also. She told of that later while giving testimony at the trial. When showed a picture of Booth, she told the court it was a poor picture, that he was better-looking than that.[4]

At the all-night meeting of the conspirators at Gautier's Restaurant in mid–March, the only time the whole group was brought together, Booth proposed capturing Lincoln at the theater. Arnold considered the plan dangerous, impractical, and doomed to failure. He was outspoken about it, and an argument developed. Arnold said he would no longer participate because the idea would not work. He also said that any attempt to capture Lincoln should be made when there was not a crowd of people around and that it should be done within a week or he would withdraw. He thought the government would get wise to the plan. Booth said that anyone who withdrew would be shot. Arnold replied that two could play that game, and the meeting broke up.[5] Booth apologized for what he had said the next day.

On March 17, 1865, Booth and Herold met Arnold and O'Laughlin and advised them that Lincoln was to attend a theatrical performance at the Soldier's Home at the edge of the city that afternoon.[6] With the failure of this attempt, Arnold was of the opinion that the government was wise to the scheme and he and O'Laughlin left Mrs. Van Tine's rooming house about March 20.

Arnold returned to his father's home in Baltimore, arriving there on March 21, as testified to in court by two of Arnold's brothers, William and Frank.[7] All would have been well for Arnold except that he wrote Booth a letter from Hookstown, Maryland, on March 27. In this letter, Arnold says among other things, "Go and see how it will be taken in R———d and ere long I shall be better prepared to again be with you." This did it. The letter tying him to Booth was found in Booth's trunk at the National Hotel on April 15.

Arnold's father had written to a friend who had two stores at Fortress Monroe. Arnold also wrote to him, asking for employment. A letter came back to Arnold from Mr. John Wharton offering employment as a clerk.

On April 1, Arnold took the afternoon boat down to Fortress Monroe. He worked as a clerk until his arrest on April 17, 1865. He was then returned to Washington and placed in solitary confinement with chains and a canvas hood over his eyes and ears onboard the *Saugus*. The man of war was lying at anchor at the navy yard, acting as a security prison now that the fighting was over.

Arnold was defended by Walter S. Cox, Esq. before the military commission. The opening of Cox's final statement may be of some interest:[8]

> I stand here not as the defender of assassins but to rescue the innocent from the opprobrium of this great crime and a death of infamy. . . .
>
> Both the accused and their counsel have labored under disadvantages not incident to the civil courts, and unusual even in military trials. In both civil courts and court-martials the accused receives not only a copy of the charge, or indictment in time to prepare for his defense, but also a list of the witnesses with whom he is to be confronted. And in the civil courts, it is usual for the prosecutor to state in advance the general nature of the case he expects to establish, and the general scope of the evidence he

expects to adduce. By this the accused is enabled not only to apply intelligently the test of cross-examination, but also to know and show how much credit is due to the witnesses who accuse him. In this case the accused were aroused from their slumbers on the night before arraignment, and, for the first time, presented with a copy of the charge.

For the most part they were unable to procure counsel until the trial had commenced; and when counsel were admitted, they came to the discharge of their duties in utter ignorance of the whole case which they were to combat, except as they could gather it from the general language of the charge, as well as, for the most part, wholly unacquainted with the prisoners and their antecedents; and the consequence is, that the earliest witnesses for the government were allowed to depart with little or no cross-examination which subsequent events show was of vital importance to elicit the truth and reduce their vagueness of statement to more accuracy....

My clients had nothing to do with the conspiracy set forth in this charge.... It imputes that the accused conspired with Jefferson Davis and others to kill and murder the President with the intent to aid and comfort the insurgents, etc. and thereby aid in the subversion and overthrow of the Constitution and laws of the United States.

I cannot for the moment suppose that the object was to inflame prejudice against the accused because of their remote connection with the authors of these evils and for want of higher victims to make them the scapegoats for all the atrocities imputed to the rebellion: to immolate them, to hush the clamors of the public for a victim....

This Commission sits by authority of the order of the President, offered in evidence, of Sept. 24, 1862, which declared martial law against all rebels and insurgents, their aiders and abettors and all guilty of any disloyal practice, affording aid and comfort to rebels against the authority of the United States.

Below the grade of treason, crimes are ranged under two general heads, viz: felonies and misdemeanors:

Felonies	*Misdemeanors*
Murder	Perjury
Arson	Battery
Rape	Libel
Robbery etc.	Conspiracies & all crime lesser than felony

Conspiracy is a lower grade of crime....

Cox argued that his clients, Arnold and O'Laughlin—and this would apply even more so to Mudd—could be charged only with conspiring to capture. They were remote from the scene of the assassination.

George A. Atzerodt

George A. Atzerodt, by trade a carriage maker at Port Tobacco before the war, was also a boatman. He found nightly passages over the Potomac to and from the Virginia shore quite remunerative. Surratt was one of his good customers. Atzerodt was a logical candidate to ferry the proposed capture party into the Confederate lines.

Atzerodt was of German extraction. He had been reared in Montgomery County, Maryland, and some of the poorer sections of Washington, D.C. His education was not extensive. A brother of his was at one time, and a brother-in-law was at the time of the assassination, on the police force of the State of Maryland.[9]

Atzerodt's expertise after the beginning of the war had become the nooks and crannies of the banks of the Potomac River south of Port Tobacco. It was very important to know where and how to hide a boat on shore in preparation for crossing and where to land on the far side without detection. Understanding and interpreting the well-developed signal codes along the shores were also of highest importance.

Early in March 1865, Atzerodt came to Washington as a member of Booth's capture team. He came to Mrs. Surratt's boarding house, where his unkempt appearance earned him the name "Port Tobacco." He imbibed too freely in his room with some of the other men one evening. When Mrs. Surratt found that he used alcohol, she put her foot down. He could not stay any longer. He checked in at the Pennsylvania House on C Street on March 18, where he remained until April 12.[10]

He was among the group taken to Ford's Theater by Booth to see Booth's last paid performance there. The group interestingly used box 7, also known as the president's box because of its previous use by President and Mrs. Lincoln.

Soon after the theater party, on March 17, according to Arnold, the men of the capture plot met at Gautier's Restaurant for the first and only time that the entire group was to be together. They wined and dined and smoked fancy cigars at Booth's expense until five in the morning. O'Laughlin and Arnold had never met the other members, except Booth, and the same held for Surratt, Atzerodt, and Payne. The latter had just recently been brought from Baltimore by Booth to get him away from the city where he had been banned.

Atzerodt lived at the Pennsylvania House at Booth's expense, waiting for his assignment, taking an occasional trip back to Port Tobacco to check on things there and making sure that the proper boat was in readiness.

When the supposed capture opportunity arose shortly after the night at Gautier's Restaurant, Atzerodt rode with Payne and met the others near the Soldier's Home. When this plan failed, he returned to the Pennsylvania House to wait for further assignment.

Union victories were making Booth's scheme to kidnap Lincoln and take him to Richmond for the exchange of Confederate prisoners less and less viable. Finally, on April 3, Richmond fell. There was no longer a

Confederate capital to which a kidnapped Northern president could be taken. The whole Southern cause was disintegrating.

About the first of April, Atzerodt entertained several friends from Port Tobacco in the lobby of his hotel. They were having drinks, and Atzerodt asked his hotel keeper to join them. He bragged to his hotel keeper, John Greenawalt, "Greenawalt, I am pretty near broke but have always got friends enough who will give me as much money as will see me through." He added, "I am going away some of these days and I will return with as much gold as will keep me all my lifetime."[11] It would fortunately turn out that the amount of gold required for this would not be very great.

Booth apparently began to see the impracticality of his impractical scheme. He began disposing of his horses and carriage.

Finally, on April 14, when Booth went to Ford's Theater to get his mail, he learned that Lincoln and Grant would be at the theater together that night.

Atzerodt said that he did not get his assignment to assassinate Vice President Johnson until the eight o'clock meeting at an unknown location on the evening of April 14. He told Booth that he had signed up to capture the president, not to kill. Booth would not release him from his assignment.

According to a clerk at the Kirkwood House where Vice President Johnson was living, Atzerodt checked into room 126 at the Kirkwood House before 8:00 A.M. on April 14, but never slept in the room.[12] This clerk did not come on duty until later in the day, however, according to his own testimony, but that was long before 8:00 P.M.

Atzerodt was a friendly fellow, not a killer, according to the testimony of many persons who knew him.[13] This is borne out by what he did on the night of April 14. He had several drinks, then rode his horse to the Kirkwood House. He stayed only a very short time.[14] The short time there may have been at the bar. He then returned his horse to the stable[15] and took public transportation, a horse-drawn car, to the area of former acquaintance near the navy yard, where he continued drinking. He then went back and took a room at the Pennsylvania House late that night and left very early the next morning without paying his bill. He did not get all "that gold." He was out of money. The drinks of the night before had used up quite a bit and the big reimbursements had not come through.

He arrived Sunday afternoon at the home of his cousin, Hartman Richter, in Montgomery County, Maryland, near Rockville about twenty miles north of Washington. He visited with neighbors and worked in his cousin's garden until arrested on Thursday, April 20.

He was placed on board the *Saugus* at anchor on the Potomac River at the navy yard, chained and in solitary confinement below deck. On April 23, a hood was placed over his head.

David E. Herold

David E. Herold, age twenty-two or twenty-three, was the youngest of the defendants tried with Mudd. He had been recommended to Booth for the capture and kidnap plot of Lincoln some months earlier by Surratt and accepted by Booth because of his knowledge of the roads of southern Maryland leading to the Potomac River.

He had worked as a druggist clerk for Francis S. Walsh for eleven months, but was recently unemployed. Walsh said he had known Herold since childhood and that during the time of employment Herold had lived with him in his house and that he knew him intimately since October 1863. There was nothing objectionable about his character. He was temperate in habits and regular in his hours. He was "trifling and juvenile." He was a boy rather than a man and tended to associate with younger people. He was quite easily influenced and led. He was fond of sports, guns, and dogs.

John Fletcher testified that Herold came to Howard's Livery Stable with Atzerodt on the afternoon of April 14 and rented a horse and saddle. He did not return at the agreed hour and Fletcher went after him about 10:30 P.M. He saw Herold riding rapidly toward the navy yard bridge. When Fletcher arrived at the bridge on another horse a little later, Sergeant Silas Cobb, the sentry, had already let Herold pass but told Fletcher if he went over he could not return. Fletcher never saw his horse again.

When Herold was captured at Garrett's tobacco barn on April 26, he was made to walk until exhausted and then tied on a horse. The party returned to Washington along with Booth's body. Herold was secreted below deck on the *Montauk* in chains in solitary confinement. He was the last to arrive.

Michael O'Laughlin

Michael O'Laughlin was one of the first people approached by Booth in the fall of 1864 to assist in his scheme to abduct Lincoln in exchange for Confederate prisoners. O'Laughlin was Booth's former neighbor on Exeter Street in Baltimore, Maryland, where they grew up. They were the same age and were schoolmates and close friends during their boyhood days.

The latter part of August or early September 1864, O'Laughlin received a note from Booth stating that he would be at Barnums Hotel in Baltimore on a certain day and asking if O'Laughlin could see him there

Opposite: **Howard Livery Stable (courtesy of the Library of Congress).**

that evening. When O'Laughlin arrived at Booth's hotel he was ushered to Booth's room, where he met Samuel Arnold for the first time. These two got along well from the start. O'Laughlin had had a brief stint in the Confederate Army according to his own declaration, as testified later by a family friend, Marshall McPhail.[16]

After an exchange of pleasantries the aroma of fine cigar smoke filled the air and wine was poured freely by Booth for both of his friends and himself. Life had been good for the actor. He had had a phenomenal rise to notoriety over the past three years. He did not hesitate to flaunt his success, even making known some of his income over the past season. He also told them about lucrative oil field speculations in western Pennsylvania. This had the desired effect on his old friends to whom dame fortune had not been so generous.

The talk soon centered on the war and the need for the release of Confederate soldiers from Northern prisons to help fight it.

Booth soon realized his judgment was correct. He was speaking to a receptive audience. His zeal for the Southern cause was not wasted. Before the evening was over both men, without further consideration, expressed their desire to cooperate. They began to form preliminary plans.

Illness of Booth, whether feigned or real, caused delay. O'Laughlin and Arnold purchased a horse and carriage at Booth's expense, which they finally drove to Washington in January 1865. After several weeks in hotels at Booth's expense, the two took a room at Mrs. Van Tine's rooming house on February 10, where they remained until March 20. The delays that occurred after they arrived in Washington were due to the fact that Lincoln was not cooperative in his trips to the Soldier's Home at the edge of the city. Booth, who was accustomed to doing his work on stage, then advocated capture at the theater. This was not accepted by Arnold and harsh words developed.

Finally, in mid–March, the group mobilized on word that the president would attend a performance at the Soldier's Home. The captors rode there in pairs. When they got to their rendezvous point, to their disappointment the president was not there. They had been foiled. O'Laughlin headed back to Baltimore. Events of the war soon made abduction to Richmond an impossibility with the fall of that city on April 3. This further complicated things.

O'Laughlin and Arnold thought the government knew of the plan and steered clear to a certain extent, but not completely. Each made a serious error. Arnold foolishly wrote a letter to Booth. O'Laughlin and three friends went to Washington for the "Illumination" of the city on April 13, 1865. This was a gala victory celebration, with all the lights of the city turned on. O'Laughlin not only went to Washington, but he went to the National Hotel and saw Booth![17] He was in Washington the night before and the night of the assassination. There was testimony at the trial that he was seen at the home of Stanton on the evening of April 13, where Grant was being serenaded.[18] A sergeant of the adjutant-general's office identified O'Laughlin at the trial and said O'Laughlin asked him if Grant was there that evening and tried to get a look at him. The sergeant asked him to leave.

On the night of the assassination, O'Laughlin stayed with a friend, John Fuller, in his hotel room downtown.[19] The testimony of this man and that of his three other traveling companions and a bartender saved him from the accusation of attempting to assassinate Grant.[20]

At the conclusion of the trial, O'Laughlin received life imprisonment, the same sentence as Arnold and Mudd. He died of Yellow Fever on September 23, 1867, at Fort Jefferson, Dry Tortugas Islands, during the epidemic there.

Lewis Payne

Lewis Thornton Powell (his true name—he was Lewis Payne in the court record) was born in Stewart County, Georgia, in 1845. His father, Reverend George C. Powell, was a planter and Baptist minister who owned slaves. Payne had two brothers and six sisters. In 1859 his family moved to Live Oak Station, Florida, along the railroad line between Jacksonville and Tallahassee.[21]

When war broke out, Payne was a lad of sixteen who had been helping his father oversee the family plantation and its slaves. His two brothers enlisted in the Confederate Army. Lewis was large and strong for his age. He enlisted in Captain Stuart's Second Florida Infantry and under Colonel Ward was ordered to Richmond. At Richmond his regiment joined the army of General Lee attached to A. P. Hill's corps.

While in Richmond the young soldier went to the theater one night. This was a new venture for him, something that his rural upbringing had not included. He was greatly impressed with the play and the acting such as he had never seen before. He was especially taken with a young actor by the name of Booth. They had something in common—perhaps a great deal more than they realized at the time. Payne was so impressed that he somehow found his way backstage and talked with Booth. They immediately found that they shared the same zeal for the Southern cause. It was an emotional experience for the young soldier and also for Booth, which neither of them forgot. After this enjoyable meeting, Payne returned to his unit.

He was involved in the Peninsular Campaign against General McClellan, saw action in the battles of Chancellorsville and Antietam, and finally was wounded at Gettysburg, where he was taken prisoner. He learned that his brothers had been killed at the battle of Murfreesboro and was devastated by the news.

While recovering from his wounds in a field hospital at Gettysburg, which cared for both Confederate and Union soldiers, he acted as a nurse for the wounded. Volunteer nurse Miss Margaret Branson testified favorably regarding his work there.[22]

From Gettysburg Payne was sent to the West Building Hospital, Pratt Street, Baltimore, and remained there until October 1863. The young man was expecting to be exchanged back to the Confederate Army but was disappointed. Finally, giving up hope, he deserted for his regiment, walking to Winchester, Virginia, and beyond. At Fauquier, Virginia, he joined up with a unit of the cavalry of Northern Virginia, with which he stayed until January 1865. At this time the fortunes of war were very poor for the South. The Southern cause began to look hopeless. Finally, Payne deserted his regiment and rode to Alexandria, Virginia, where he sold his horse to obtain funds and took an oath of loyalty to the Union.

He then thought of his friend, Miss Margaret Branson, and went to the young lady's home in Baltimore, Maryland. Miss Branson's mother was running a room and boarding house in Baltimore during the war. He took a room at her house, where he expected to wait for peace to occur. He actually remained there only until March 1865. During this stay he became involved in a violent argument with a Negro maid, who became insolent regarding the cleaning of his room. It was a physical encounter in which he struck her and supposedly stomped on her. She brought legal action against him and he was required by law to leave Baltimore.

He was put out on the street. By this time his funds had run out and he was destitute. He somehow met Booth a second time. This was either by chance, or by looking him up at the theater where he was playing. Their friendship was immediately rekindled by their zeal for the Southern cause and Payne's destitute condition. Booth at this time was looking for a strong Confederate such as Payne and Payne needed friendship and money badly. Payne swore loyalty to Booth in exchange for money, food, and lodging. Booth immediately took him out of Baltimore to Washington, D.C., where, at the Herndon House, he held him in readiness.

On approximately March 17, 1865, the attempt to kidnap Lincoln near the Soldier's Home was finally made. Payne and Atzerodt rode together during that escapade. When Lincoln did not show up, Payne rode back into town as did Atzerodt to await further assignment.

As it turned out, with the terminal events of the war fast approaching, this one and only mobilization of the kidnap group ended the attempts to abduct Lincoln. Payne's next assignment—to assassinate Secretary of State Seward—did not succeed, but cost him his life.

Edward (Edmund) (Ned) Spangler

Ned Spangler was a long-time friend of Booth's. Spangler had worked for Booth's father as a carpenter at Bel Air, the Booth country home thirty miles north of Baltimore during Booth's teenage period.

Spangler was forty-three years old in 1865, about fifteen years older than Booth. Following his employment with the Booths, he began working at theaters in Baltimore and Washington. According to John T. Ford, proprietor of Ford's Theater, he had been an employee at Ford's Theater nearly four years. The first part of this employment was of an intermittent nature but the last two years were continuous.[23] It is probable that Booth helped Spangler get the job at Ford's Theater.

Spangler considered Baltimore his home and spent his summers there. His wife had died about one year previously. He was a stage hand at night, moving scenery between acts and bringing whatever was needed. During the day he worked as a carpenter under James Gifford, the stage-carpenter in charge of scenery and other things needed for productions. Spangler had great admiration for Booth. The two were very good friends.

Spangler was a good-natured, willing worker who only occasionally drank more than he should. He rarely slept in bed and usually slept at the theater. He had few associates. In 1865 he boarded at a nearby boarding house at 7th and G streets, but did not have a room there. He kept his trunk at the theater. He apparently was an avid crab fisherman. A rope found among his belongings caused speculation as to its purpose. From the testimony of several other employees, it was finally identified as a rope used for scenery that he may have used for crab fishing.

In April 1865 Spangler was the scene shifter stationed in the left wing of the theater looking toward the audience. This was just below the president's box. Jacob (Jake) Ritterspaugh was the scene shifter in the right wing. Both of these men were carpenters and took their meals at the same boarding house, Mrs. Scott's, at 7th and G streets.

After Booth jumped to the floor of the stage, he ran toward the rear and to the left side of the stage from the audience, where Ritterspaugh was stationed. After Ritterspaugh testified that he was at the theater on the night of the assassination he stated that during the second scene of the third act he heard a pistol shot and soon after that someone cried out that the president had been shot. Very soon after that he saw a man with his head down, wearing no hat and carrying a knife in his hand, running toward the rear door. "I made for him and as I came up to him he tore the door open and struck at me with his knife and I jumped back. He then ran out and slammed the door shut. I then went to get the door open quick. It stuck. I could not get it open. A moment later I was able to get the door open. The man had gotten on his horse and was riding out the alley to F Street."

In a few minutes he went back into the theater to the wings, where Spangler was still standing. Spangler was pale and looked scared. Ritterspaugh told Spangler that it was Booth, and that Booth had ridden out the alley. Spangler then slapped Ritterspaugh on the face with the back of his hand and said, "Don't say which way he went." Ritterspaugh asked him what he meant by slapping him in the mouth. Spangler said, "For God's sake, shut up."[24] Ritterspaugh said a tall stout man went out the rear door right after he did.

Spangler had done many things for Booth during their relationship at the theater. In January 1865 he made a stable for Booth's horses behind the theater and fed and cared for them there. Sometimes Joseph Burroughs ("Peanuts") helped with this. About a month later Spangler altered the stable to accommodate a buggy that Booth had bought. In April, after the fall of Richmond and about a week before the assassination, Booth had Spangler sell the horse and buggy to a liveryman.[25]

Joseph Burroughs testified that he carried bills in the daytime and stood by the stage door at night during performances to see that only authorized persons entered. When Spangler called him about 9:30 P.M. on April 14 to hold Booth's horse, he said he could not do it because he had to watch the stage door. Spangler said it was okay, that he would take the responsibility.

Burroughs testified to something else of interest.[26] He said that he was in the president's box when Mr. Harry Ford, the manager of the theater, was draping flags about the openings on the stage side of the box. Ford told him to go up with Spangler and help take the partition out of the president's box since General Grant would also be there that evening. Thomas J. Raybold testified that he thought that Booth had personally occupied box 7, the one occupied by Lincoln on April 14, two weeks earlier.[27]

Booth had personally occupied the president's box two weeks earlier; Spangler was in the president's box the afternoon of April 14; and Booth was in and out of the theater several times that day with full access to all parts of the theater, beginning in the morning when he picked up his mail. There was ample opportunity to make alterations.

Spangler was arrested at his boarding house on 7th and G streets on April 19, 1865. He was incarcerated with the other suspects on a monitor at anchor off the pier of the navy yard and brought to trial before the military commission on May 9, 1865, with the other seven defendants.

Mrs. Mary E. Surratt

Of those who paid the supreme sacrifice for the death of Lincoln, none is more pathetic than Mary E. Surratt, the lone woman tried before the military commission. At the outbreak of the war she was living comfortably with her husband and three children in the small cross-roads town of Surrattsville, thirteen miles south of Washington and about seventeen miles north of Bryantown, Maryland.

As a young man John H. Surratt, Sr., inherited a farm from an uncle. He had been working on the Virginia Railroad prior to that. Soon after inheriting the farm he married a beautiful young lady in 1835, named Mary E. Jenkins, daughter of Samuel I. Jenkins. To supplement farm income and help finance his new responsibilities, he and Mary built a store on the premises that was soon expanded into a tavern. A bar where liquor was sold to weary travelers increased traffic and income and since they were on a main road to Washington some rooms for overnight guests were added.

The area developed and the cross-roads was named Surrattsville in Surratt's honor with him as postmaster. The tavern became a popular stopping place for those on the way to the nation's capital.

A family was soon on the way for the Surratts. The first child was a son whom they named Isaac after his grandfather. A few years later a daughter named Anna E. joined the family, and in 1844 a second son, John Harrison Surratt, was born, named after his father. The Surratts were good Catholics and Mrs. Surratt practiced her religion faithfully. The children attended the local parochial school. John went away to divinity school at age fifteen to Saint Charles College just west of Baltimore. While John was at Saint Charles College, he became acquainted with another young divinity student named Louis J. Wiechmann. These two formed a very close, warm relationship, which was soon to turn more cold than it had been warm.

Mrs. Surratt raised her family in an exemplary way. According to some sources, John Surratt, Sr., became a good customer at his own bar but other than that things went well.

The Surratt family, like the majority of families in southern Maryland, were quite sympathetic to the Southern cause. When war broke out these sentiments were strengthened and shared by all members of the family. Isaac joined the Confederate Army in 1861 and was sent to Texas under General Magruder.

Postmaster Surratt was in an excellent position to do his part for the Confederate cause. He acted as go-between on courier routes from Richmond and points north. Contraband articles and mail smuggled across the Potomac River from Virginia and particularly Richmond were readdressed and sent onward to desired destinations. The Surratt Tavern, which had become a popular and friendly place to stop at on the way to Washington, became a friendly stopover for Confederate travelers. The latest in Confederate information was available there.

All went well until John Surratt, Sr., died suddenly in 1862. This threw a tremendous burden on Mrs. Surratt—more than she and young Anna could handle.

To fill the void, young John came home from college to help his mother. Three years later, when the stakes were higher, he was not so chivalrous.

Surratt's character at Saint Charles College was excellent; he shed tears on leaving.[28] The president of the college approached him and told him not to weep, that he would always be remembered by those who had charge of the institution.

Surratt came home from college when his father died. He was then eighteen years old. He took over many of the duties of his father, including the postmastership. He was not experienced but necessity is a great instructor for an apt student. Surratt learned fast.

An exciting aspect of the business that especially appealed to Surratt was the underground intelligence that his father had started and that was increasing as the war progressed. The Surratt Tavern became known as a "safe house" for undercover agents.

Surratt lost the postmastership about a year later. There were charges of tampering with mail. It was no great loss for him, however, since he now had connections in Richmond. Good couriers were in demand, and he took up the trade. It was exciting for a young man and paid well. The irregular hours were no bother to him. He knew the ropes of passing back and forth over the Potomac River without detection. He had found a carriage maker in Port Tobacco who was an excellent boatman, a German named Atzerodt, who could safely make the passages back and forth. This was not easy because Union gunboats patrolled the river regularly. After one passed, there was a scurry of activity along both banks aided by high-cliff on-shore signals.

John and Anna were a great help at home for Mary Surratt. Isaac was off in Texas. They were able to handle the tavern but the farm work was too much. Mrs. Surratt also owned a house in Washington, on H Street. This was an eight-room three-story row house right on the sidewalk with steps going up to the front entrance elevated above the sidewalk level. It was not far from downtown. Mrs. Surratt felt that she could operate this house in the city better by renting rooms and taking in boarders. She then would not have the responsibilities of the farm. She proceeded to make plans to do that.

She finally was able to find a retired Washington policeman by the name of John M. Lloyd who was willing to rent the tavern and the farm at Surrattsville. Anna could help with the house and John was quite busy with his work. This would free him more for the activities that he was interested in.

In the fall of 1864 Mrs. Surratt began moving household things to 541 H Street. On November 1, 1864, she began taking in roomers. On December 1 Mrs. Surratt moved her residence there and John Lloyd took over the tavern at Surrattsville. One of the first roomers to take up residence at the new location was John's college schoolmate, Louis J. Wiechmann, who held a government job. He was clerk in the office of General Hoffman, commissary-general of prisoners for the Union Army. Other boarders at Mrs. Surratt's house were Miss Honora Fitzpatrick and Miss Dean. The presence of a "safe house" in Washington was soon well known to those desiring one.[29]

After Booth and Surratt met on 7th Street, Booth became a frequent visitor at the Surratt house. Usually his visits were brief.[30] Sometime in March 1865 Payne came to the Surratt house. Three weeks later he came again and stayed three days.[31]

Atzerodt came to the Surratt house also about three weeks after Wiechmann made the acquaintance of Booth. He was called "Port Tobacco" by the ladies of the house because of his unkempt appearance. Mrs. Surratt and her daughter Anna both objected to Atzerodt and he found quarters elsewhere, at the Pennsylvania House. Herold came on one occasion to H Street and Wiechmann had met him at the tavern in Surrattsville in the spring of 1863.[32]

In the testimony of Wiechmann before the military commission on May 18, 1865,[33] Mrs. Surratt was described as always hospitable. She had many acquaintances. Many people came from the country and stayed at her house. Her conduct was always of the highest quality and moral character. She was religious and attended Catholic services regularly. Wiechmann said that he accompanied her to church on Sunday generally. During the winter of 1864/65 Surratt was frequently away from home. During November 1864 he was down in the country "almost the whole time."

Wiechmann and Surratt roomed together and ate at the same table. They were on intimate terms and saw each other every day when Surratt was in town. Surratt once talked of going to England on a cotton speculation and on another occasion about going on the stage like Booth.

About the middle of March 1865, Booth had an acting performance at the Ford's Theater that, as it turned out, would be his last. He played Pescara in *The Apostate* and evidently engaged the right hand upper box that would be occupied by Lincoln on the night of April 14 for his guests.[34] According to Wiechmann's testimony, he gave tickets to Surratt and O'Laughlin, who gave one to his landlady, Mrs. Van Tine, and must have given out quite a few others. The young ladies from the Surratt house attended but there is no mention that Mrs. Surratt did, which seems strange.

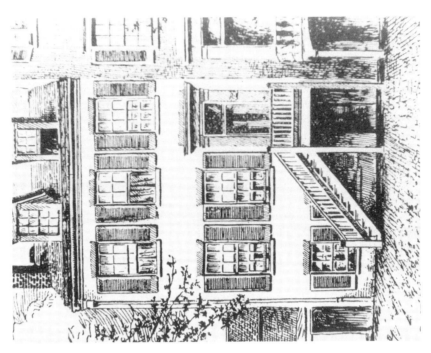

At any rate it was a gala event for the young ladies and an instructive one for the members of Booth's capture group, who were able to study the theater first-hand. Payne, Atzerodt, Surratt, O'Laughlin, Arnold, Herold, and Wiechmann were all there and Spangler was shifting scenery. Booth was acting and he came into the box and spoke to the group during the course of the evening. It was a "shakedown cruise" if there ever was one.

After the play was over, the group left together. When Atzerodt and Herold did not follow, Wiechmann turned and went back and found Atzerodt and Herold talking to Booth in the restaurant next to the theater. They then, according to Weichmann, "all rejoined the group and went to Kloman's for some oysters following which we separated, Surratt, Holahan and myself going home and the others down Seventh Street." Holahan, who boarded with Mrs. Surratt, had also been in the audience.

About mid–March 1865, while Payne was staying at the house, Wiechmann said he went to the third floor on returning from work one day and found Surratt and Payne seated on a bed playing with bowie knives and two revolvers. There were four sets of new spurs on the bed also.[35]

During Payne's second visit about March 16, Wiechmann came home from work and, since Surratt was not there, he asked Dan, the servant, where he had gone. He was told that Surratt, with six others, had left the front of the house on horseback about two-thirty that afternoon. On going down to dinner later, he met Mrs. Surratt "weeping bitterly" in the passage. He asked her what the trouble was and she said, "John has gone away; go down to dinner and make the best of your dinner you can."

After dinner when Wiechmann was in his room reading, Surratt rushed into the room very excited with a pistol in his hand, saying, "I will shoot any one that comes into this room. My prospects are gone; my hopes are blighted. I want something to do. Can you get me a clerkship?" Ten minutes later, Payne came in also excited and he had a pistol. About fifteen minutes after that, Booth came in with a whip in his hand and frantically paced up and down the room several times before he saw Wiechmann.[36] They then went to the third floor back room and stayed there about thirty minutes, then left the house together.

This is certainly the same episode described by Arnold as the capture attempt of Lincoln in which Lincoln did not appear at the Soldier's Home on March 17.

Afterward Wiechmann was told that Payne had gone to Baltimore and that Booth had gone to New York. According to Arnold, he and O'Laughlin went to Baltimore so that the group was quite dispersed for a while. Booth had Spangler sell his horses and carriage. He also told his

Opposite: **Surratt house: (left) in 1865; (right) in 1990.**

friend Chester in New York that the capture plot was off due to some persons withdrawing. What else was going on in Booth's mind at this stage is only conjecture.

On April 2 Mrs. Surratt asked Wiechmann to take a message to Booth; she wished to see him on "private business." He came to the house that evening.

Wiechmann testified that he was asked by Mrs. Surratt on April 11, the Tuesday before the assassination, to go to the National Hotel and ask Booth if his buggy could be used to make a trip to the Surratt Tavern in the country. Booth said he had sold his buggy but gave Wiechmann $10 to rent one for her. Wiechmann then drove her to the country, leaving at nine and arriving at Surrattsville about noon. Mrs. Surratt was trying to collect a bill of $479 of thirteen years' standing owed to her by a Mr. Nothe. They had dinner at Captain Gwynn's place before returning home.[37] On this trip down they passed John Lloyd, the proprietor of the Surratt Tavern, on the road from Uniontown to Washington. It had been raining and the road was muddy. They backed up and Mrs. Surratt had a conversation with Lloyd leaning out of the buggy. Lloyd testified[38] that Mrs. Surratt broached the subject about articles at his place, which he said he at first did not understand. She then came out plainer and asked him to have the "shooting irons" ready because they would be needed soon.

On the afternoon of Friday, April 14, Mrs. Surratt rapped on Wiechmann's door and said she had to go to Surrattsville again, that she had received a letter about the money owed her. Wiechmann rented a buggy at Howard's Livery Stable, this time at her expense, and they again drove down together. Mrs. Surratt brought along a package wrapped in paper that was placed in the bottom of the buggy. They arrived there in the late afternoon.

In Lloyd's testimony,[39] he states that Mrs. Surratt was at his place when he returned in the evening. She met him as he got out of his buggy and told him to have those shooting irons ready, that someone would call for them that night. She gave him a package wrapped in paper, which he found to be a field glass. She told him to have two bottles of whiskey ready to go with the other things.

Mrs. Surratt and Wiechmann returned by about eight-thirty or nine o'clock that evening. Shortly after their return, while Wiechmann was in the dining room, the door bell rang. It was answered by Mrs. Surratt. He heard footsteps go into the parlor, immediately out again, and down the steps.

Detectives came to the Surratt house at 3:00 A.M. Saturday. At this time those in the house learned that Lincoln had been shot and that Seward had been badly wounded. They came in search of Surratt. He was not there.

The testimony of Major H. W. Smith was heard on May 19. He stated that he was in charge of the party that went to Mrs. Surratt's house the night of Monday, April 17.[40] He arrested Mrs. Surratt, Miss Anna Surratt, Miss Fitzpatrick, and Miss Jenkins. When Smith was at the door, he asked, "Are you Mrs. Surratt?" She said, "I am the widow of John H. Surratt," and he added, "The mother of John H. Surratt, Jr.?" She replied, "I am." He then said, "I came to arrest you and all in your house and take you for examination to General Augur's headquarters."

Payne came to the house. The major questioned him as to his occupation and what he was doing there at that hour. He stated that he was a laborer and had come to dig a gutter at the request of Mrs. Surratt. When Mrs. Surratt was asked if she knew this man and whether she had asked him to dig a gutter for her, she replied, raising her right hand, "Before God, sir, I do not know this man and have never seen him, and I did not hire him to dig a gutter for me." Payne said nothing. He was placed under arrest and sent to Colonel Wells at General Augur's headquarters for further interrogation.

Payne was dressed that night in an old grey coat. His black pants had one leg rolled up and the other stuffed into the top of his boot. On his head was a shirtsleeve, which hung down to one side, and on his shoulder was a pickaxe.[41] His appearance was most bizarre. Mrs. Surratt may have not recognized him in an effort to help him.

The interrogation of Mrs. Surratt at the general's headquarters has not come to light.[42] After it was completed, the ladies of the group were confined at Carroll Prison, where Mudd was taken on April 24, one week later. Payne, after his identification by one of the servants at Seward's home as the wild man who slashed and nearly killed members of that family, was placed aboard the *Saugus* at anchor midstream in the east branch of the Potomac River. He was soon to be joined in this floating security prison by Arnold, O'Laughlin, Spangler, Atzerodt, and Herold.

Two monitors were at anchor in the river to share the confinement of the conspirators. It was in the confined quarters of these two monitors that canvas hoods were ordered over the heads of the prisoners by Stanton. These were first placed over the heads of the captives on April 23 to make their isolation more complete. These hoods covering the eyes and ears of the prisoners not only made their confinement solitary and complete, but also made them miserable in the extreme summer heat.

Here the captives awaited their fate. Mrs. Surratt and Mudd fared a little better in the Carroll Annex until the end of April. On May 1 all the prisoners were taken to the austere Arsenal Prison, at now Fort McNair down near Greenleaf Point about a mile south of the Capitol. A courtroom was prepared on the northeast corner of the third floor of the building for the trial before the military commission.

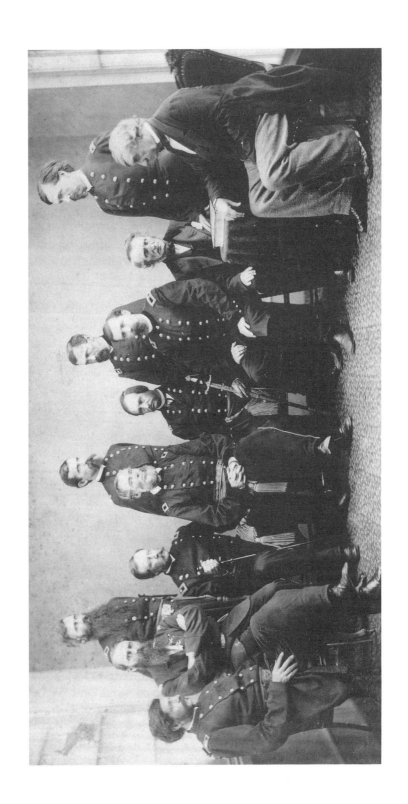

The Trial Begins

The trial was held in a refurbished room on the third floor of Arsenal Prison. The eight prisoners were seated at the west end of the room in their chains with guards seated alternately between them. Their hoods were removed while in the courtroom. There were tables for defense counsel in front of them.

The nine-man military commission was seated on the north side of the room with the three judge-advocates.

The witness stand was in the center of the room between two posts, with a table on either side. There was a table for reporters on the south side of the room opposite the military commission.

There was very little room for spectators. In fact they were not admitted in the beginning.

The first three days of the trial (May 9–11, 1865) were taken up with appointing and swearing in counsel and other preliminaries. Three attorneys declined to represent Mudd for various reasons. This was fortuitous. Mrs. Mudd somehow obtained the services of Brigadier General Thomas Ewing, Jr., just mustered out of the Union Army. She did not say how she accomplished this. He was assisted by Frederick Stone of Port Tobacco. The two made a strong team.

On May 12, 1865, the final introduction of counsel for the accused was made. This was on the third day of the trial. Next the accused offered a plea to the jurisdiction of the commission because none of the accused had been in the military service of the United States. The pleas of the accused were overruled by the commission. Pleas for severance were then made by each defendant. The commission was asked to try them separately. This was denied. The accused then each pleaded "Not Guilty."[43] Testimony relating to the general conspiracy was then heard.

Testimony for the Prosecution

Witness for the prosecution. Richard Montgomery. In the service of the United States Government (Secret Service). Montgomery operated under

Opposite: **Members of the military commission for the Lincoln murder trial. Seated, left to right, are: Col. D. R. Clendenin, Col. C. H. Tompkins, Gen. A. P. Howe, Gen. J. A. Ekin, Gen. D. Hunter, President of the Commission, Gen. R. S. Foster, Asst. Judge-Adv. Gen. J. A. Bingham (Ohio congressman, the only civilian), and Judge-Advocate J. Holt. Standing are Gen. T. M. Harris, Gen. L. Wallace, Gen. A. V. Kautz, and Asst. Judge-Advocate Gen. H. L. Burnett. The three at the extreme right were the prosecutors. (Courtesy of the Library of Congress.)**

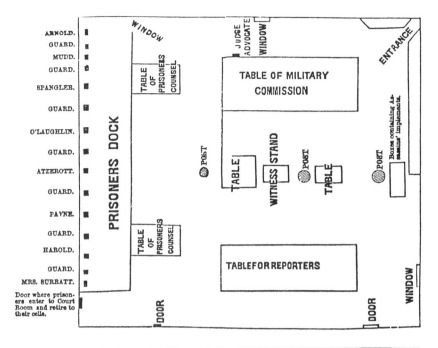

Top: Floor plan of the courtroom; *bottom:* the military court in session (courtesy of the National Archives).

the name James Thompson. He led the Confederate agents to believe this was his correct name and registered under other names at any hotel at which he stopped.

[The testimony has been transposed to narrative form by Pitman.]

Montgomery stated that he visited Canada in the summer of 1864 and except for travel time had remained there until about two weeks previously.

He knew the Confederate agents in Montreal, Jacob Thompson [former secretary of interior in the Buchanan administration], George N. Sanders, Clement C. Clay, Professor Holcomb, Beverly Tucker, W. C. Cleary, and Harrington. He had frequently met these persons since the summer of 1864 in Niagara Falls, Toronto, St. Catherines, and Montreal. Jacob Thompson went by several other names, one of which was Carson. Clay went by the name of Hope, Tracy, or T. E. Lacey.

In talking with Jacob Thompson in the summer of 1864, he said he [Thompson] had "friends" (Confederates) all over the Northern states, who would go to any lengths to serve the cause of the South. He stated that he could at any time have Lincoln and any of his advisors that he chose put out of the way. His "friends" would not let him know anything about it if necessary and would not consider it a crime when done for the Confederacy.

He talked with Clement C. Clay about this and his reply was, "That is so, we are all devoted to our cause."

Montgomery saw Jacob Thompson several times in January 1865 in Montreal. On one of these occasions Thompson had said a proposition had been made to him to rid the world of the tyrant Lincoln, Stanton, Grant, and some of the others. He said he was in favor of the proposition, but had determined to defer his answer until he had consulted with his government at Richmond. He was awaiting approval. Montgomery did not know whether this approval was ever given. W. C. Cleary was described as a sort of confidential secretary to Thompson. Cleary told Montgomery that Booth was one of the parties to whom Thompson had reference and that Booth had been there twice in the winter; he thought the last visit was in December. He had also been there in the summer. Montgomery stated he was familiar with the two secret cipher codes used by the Confederates. He was entrusted with dispatches, which he took to Richmond and back to Canada, leaving copies in Washington.

He gave advance information regarding the "firing" of theaters in New York City. He also gave some information in advance about the St. Albans, Vermont, raid although he did not have exact details of the strike. [This was a raid of about twenty-five Confederate soldiers, nearly all escaped prisoners, led by Lieutenant Bennet H. Young. They failed to burn the town but robbed three banks of $200,000.]

May 12. Samuel Knapp Chester. For the prosecution. Chester was a fellow actor whom Booth attempted to recruit. He stated that he had known Booth a great number of years and that he had known him intimately for six or seven years. About the latter part of December or early January, Booth called at his home in New York City.

Booth had previously spoken to Chester about a speculation. On this occasion, during a walk in the neighborhood, Booth told Chester that his speculation consisted of a large conspiracy to capture the heads of the government, including the president, and take them to Richmond. He asked Chester to join but Chester refused. Booth was insistent and talked for a half-hour. Chester stood firm. Booth then said to Chester, "You will at least not betray me," and added "You dare not."

Booth told Chester that the affair was to take place at Ford's Theater in Washington and that a large number of people were involved. He approached Chester again in February and was again turned down. Chester at this time told him not to mention the affair to him again. Chester returned fifty dollars to Booth that the latter had sent him in a letter as an inducement to join. Booth commented that he or some other party must go to Richmond to obtain means to carry out their designs. On Friday, April 7, one week before the assassination, Booth was again in New York and stated that he was selling his horses, that he had abandoned the idea of capturing the president owing to some parties backing out. On this visit while they were at a table at the House of Lords Restaurant, Booth remarked, "What an excellent chance I had to kill the president on inauguration day!"

May 13. For the prosecution. Louis Wiechmann (reporters spelled it Weichmann), a government clerk and former schoolmate of John H. Surratt, son of Mrs. Mary Surratt, had previously boarded at the Surratt boarding house at 541 H Street up to the time of the assassination. He now acted as a government witness for the prosecution. Many people were of the opinion that he was involved in the plot and should have been tried. His action as a government witness saved him from this. The truth of his testimony was questioned also by some people. Certainly it was disturbing for many, including Mudd. It was especially damaging for Mrs. Surratt. He wrote a book, which was published by Knopf in 1975. He died in Anderson, Indiana, in 1902.

He testified as follows:[44]

> Q. When did you begin to board at the house of Mrs. Surratt, a prisoner here?
> A. The first of November, 1864.
> Q. In this city?
> A. Yes, sir.

Q. In what part of the city?

A. H Street, between Sixth and Seventh, No. 541.

Q. You speak of Mrs. Surratt that is sitting near you there?

A. Yes, sir. She is the lady.

Q. State when you first made the acquaintance of the prisoner, Dr. Samuel A. Mudd?

A. It was about the 15th of January, 1865. [This was established by later testimony as December 23, 1864.]

Q. State under what circumstances.

A. I was passing down Seventh Street, in company of John Surratt; and when opposite Odd Fellows Hall, someone called, "Surratt, Surratt!" and on turning around, Mr. Surratt recognized an old acquaintance of his, Dr. Samuel A. Mudd of Charles County, Maryland.

Q. The prisoner at the bar?

A. Yes, sir. That is the gentleman there [pointing to Mudd]. Mr. Surratt introduced Dr. Mudd to me; and Dr. Mudd introduced Mr. Booth, who was in company with him, to both of us.

Q. He and Booth were walking together in the street?

A. Yes, sir. They were coming up Seventh Street and we were going down.

Q. You mean J. Wilkes Booth?

A. Yes, sir. J. Wilkes Booth.

Q. Where did you go to from there when you went?

A. Booth then invited us to his room at the National Hotel.

Q. What occurred there?

A. Booth told us to be seated; and he ordered cigars and wines to the room for four. Dr. Mudd then went out into the passage and called Booth out, and had a private conversation with him. Booth and Mudd came in, and they then called Surratt out.

Q. Both of them called him out?

A. No, sir. Booth went out with Surratt; and then they came in, and all three went out together, and had a private conversation in the passage, leaving me alone.

Q. How long did the conversation last?

A. It must have been about fifteen or twenty minutes.

Q. Did you hear what it was?

A. No sir. I do not know the nature of the conversation. I was seated on a lounge at the time, near the window. On returning to the room the last time, Dr. Mudd came to me, and seated himself by my side on the settee and he apologized for his private conversation, stating that Booth and he had some private business; that Booth wanted to purchase his farm.

Q. Did you see any maps or papers of that sort used?

A. No, sir. Booth at one time took out the back of an envelope, and made marks on it with a pencil. I should not consider it writing but more in the direction of roads or lines. Surratt and Booth and Dr. Mudd were at that time seated round the table—a center table—in the center of the room.

Q. Did you see the marks?

A. No, sir. I just saw the motion of the pencil. Booth also came to me and stated that he wished to purchase Dr. Mudd's farm. Dr. Mudd had previously stated to me that he did not care about selling his farm to Booth because Booth was not going to give him enough.

Q. But did you hear a word spoken yourself in regard to the subject of their conference?

A. No, sir. I did not.
Q. You only saw the motion of the pencil as they were marking?
A. No, sir [sic]. What their conversation was I do not know.
Q. You continued to board at the house of Mrs. Surratt, the prisoner?
A. I boarded at Mrs. Surratt's house up to the time of the assassination.

This second meeting between Mudd and Booth brought out at the trial was verified by the testimony of Jeremiah Theodore Mudd, Dr. Mudd's cousin, when called for the defense.[45] Jeremiah Mudd had a very strong resemblance to Abraham Lincoln and was frequently mistaken for him.[46] The two, Jeremiah and Sam, had come to Washington together for Christmas shopping and to meet friends from Baltimore at the Pennsylvania House Hotel, where they both registered. This was verified by reference to the Pennsylvania hotel register at the trial. When walking in front of the National Hotel that evening, Mudd ran into John Wilkes Booth on the street. Booth asked him to introduce him to John Harrison Surratt, son of a friend of Mudd's who formerly ran a tavern in Surrattsville, near his farm. The friend had died in 1862 and his widow had recently moved to a house on 541 H Street, where she ran a boarding house and lived with her daughter and son. It was on their way to Mrs. Surratt's boarding house that they ran into John Surratt walking with Louis Wiechmann.

Mudd had not mentioned this before. In his statement to Colonel Wells at Bryantown he had stated that he had met Booth on only one occasion prior to April 15.

Wiechmann had given the wrong date but the fact that a second meeting between Mudd and Booth had occurred in Washington was established in the testimony.

This of course was sensational news. The newspapers across the country headlined it. Wiechmann's testimony was not only damaging to Mudd, it was also very damaging to Mrs. Surratt, who ran the rooming house at 541 H Street and owned the tavern at Surrattsville. She made periodic trips to the latter place to look after her property, then rented to John M. Lloyd. On two of these trips, Wiechmann, one of her young roomers at 541 H Street, accompanied her when she went there by buggy. On the last trip that, ominously, was on April 14, the afternoon of the day of the assassination, she took along a package of Booth's and gave it to John Lloyd the innkeeper. This turned out later to contain John Wilkes Booth's field glasses. This strongly implicated her in Booth's scheme. She probably thought she was aiding in the capture attempt if she indeed gave it a second thought. When Booth changed his plan to assassination instead of capture is not definitely known, but it was very late. Although he may have had the possibility in the back of his own mind for some time, he did not tell anyone. The evidence indicates that he made up his mind on the morning of April 14, when he learned that both Lincoln and Grant planned to attend the theater that evening. He learned this when he picked up his mail there. The final assignments for his accomplices were made at a meeting about 8:00 P.M. at the Herndon House. They may not have all been together at one time but Atzerodt was there. It was the first Atzerodt knew that he was to shoot Vice President Johnson and he objected strenuously. He told Booth that he agreed to help kidnap but not to kill but he was not released from his assignment. He never attempted to fulfill it. Did Mrs. Surratt know about Booth's hideous intent on the day she took his field glasses to Lloyd at the tavern in Surrattsville? Lloyd's testimony indicates that she did. It was very strong evidence against her. These things point out the cruel, thoughtless things that Booth, in his depraved state of mind, was doing and allowing to happen. He played the lead role as he did on the stage, in an egotistical manner, drawing others into the plot without regard for their safety and not keeping them informed of changes in plans. Chester escaped only because of his own good judgment.

The proceedings at the trial were very complicated. This was, first, due to the fact that eight people were being tried as a group. Second, the limits of the conspiracy were indefinite. Third, the accused were not allowed to testify in their own behalf. Many witnesses were called to tell what an accused person said or did. In the beginning testimony was of a general nature. Later testimony did not proceed in an orderly manner for each of the accused. The testimony of Wells and Lovett regarding their interviews with Mudd on April 18 through April 21 has already been given.

After Wiechmann's testimony, there was a short relief, but on May 25, several of Mudd's former slaves came to the stand.

First was Mary Simms for the prosecution. May 25. She said that she had been Dr. Mudd's slave for four years and left about November 1864. She had heard Dr. Mudd talk about President Lincoln. He said that he stole in there at night, dressed in woman's clothes; that they lay in watch for him, and if he had come in right, they would have killed him. He said nothing about shooting him; they would have killed him, she said, if he had come in right, but he could not; because he was dressed in woman's clothes. She said that John Surratt visited frequently. He would go to Virginia and stop on the way back and give the news. Strange people hid in the woods and slept there. Bed clothes were taken to them. She gave the names of a lot of people who visited the Mudd home.

Mr. Ewing later brought evidence through other witnesses that many of these visitors were in the early stage of the war, in 1861, when there was much confusion and shifting of loyalties in Charles County. The reference to Lincoln wearing woman's clothes referred to a rumor that Lincoln did this on his way to Washington in February of 1861. Conditions were very bad in Baltimore on that trip and several plots against Lincoln were known to exist. For safety's sake Lincoln's train left Philadelphia early and went through Baltimore without stopping. Those who were foiled by this security measure may have spread the rumor that Lincoln wore woman's clothes. It was a rumor of 1861, prior to Lincoln's first inauguration.

Elzee Eglent for the prosecution. May 25. This young man was a former slave with whom Dr. Mudd had had some difficulty. Dr. Mudd had put a little buck-shot into his thigh a year or so earlier when he had been unruly.

He testified: I know Dr. Samuel Mudd; he was my boss; yonder he is. [Pointing to the accused] I was his slave and lived with him until the 20th of August before the last.

Q. Did he say anything to you before you left him about sending you to Richmond?

A. Yes, sir. He told me the morning he shot me that he had a place in Richmond for me.

Mr. Ewing: I object to that question and the answer.

The Judge-Advocate: The object to the question is to show disloyalty. Objection overruled.

Witness: He told me he had a place in Richmond for me when I should be able to go away. He did not say what I was to do there. He named four more that he said he was going to send to Richmond—Dick and my two brothers, Sylvester and Frank. I saw men come to Dr. Mudd's dressed some in black clothes and some in gray; grayjackets, coat-like, and gray breeches. . . . They used to sleep in the woods, about a quarter of mile off, I reckon, and would come to the house at different times, and go back to the woods. I don't know where they got their victuals, but I have seen victuals going that way often enough; I have seen my sister, Mary Simms, carry them. That was in the June and July before the last.[47]

Sylvester Eglent for the prosecution. May 25.

I used to live about a quarter of a mile from the house of Dr. Samuel Mudd; I lived with his father.

Q. State whether you heard him say anything, at any time, about sending men to Richmond.

A. Last August, a twelvemonth ago, I heard him say he was going to send me, Elzee, my brother Frank and Dick Gardner and Lou Gardner to Richmond to build batteries.

Mr. Ewing objected to the question and the answer.

The commission overruled the objection.

Witness: That was the last Friday in the August before last, and I left the next night. Forty head of us went in company.[48]

Melvina Washington for the prosecution. May 25.

I used to live with Dr. Mudd. [Pointing to the accused] I left him this coming October two years. The last summer I was there I heard say that President Lincoln would not occupy his seat long. There was a heap of gentlemen in the house at the time. Some had gray clothes and some had little short jackets with black buttons.

Sometimes they stayed in the house and sometimes slept in the pines not far from Dr. Mudd's spring. Dr. Mudd carried victuals to them sometimes and once he sent them by Mary Simms. I was at the house one day when they were sitting down to dinner with two boys watching. When they were told somebody was coming, these men rushed from the table to the side door and went to the spring.

Cross-examination by Mr. Ewing.

Witness: Those men stayed in the woods a week or more and were at the house seven or eight times. I did not stay about the house but went up when there was company. I had to go up on account of the milking, and that is how I happened to see them.

Milo Simms for the prosecution. May 25.

I was a slave of Dr. Samuel Mudd and lived with him. [Pointing to the prisoner] I left his house the Friday before last Christmas.... I worked mostly in the field but sometimes at the house to take care of the horses.... Mr. Surratt was not shown to me by anyone. Dr. Mudd came out to me and said, "Take Mr. Surratt's horse to the stable and feed him." He stayed all night that time.

Rachel Spencer for the prosecution. May 25. A former slave who left the Mudd household January last. She also said men stayed in the woods last summer and that food was taken to them.

William Marshall for the prosecution. May 25.

I was a slave until 1863.

Q. State whether you heard any conversation between Benjamin Gardiner and Dr. Mudd about the rebels and their battle with Union forces at the Rappahannock.

Mr. Ewing objected to the question but was overruled.

A. Yes, sir. I did. Soon after the battle of the Rappahannock I happened to be home. Mr. Gardiner said to the doctor when he was making a call, "We gave them hell down on the Rappahannock." The doctor said, "Yes we did."

Daniel J. Thomas for the prosecution. May 18. This witness claimed that Dr. Mudd made disparaging remarks about Lincoln and his cabinet during a political discussion about two months earlier and even predicted the death of Lincoln. This was devastating testimony against Dr. Mudd if it stood. It indicated that Dr. Mudd knew about the assassination plot two months before it occurred. There was no other evidence of this nature. It was brought out by further questioning and by other witnesses that this witness was interested in the ten thousand dollar reward. He was also said to be unreliable by others. Mr. Ewing called eight witnesses to discredit D. J. Thomas. His brother, a physician, testified he had cared for Mr. Thomas medically and that he was at times unstable mentally. With this, the value of his testimony dropped to zero.[49]

Marcus P. Norton for the prosecution. June 3. Mr. Norton was stopping at the National Hotel in Washington about the 3rd. of March just prior to the second inauguration of President Lincoln. He occupied room 77. He stated that he saw Booth whom he knew from stage performances talking to Atzerodt in the lobby of the hotel on one occasion. On the morning of March 3rd a man entered his room by mistake, apologized saying he was looking for Booth and quickly left. He said the man was Dr. Mudd or someone that looked exactly like him. This testimony was discredited by other witnesses who testified that Dr. Mudd was not in Washington on March 3rd.

William A. Evans for the prosecution. June 5. This witness testified that he saw Dr. Mudd enter Mrs. Surratt's boarding house on H Street on the 1st or 2nd of March. This was not verified by the testimony of Wiechmann or other boarders who said they had never seen Dr. Mudd there. It was discredited on this basis and also on the fact that he said that he had been very confused and disturbed since the death of President Lincoln. He was a very garrulous witness.

John W. Ward for the prosecution. May 20. This witness was a resident of Bryantown, Maryland. He went down town in the village about 1 P.M. April 15th and observed that the military was in town and that there was excitement.

> When I returned home a neighbor said the president had been shot. I immediately went back to town where I heard of the assassination. I also heard that the assassin's name was Booth. It was spoken of by everybody. This was between one and two o'clock. The village was put under martial law. I think I saw Dr. Mudd there but the excitement was so great that I cannot be sure. "Boose" was the name given by the soldiers.

Frank Bloyce for the prosecution. May 20.
> I was in Bryantown on Saturday after the murder of President Lincoln. I saw Dr. Mudd there between 3 and 4 o'clock.

Mrs. Eleanor Bloyce for the prosecution. May 19.
> I know Dr. Mudd. I saw him riding toward Bryantown with a gentleman with him. In a short time Dr. Mudd returned alone. After that I went into Bryantown myself. On arriving there I found the soldiers from Washington and heard that the president had been shot the night before at the theater. I did not hear who shot him.

Mrs. Becky Briscoe for the prosecution. May 19.
> I live about a quarter of a mile from Bryantown. On the Saturday after President Lincoln was murdered, I was by the door and saw Dr. Mudd riding into town with a strange gentleman about 3 o'clock. The gentleman went toward the bridge and Dr. Mudd kept on toward Bryantown. This gentleman came back and went toward the swamp. The bridge is in sight of Bryantown. He stayed in the swamp until the doctor came back in a little while. I went to town and heard the president had been

murdered. I didn't know for two or three days that the man who killed him was Booth.

Other witnesses testified for the prosecution in regard to other defendants. The testimony for the prosecution closed at the end of May 23. The June 3 testimony of Marcus Norton and the June 5 testimony of William Evans were actually made during the defense testimony. There were 131 witnesses for the prosecution. Nineteen of these were against Mudd.

The weather was hot and humid in the city of Washington. The trial room was an oven. White curtains blew in and out of the three small windows, exchanging the highly heated outside air for that of the inside without giving relief. The trial wore on with a confusing sequence of witnesses relating to one defendant, then another in no definite order. The press corps described Mudd as one of the most composed. He rested his hands on a railing in front of the prisoner's dock. This helped relieve the weight of his handcuffs joined by a chain. The other male defendants were even worse off. Their hands were joined by rigid iron manacles. Their hands were thus held about twelve inches apart so that they could not be joined.

Mrs. Surratt wore handcuffs joined by a chain. Atzerodt and Payne each had a fifty-pound iron ball attached to one leg that was carried by a guard when they entered or left the courtroom. At least they were free of their terrible hoods while they were in the courtroom.

At this point in the trial, before the defense was heard, the case for Mudd might have been summed up somewhat as follows:

1. Mudd had pro–Southern sympathies at least early in the war but had taken the oath of allegiance to the United States and had voted for a Union candidate in the November 1864 elections.

2. It was claimed that he had made derogatory statements regarding President Lincoln. One witness said he predicted the death of the president.

3. He had not told of a second meeting with Booth in Washington in December 1864.

4. He had not immediately reported the visit of the two strangers on April 15.

5. He had treated the injured stranger, which any good doctor should have done. He said he did not recognize the injured man.

6. He had stabled Booth's horses and allowed his patient to rest upstairs in his home on April 15.

7. When questioned about the events of April 15 his interrogators thought him evasive and nervous, as though he was withholding information.

Testimony for the Defense of Mudd

J. C. Thompson. May 26.[50] This witness, son-in-law of Dr. Cox, Charles County, Maryland, told of introducing John Wilkes Booth to Dr. Mudd at St. Mary's Catholic Church on a Sunday morning in October or November 1864. Booth came as a stranger with a letter of introduction from a man named Martin in Montreal. He was interested in buying land, he said, and also horses. In response to a question of Booth making a second visit to Charles County, the witness said that Booth made a second visit about the middle of December. (This answer was not followed up at the trial. It will come up later.) He said he lived about seven or eight miles from Dr. Mudd.

William T. Bowman. May 27.

I live in Charles County, Maryland. Sometime in December last I met John Wilkes Booth at church near Bryantown. I was told it was Booth, the tragedian. After talking with several people, he asked me if I had land for sale. I told him I did and pointed some of it out to him through the window. He also asked about horses for sale and I said I had several. He said he would be down in a couple of weeks and look at my land. I had heard Dr. Mudd say he would sell his land last summer when he could get no hands. I asked him what he expected to do if he sold his land. He said he thought of going into business at Benedict on the Patuxent River. Some five days later, I saw Dr. Mudd and told him. He said, "That fellow promised to buy my land." It is about eighteen miles from Bryantown to Pope's Creek, which is opposite Mathias Point.

Jeremiah Dyer. May 27.

I have lived in Baltimore for two years. Before that I lived one-half mile from Dr. Samuel Mudd. In 1861 Colonel Dwight's regiment was passing through and arresting people. I was in the neighborhood of Dr. Mudd's home for about a week with Andrew Gwinn and his brother Benjamin. A lot of people were being arrested and we had heard that they wanted to arrest us. We slept in the pines. Dr. Mudd supplied us with some bedding and he or Mary Simms brought us food.

I have known Daniel J. Thomas since he was a boy. His reputation is so bad that I would not believe him under oath.

I have known Dr. Mudd since he was a boy. He has always been regarded as a good citizen. I have always considered him a good and humane slave master. He told me of shooting one of his servants who was unruly and was sorry he had done it.

Q. In 1861 was the subject of the Legislature of Maryland passing an ordinance of secession much discussed among you?

A. I heard it spoken of in crowds but I have no recollection of speaking with any particular person.

I do not know that I particularly rejoiced at the success of the rebels at the first battle of Bull Run. When Richmond was taken, my sympathies were on the side of the government. I wanted to see the war stopped. I believe the United States were pursuing the right course, except in emancipating the slaves. I thought that was wrong.

By Mr. Ewing: I know that Mr. Thomas has not borne a good reputation for truth and veracity since he was a boy. The military organization to which I belonged in 1859 was not regarded as a disloyal organization. We never drilled after the war broke out.

By Mr. Stone: Dr. Mudd does not live on any of the direct roads from Washington to the Potomac. It would be seven or eight miles out of the way to go past Dr. Mudd's place.

By Assistant Judge-Advocate Bingham: In September 1861 I accompanied Benjamin and Andrew Gwinn to Richmond, Virginia, after spending four or five days in the pines at Dr. Mudd's.

By Mr. Ewing: I am a brother-in-law to Dr. Mudd. When I returned from Virginia, I took the oath of allegiance and have never to my knowledge, violated it.

Allen J. Brook. May 27.

By Mr. Ewing: I worked for Dr. Mudd from January to September 1864. I know Andrew Gwynn and Benjamin Gwynn. I did not see either of them at Dr. Mudd's. I was in the stable morning, noon, and night and I never saw any strange horses there. I stayed at Dr. Mudd's house while I worked there and took my meals there. I never saw any one staying in the woods since the beginning of the war in 1861. Then I saw Jerry Dyer, Benjamin and Andrew Gwynn but I have not seen them since.

Assistant Judge-Advocate Bingham: The witness was shown a picture of John Surratt. He said, "I know that man, it is John Surratt." He said he saw him August last sixteen miles from Dr. Mudd's and that he never saw him at Dr. Mudd's.

Frank Washington. May 27. [This is Dr. Mudd's trusted hired hand who was referred to previously on April 15.]

By Mr. Stone: I was with Dr. Mudd all of last year. I was his plowman. I still work for him. I was there every day except Sundays and holidays. I took my meals in Dr. Mudd's kitchen. I was in the stable night and morning and at noon. I was often at the spring. I know Andrew and Benjamin Gwynn by sight. It has been four years since I saw them. There have been no strange horses in the stable. I never saw any one there called Captain Perry or Lieutenant Perry or Captain White. I know Mary Simms.

Q. What do the servants in the neighborhood think of her character for telling the truth?

A. She was never known to tell the truth.

Q. Would you believe her on oath?

A. No, sir.

Q. How did Dr. Mudd treat his servants?

A. He treated them pretty well.

Q. How did he treat you?

A. He treated me first rate. I have no fault to find with him.

[A photo of John Surratt was shown to the witness.] I do not know him. I never saw him.

By the Judge-Advocate: I have known Mary Simms since she was a small girl. Others on the place think of Mary Simms as I do. I was not on the place when Dr. Mudd shot one of his servants. I knew him but have not seen him since the second year of the war.

[The witness was asked to look at David Herold, one of the accused.]

A. I never saw him. I do not know any of the prisoners except Dr. Mudd.

Witness: I was home on Saturday the morning after the president was killed when two men called at Dr. Mudd's. I took their horses. I got a glimpse of one of them as he was standing in the door just as day was breaking.

By Assistant Judge-Advocate Burnett: Two stray horses came there the day after the assassination. I put them in the stable and fed them. One was a bay and the other was a large roan. At noon the bay was gone and Dr. Mudd's gray one.

Q. Did the little man on the end of the seat there [Herold] ride the bay one or the Doctor?

A. I do not know. I never saw him on a horse.

Q. You know you took out the bay one and Dr. Mudd's gray?

A. Yes, sir.

I do not know where they went. When I brought out the horses, I went to the field and did not come back until sundown. Both horses were then gone. Dr. Mudd has only two servants now, myself and Baptist Washington, a carpenter. I get $130 a year wages. I do not know that I shall get any thing extra for coming here. I do not know anything about any arms being brought to Dr. Mudd's at any time.

Baptist Washington. May 27.

By Mr. Stone: I worked for Dr. Samuel Mudd last year. I put up a room between his house and the kitchen. I was there from January or February until August. I never heard of anybody being camped at the spring or in the woods. I knew Mary Simms. Nobody put much confidence in what she said. Mary Simms took care of the children and waited on the table sometimes.

Q. How did Dr. Mudd treat his servants?

A. He always treated his servants very well.

Q. How did he treat you?

A. He treated me very well. I was always very satisfied with the accommodations he gave me when I was there.

[The witness was shown a photograph of John Surratt.] I do not know that man. I never saw him at Dr. Mudd's that I know.

Mrs. Mary Jane Simms. May 27.

I lived with Dr. Samuel Mudd last year except for three weeks. I know Captain Bennett Gwynn and Mr. Andrew Gwynn, also John Surratt. I saw none of these people at Dr. Mudd's last year.[51]

Bennett F. Gwynn. May 20.

By Mr. Ewing: My name is Bennett F. Gwynn. I am sometimes called Ben Gwynn. Andrew and George are my brothers. In August 1861 I was with my brothers at Dr. Mudd's place. At that time General Sickles came to Maryland and was arresting nearly everybody. We came down to Charles County and stayed more than a week.

Q. Where did you and those with you sleep when you were near Dr. Mudd's home?

A. We slept in the pines near the spring. We had some counterpanes there that were brought by Dr. Mudd who brought us meals. While we were there, we went to Dr. Mudd's house nearly every day. I have not been to Dr. Mudd's home since November 1861.[52]

Fourteen witnesses were called to testify about the reliability of Daniel Thomas, who had testified for the prosecution that Mudd had predicted the death of Lincoln by several weeks, a very serious charge. These witnesses testified that Thomas was not trustworthy and there was no basis for his testimony. Downing, in whose home the conversation was said to have taken place, denied that it happened. This subject was climaxed by the testimony of Dr. John C. Thomas. Dr. Thomas was a practicing physician and stated that he had attended his brother professionally for several serious attacks. He had had a serious attack of depression six years previously and sometimes he was mentally affected. Several other witnesses testified that he wished to obtain reward for his testimony. Ewing labored long and hard to counter the charge of prophecy of Lincoln's death. The defense witnesses discredited Thomas to such an extent that his testimony was of little value. If that had not been true, the array of defense witnesses would have been enough to wear down any resistance to Mudd's innocence.

Jeremiah Mudd testified at length about the trip to Washington on December 23, 1864, with Mudd. They went to make purchases. Mudd bought a stove and made arrangements to have it hauled to his residence. The meeting with Booth in front of the National Hotel was incidental. Ewing called Francis Lucas, who testified that Mudd contacted him to bring his newly purchased stove home.[53]

Samuel McAllister, the clerk at the Washington House Hotel, was called to testify that Mudd was at the Washington House with Jeremiah Mudd on the night of December 23.

Thomas L. Gardiner for defense. May 29.[54]

By Mr. Ewing: On the 23rd of March last, Dr. Samuel Mudd and I came to Washington. We left home about 8 A.M. and came to Washington to attend the sale of government condemned horses. The date of the sale was changed and we were disappointed.

Dr. Charles Allen and Mr. Henry Clark both testified that they met Mr. Gardiner and Dr. Mudd on their trip to Washington on the 23rd of March. Mr. Clark testified that they stayed at his home that night.

There was testimony that Mudd had been seen entering Mrs. Surratt's boarding house at 541 H Street early in March and also Marcus Norton thought he had entered his room by mistake at the National Hotel on March 3 looking for Booth.

To counter these charges, Ewing called many witnesses who testified about Mudd's whereabouts in early March. Fannie Mudd testified that Mudd treated her for suspected smallpox on March 3. She also testified that Mudd was at home from March 1 to March 5. Emily Mudd also testified that Mudd treated her sister the first week of March.

Ewing used the same tactics as he had to discredit Thomas to show that no additional meetings between Mudd and Booth occurred between

December 1864 and April 15, 1865. He called multiple witnesses, one after the other. Seventeen witnesses were called to testify as to Mudd's whereabouts during this interval. There were two trips to Washington to buy horses, one of which is referred to above. The witnesses testified precisely as to Mudd's whereabouts during these absences from home. Betty Washington testified that Mudd was very busy with the tobacco planting the first week of March and was not away during that time. Thomas Davis testified that Mudd treated him while he was sick in bed the first week of March and that he came to see him on Ash Wednesday. The testimony covered the complete period up to April 15.

The testimony of Dr. George Mudd, a practicing physician in Bryantown and Mudd's second cousin, was very important in regard to the delay in reporting the presence of two strangers at the Mudd home on April 15. It led to several caustic verbal exchanges between Ewing and Bingham.

Dr. George D. Mudd for the defense. May 29.[55]

By Mr. Ewing: I am a practitioner of medicine in the village of Bryantown, Charles County, Maryland. Dr. Samuel Mudd was a student of medicine under me for many years. His father and my father were first cousins. I know his reputation in the neighborhood for peace, order and good citizenship and I know of none whose reputation is better. I have always considered him a humane man to his servants, as well as to others. He always clothed and fed his servants well and treated them kindly as far as I know.

I was at Bryantown Saturday April 15 when the news of the assassination of the President reached there and remained there all evening. Lieutenant Dana, upon whom I called for information, told me that the party who had attempted the assassination of Secretary Seward was named Boyle and claimed him to be the same party who assassinated Captain Watkins and that the party who assassinated the President was supposed to be a man by the name of Booth. He thought that he had not yet gotten out of Washington. Boyle, who was known in our region of country and had been there three or four weeks before, was a noted desperado and guerrilla.

I was at church Sunday the 16th. It was then known that the President had been assassinated, but no one, to my knowledge, supposed that Booth had crossed the river; this at least is my impression; I did not make much inquiry in that regard. I saw Dr. Samuel Mudd at church. On returning home he overtook me and I rode with him as far as his house.

Q. State whether he said anything to you about any persons having been at his house?

The Judge-Advocate: You need not answer that question. The government has not introduced the declarations of the prisoner, Dr. Mudd at that time.

Mr. Ewing: I propose to offer that statement for the purpose of showing that Dr. George Mudd, a resident of Bryantown, and whom I will prove is a man of unquestionable loyalty, was informed by the prisoner at the bar that there were two suspicious persons at his house on Saturday morning. He told him of the circumstances of their coming there; expressed to him a desire that he should inform the military authorities, if he thought it advisable, of the fact of their having been there; stated to him that he wished him to take it directly to the military authorities, and not tell it at large about the streets, lest the parties or their friends might assassinate him for his disclosure.

I can imagine no declaration of a prisoner more clearly admissible than this. It accompanies, or is connected with acts which they have shown of the preceding day, and subsequent days. It is a part of the very gist of acts and omissions by which he is sought to be implicated here and to refuse to allow him to show that he informed the government, through one of its most loyal friends, of the presence of these men in his house and his suspicions in regard to them, would be to strip him of a complete and admissible defense. On the subject of such actions—for this statement was an act—I read an authority from Russell on crimes, vol. 2, page 750. [An appropriate paragraph was read from this source. Following this, two additional sources were referred to and read to the court. Following this Ewing continued.]

It is to explain his silence up to the time of his making the communication to Dr. George Mudd and to rebut the evidence of detective Lloyd as to his concealment, on the Tuesday following, of the fact that these two men had ever been at his house, that I propose to introduce that statement in evidence. This statement was made before he could have known that any suspicions were directed against him. It was an act done during the time of that silence and alleged concealment, by reason of which they seek to implicate him as an accessory before and after the fact in the assassination. That conversation with Dr. George Mudd accounts for the silence; that conversation broke the silence. If the fact of his having been silent is to be urged against him, may not the fact that he broke the silence, and communicated all the facts to the military authorities, be introduced in his behalf? [Other authorities were quoted to the court.]

The Judge-Advocate: The res gestae consisted in his having received and entertained these men and sent them on their way rejoicing, having fed them, having set the leg of the one whose leg was broken, having comforted and strengthened and encouraged them, as far as his hospitality and professional skill could do, to proceed on their journey. This is the res gestae and it was complete at 4 o'clock Saturday evening. . . . The great principle which says that a criminal shall not manufacture testimony for his own exculpation, intervenes and forbids that this Court shall hear the testimony.

Assistant Judge-Advocate Burnett suggested that the witness be asked if Mudd directed him to notify the authorities.

Mr. Ewing: State whether you communicated to the military authorities in Bryantown the fact of any suspicious persons having been at the house of Dr. Samuel A. Mudd on Saturday.

A. I did to Lieutenant Dana, who was the principal in command of the military there at that time.

Q. When did you communicate it to him?

A. I think it was on Monday morning.

Q. Did you make any communication to any other military authorities?

A. Yes, sir. Tuesday afternoon to four detectives. They questioned me very particularly about the affair. I then escorted them to Dr. Mudd's home.

Later Ewing tried again.

Q. Did you have any conversation with Dr. Samuel Mudd at the church, or hear his conversation, as to what he knew of the assassination?

A. No, sir; I heard. . .

Assistant Judge-Advocate Bingham: You need not state anything you heard him say there.

Ewing: I think it admissible, as explanatory of the conduct of the accused during the very time of the occurrence of the offenses charged—because, as I said before, one of the offenses charged is concealment, which relates beyond that Saturday—as showing his frame of mind, his information, his conduct.

Ewing and Bingham argued at great length on this point of admission of the evidence that Mudd asked to have the authorities notified on Sunday.

The objection was upheld by the commission but in the course of the arguments Ewing introduced the gist of the facts. In this way he got his points across although the witness was not allowed to give testimony. It was almost universal that any objection was upheld by the commission. In this case, however, Dr. George Mudd was recalled as a defense witness on June 9 and allowed to testify in regard to these matters. At that time he testified that Dr. Samuel Mudd had taken the Oath of Allegiance to the United States of America under his administration in June or July 1864. This was in regard to framing a new constitution for the State of Maryland. Dr. George Mudd was improvised by two of the judges as the chief judge of the election that day.

Ewing then questioned Dr. George Mudd about Daniel J. Thomas. The witness testified that Thomas's reputation for veracity was very bad and at times the man was not of sound mind.

Testimony for the defense closed on June 10 with some additional witnesses for the prosecution being heard on June 12. There were 131 witnesses for the prosecution. Nineteen of these were against Mudd, seventeen against Payne, ten against Atzerodt, eleven against O'Laughlin, eight against Arnold, four against Spangler, and seven against Mrs. Surratt.[56]

There were 128 witnesses for the defense, seventy-three of which had bearing on Mudd.

Arguments of counsel began on June 16 and Ewing's arguments for Mudd, Spangler, and Arnold on June 23.

The Summation of General Thomas Ewing, Jr.[57]

The first argument presented by Ewing was that the military court did not have jurisdiction over civilians when civil courts were intact. (The civil courts were intact in Washington, D.C., in 1865.)

MAY IT PLEASE THE COURT: The first great question—a question that meets us at the threshold—is do you, gentlemen, constitute a court, and have you jurisdiction, as a court, of the persons accused, and the crimes with which they are charged? If you have such jurisdiction, it must have been conferred by the Constitution, or some law consistent with it and carrying out its provisions.

1. The 5th article of the Constitution declares: "That the judicial power of the United States shall be vested in one Supreme Court and in such inferior courts as Congress may from time to time ordain and establish"; and that "the judges of

both Supreme and inferior courts shall hold their offices during good behavior."

Under this provision of the Constitution, none but courts ordained or established by Congress can exercise judicial power and those courts must be composed of judges who hold their offices during good behavior. They must be independent judges, free from the influence of executive power. Congress has not "ordained and established" you a court, or authorized you to call these parties before you and sit upon their trial and you are not "judges" who hold your offices during good behavior. You are, therefore, no court under the Constitution and have no jurisdiction in these cases, unless you obtain it from some other source, which overrules this constitutional provision.

The president cannot confer judicial power upon you, for he has it not. The executive, not the judicial, power of the United States is vested in him. His mandate, no matter to what man or body of men addressed, to try and, if convicted, to sentence to death a citizen, not of the naval or military forces of the United States, carries with it no authority which could be pleaded in jurisdiction of the sentence. . . .

2. The president, under the 5th amendment to the Constitution, may constitute courts pursuant to the Articles of War, but he cannot give them jurisdiction over citizens. This article provides that "no person shall be held to answer for a capital or otherwise infamous crime unless on a presentment or indictment of a grand jury, except in cases arising in the land or naval forces, or in the militia when in actual service in time of war or public danger."

The presentment and indictment of a grand jury is a thing unknown and inconsistent with your Commission. You have nothing of the kind. Neither you nor the law officers who control your proceedings seem to have thought of any such thing. These defendants did not and do not belong to the "land or naval forces" of the United States—nor were they "militia in time of war or public danger, in actual service."

Ewing's arguments continued at great length. He clearly pointed out that the military court did not have jurisdiction over private citizens when the civil courts were intact. His previous record in the Union Army as major-general gave him stature among the members of the military commission.

Next he complained strenuously that the crime of which his client was accused was not clearly stated.

Argument on the LAW AND EVIDENCE IN THE CASE OF DR. SAMUEL A. MUDD by Thomas Ewing, Jr.

May it please the court: If it be determined to take jurisdiction here, it then becomes a question vitally important to some of these parties—a question of life and death—whether you will punish only offenses created and declared by law, or whether you will make and declare the past acts of the accused to be crimes, which acts the law never heretofore declared criminal: attach to them the penalty of death, or such penalty as may seem meet to you; adapt the evidence to the crime and punish. This, I greatly fear may be the purpose, especially since the Judge-Advocate said in reply to my inquiries, that he would expect to convict "under the common law of war." This is a term unknown to our language—a quiddity—wholly undefined and incapable of definition. It is in short just what the Judge-Advocate chooses to make it.

I will now proceed to show you, that on the part of one of my clients—Dr. Mudd—no crime known to the law and for which it is pretended to prosecute, can possibly have been committed. Though not distinctly informed as to the offense for which the Judge-Advocate claims conviction, I am safe in saying, that the testimony does not point to treason and if he is being tried for treason, the proceedings for that crime are widely departed from.

The prosecution appears to have been instituted and conducted under the proclamation of the Secretary of War of April 20, 1865. This makes it a crime punishable with death, to harbor or screen Booth, Atzerodt, or Herold, or to aid or assist them to escape. It makes it a crime to do a particular act and punishes that crime with death. I suppose we must take this proclamation as law. Perhaps it is part of what the Judge-Advocate means when he speaks of the "common law of war." If this be so, my clients are still safe, if we are allowed to construe it as laws are construed by courts of justice.

Mr. Ewing: I will show, first, that Dr. Mudd is not, and cannot possibly be, guilty of any offense known to the law.[58]
1. Not of Murder. The overt act attempted to be alleged is the murder of the president. The proof is conclusive, that at the time the tragedy was enacted Dr. Mudd was at his residence in the country, thirty miles from the place of the crime. . . .

2. Not of Treason. For the law is clear, that, in cases of treason, presence at the commission of the overt act is governed by the same principle as constructive presence in ordinary felonies and has no other latitude greater or less, except that in proof of treason two witnesses are necessary to the overt act and one only in murder and other felonies. . . . Persons not sufficiently near to give assistance are not principals. And although an act be committed in pursuance of a previously concerted plan, those who are not present, or so near as to be able to afford aid and assistance, at the time when the offense is committed, are not principals, but accessories before the fact.

It is, therefore, perfectly clear, upon the law as enacted by the Legislature and expanded by jurists, that Dr. Mudd is not guilty of participating in the murder of the president; that he was not actually or constructively present when the horrid deed was done, either as a traitor, chargeable with it as an overt act, or a conspirator, connected as a principal felon therewith.

3. The only other crimes defined by law for the alleged commission, of which the Judge-Advocate may, by possibility, claim the conviction of the accused, are: 1st the crime of treasonable conspiracy, which is defined by the law of 21st July, 1861 and made punishable by fine not exceeding $6,000 and imprisonment not exceeding six years. . . .

4. Admitting the War Secretary's proclamation to be law, it, of course, either supersedes or defines the unknown something or nothing which the Judge-Advocate calls "the common law of war." If so, it is a definite, existing thing and I can defend my clients against it and it is easy to show that Dr. Mudd is not guilty of violating that proclamation. He did not, after the date of the proclamation, see either of the parties named therein—dress the wound of Booth or point out the way to Herold—and the proclamation relates to future acts, not to the past.

I now pass to a consideration of the evidence which I think will fully satisfy the

Court that Dr. Mudd is not guilty of treasonable conspiracy, or of being an accomplice, before or after the fact in the felonies committed.

Ewing then proceeded to summarize the evidence, pointing out that the accused was a practicing physician residing five miles north of Bryantown, nearly thirty miles from Washington. His home was four or five miles east of the road from Washington to Bryantown. It was pointed out that the accused was of exemplary character—peaceable, kind, upright, and obedient to the law. His family were slave holders; he did not like the antislavery measures of the government, but was respectful and temperate in his discussions of the issue. He took the oath of allegiance prescribed for voters and voted for a Union candidate in 1864.

His meeting with Booth in November 1864 was described and the testimony of nearly all the witnesses was referred to individually. Mudd knew Surratt's father before his death in 1862. He had had only brief contact with Surratt in 1864. In going over the contacts with Booth prior to April 15, Ewing did not accept the testimony of Wiechmann, referring only to the meetings between Booth and Mudd at church and on the following day when the one-eyed horse was purchased. He referred to Wiechmann's testimony as describing a possible third meeting. The relationship between the two was portrayed as accidental and brief. Knowing Booth should not be held against Mudd. He was a well known stage personality whose acquaintance was courted by many respectable people.

Mr. Ewing:[59] I then confidently conclude that Dr. Mudd cannot be convicted as a principal in the felony. He did not participate in its commission, and was more than thirty miles distant from the scene when it was committed. He cannot be convicted as an accessory before the fact, for the evidence fails to show that he had any knowledge or suspicion of an intention to commit it.

If then he is to be held responsible at all, it is as an accessory after the fact. Does the evidence implicate him in that character?. . .

On the morning after the assassination, about daybreak, Booth arrived at Dr. Mudd's house. He did not find the doctor on watch for him as a guilty accomplice, as expecting his arrival would have been. All his household were in profound sleep.

An accessory after the fact occurs when a person knowing a felony to have been committed, receives, comforts, or assists him whom he knows to be a felon. He must know that the felon is guilty to make him an accessory (1 Chitt. Crim. Law, 264). Any assistance given to him to hinder his being apprehended, tried, or punished, is sufficient to convict the offender—as lending a horse to escape his pursuers; but the assistance or support must be given in order to favor an illegal escape. Now let us apply the facts to the law, and see whether Dr. Mudd falls within the rule.

On the morning after the assassination, about daybreak, Booth arrived at Dr. Mudd's home. Dr. Mudd is awakened from his sleep by a loud knock at his door. He is told by Herold that his partner had suffered a broken leg because of a fall of his horse. The doctor arose from his bed, assisted the injured man into his house, laid him upon a sofa, took him upstairs to a bed, set the fractured bone, sent him a razor to shave himself, permitted him to remain there to sleep and rest and had a crude crutch improvised for his use. For all this he received the usual compensation for services rendered. He then went to his fields to work until noon. After dinner, while Booth was disguised in his chamber, Mudd left the house with Herold. Even though he had known of the assassination and that his patient was the assassin, none of these acts of assistance would have made him an accessory after the fact.

"If a person supply a felon with food, or other necessities for his sustenance, or professionally attend him sick or wounded, though he knows him to be a felon, these acts will not be sufficient to make a party an accessory after the fact" (*Wharton's American Criminal Law*, p. 73). But he did not know and had no reason to suspect, that his patient was a fugitive murderer. . . . Down then to the time Mudd left home with Herold, after dinner, the evidence affords no pretext for asserting he was an accessory after the fact.

But if he was not then an accessory, he never was. It is shown that Herold turned back on the way to Bryantown, and when Mudd returned, he and Booth had gone. And the evidence does not show that he suspected them of having been guilty of any wrong, until his wife told him, after they had gone, that the whiskers of the crippled man fell off as he came down stairs to go. . . .

The conclusion most unfavorable to Mudd which the evidence can possibly justify is, that, having had his suspicions thoroughly aroused Saturday night, he delayed until Sunday noon to communicate them to the authorities. . . .

Can, then, Dr. Mudd be convicted as a conspirator, or an accessory before or after the fact, in the assassination? If this tribunal is to be governed in its findings by the just and time-honored rules of law, he cannot. If by some edict higher than constitutions and laws, I know not what to anticipate or how to defend him. With confidence in the integrity of purpose of the Court and its legal advisors, I now leave the case to them.

Defense counsel summed up and gave arguments for each of the defendants.

A list of defense counsel for each defendant is as follows:

Samuel Arnold	Walter S. Cox, Esq.
George A. Atzerodt	William E. Doster, Esq.
David Herold	Frederick Stone, Esq.
Michael O'Laughlin	Walter S. Cox, Esq.
Dr. Samuel Mudd	Major General Thomas Ewing, Jr., Esq.
	Mr. Frederick Stone, Esq.
Lewis Payne (Powell)	William E. Doster, Esq.
Edward Spangler	Major General Thomas Ewing, Jr.
Mrs. Mary Surratt	Frederick Aiken, Esq.
	John W. Clampitt, Esq.
	Senator Reverdy Johnson, Esq.

Following the presentations of defense counsel, Honorable John A. Bingham, Special Judge-Advocate, gave a fifty-page argument in reply to the several arguments in defense of Mary E. Surratt and others charged with conspiracy and the murder of Abraham Lincoln, late president of the United States.[60]

May it please the Court:

The conspiracy here charged and specified, and the acts alleged to have been committed in pursuance thereof, and with the intent laid, constitute a crime the atrocity of which has sent a shudder through the civilized world. All that was agreed upon and attempted by the alleged inciters and instigators of this crime constitutes a combination of atrocities with scarcely a parallel in the annals of the human race. Whether the prisoners at your bar are guilty of the conspiracy and the acts alleged to have been done in pursuance thereof, as set forth in the charge and specification, is a question the determination of which rests solely with this honorable Court and in passing upon which this Court are the sole judges of the law and the fact.

In presenting my views upon the questions of law raised by the several counsel for the defense and also on the testimony adduced for and against the accused, I desire to be just to them, just to you, just to my country and just to my convictions. The issue joined involves the highest interests of the accused, and, in my judgment, the highest interests of the whole people of the United States....

The crime charged and specified upon your record is not simply the crime of murdering a human being, but is the crime of killing and murdering, on the 14th day of April, A.D. 1865, within the military department of Washington and the intrenched lines thereof, Abraham Lincoln, then President of the United States, and Commander-in-Chief of the army and navy thereof; and then and there assaulting, with intent to kill and murder, William H. Seward, then Secretary of State of the United States. Then and there lying in wait to kill and murder Andrew Johnson, then Vice President, and Ulysses S. Grant, the Lieutenant-General in pursuance of a treasonable conspiracy entered into by the accused with one John Wilkes Booth and John H. Surratt, upon the instigation of Jefferson Davis, Jacob Thompson, George Sanders and others, with the intent thereby to aid the existing rebellion and subvert the Constitution and laws of the United States....

It is charged that in aid of this existing rebellion a conspiracy was entered into by the accused, incited and instigated thereto by the chiefs of this rebellion, to kill and murder the executive officers of the government partially executed by the murder of Abraham Lincoln....

The civil courts, say the counsel, are open in the District. I answer, they are closed throughout half of the Republic and were open in this District on the day of this confederation and conspiracy, on the day of the traitorous assassination of your president and are only open at this hour by force of the bayonet. Does any man suppose that if the military forces which garrison the intrenchments of your capital, fifty thousand strong, were withdrawn, the rebel bands who this day infest the mountain passes in your vicinity would allow the Court, or any court, to remain open in this District for the trial of these their cofederates, or would permit your executive officers to discharge the trust committed to them, for twenty-four hours?

At the time this conspiracy was entered into and when this Court was convened and entered upon this trial, the country was in a state of civil war. An army of insurrectionists have, since this trial began, shed the blood of Union soldiers in battle. The conspirator, by whose hand his co-conspirators, whether present or absent jointly murdered the president was not arrested upon civil process, but was pursued by the military power of the Government, captured and slain.

It is a sufficient answer to say to the gentleman, that the power of this Government to try and punish military offenses by military tribunals is no part of the judicial power of the United States, under the 3rd article of the Constitution, but a power conferred by the 8th edition of the 1st article and so it has been ruled by the Supreme Court in Dyres vs. Hoover, 20 Howard, 78. If this power is so

conferred by the 8th section, a military court authorized by Congress and constituted as this has been, to try all persons for military crimes in time of war, though
not exercising "judicial power" provided for in the 3rd article, is nevertheless a
court as constitutional as the Supreme Court itself. . . .

Military Law is a system of regulations for the government of the armies in the
service of the United States, authorized by the act of Congress of April 10, 1806,
known as the Articles of War, and naval law is a similar system for the government
of the navy, under the act of Congress of April 23, 1800. . . .

Martial law and military tribunals are as essential to the successful prosecution
of war as are men, arms and munitions. The Constitution has vested the power to
declare war and raise armies and navies exclusively in the Congress and the power
to prosecute the war and command the army and navy exclusively in the President. . . .

These extracts are made from the first twenty pages of Bingham's fifty-page
summation.[61] These pages have largely to do with the authority of the
military commission in answer to Ewing and Johnson's accusations that the
president did not have authority to appoint it. These extracts refer to the
powers of the president in time of war, indicating that the president has full
power.

Bingham's report has thirty more pages in which he takes up the
testimony of witnesses. He is impressed that the assassination was known
of and approved by Jefferson Davis. Clear evidence of that approval is lacking. Booth tried to get it on his trips to Montreal, but whether he actually
did is open to question. Jacob Thompson's account showed deposit
receipts for $180,000. On April 6 this amount was withdrawn from the ac-
count at the Ontario Bank of Montreal. This indirect evidence was pointed
out by the special judge-advocate. Booth had on his person at the time of
his death a bill of exchange drawn on the Ontario Bank, Montreal, for 61
pounds, 12 shillings, and 10 pence. It was dated October 27, 1864, not April
1865.

On June 14, Ewing made his final appeal to the judge-advocate to
clarify the charges against his clients. He asked that the charge and
specification of the crime be relieved of ambiguity. He pointed out that
there was but one charge, in form, against the accused, but in fact there
seemed to be four:

1. Maliciously, unlawfully, and in aid of the existing armed rebellion against the
United States.
2. In pursuance of said malicious, unlawful and traitorous conspiracy, maliciously, unlawfully and traitorously murdering the said Abraham Lincoln,
President.
3. Maliciously, unlawfully and traitorously assaulting with intent to kill and
murder, the said William H. Seward, Secretary of State.
4. Lying in wait with intent maliciously, unlawfully, and traitorously to kill and
murder the said Andrew Johnson, then Vice President, and Lieutenant-General
Ulysses S. Grant.

The offenses enumerated, as aforesaid, in the said charge, are separate and distinct, and we, therefore ask that the Judge-Advocate should state, in regard to those of the accused whom we represent, of which of said offenses, under the evidence, he claims they should be convicted.

It was to no avail. The judge-advocate again repeated what he had said before: "They are all alleged to have participated in the general conspiracy, and in the execution of that conspiracy, so far as the assassination of the President is concerned; and the particular parts which each one performed therein afterward, either in execution or in the attempt to execute, are set forth. It is for the Court to determine how far the proof sustains these allegations."[62]

The hearing of witnesses was completed on June 14. The court was reconvened on June 27 to hear the testimony of Sanford Conover, an undercover agent reporting for the prosecution. This man was later discredited.

The prisoners were returned to their cells each night, hooded and chained, not knowing what was coming next. It was a very hot summer in Washington and everyone sweltered in the courtroom and at night. This was worst of all for the prisoners in their small, poorly ventilated cells. With their uncomfortable hoods in place, they must have nearly suffocated. This was in addition to the discomfort of their restraining irons.

During this time, counsel for each of the defendants presented a summation of evidence for his client.

The final argument of Special Judge-Advocate John A. Bingham, according to military procedure, closed the presentations of counsel.

On June 29, again according to military procedure, the commission with the three judge-advocates met behind closed doors. All were excluded, including the court recorder and defense counsel. The inclusion of the judge-advocates during deliberation of the commission has been likened to including the prosecuting attorney with a civil jury during deliberation. What transpired behind the closed doors from ten A.M. until six P.M. on that hot day has been subject to much speculation and debate.

Many opinions have been given but the people who made them were not there. The commission made its own meager court record about what transpired. All except Spangler were found guilty of the charge of conspiracy.

Sentencing

The death penalty required a 6/3 majority of the nine commissioners. This they agreed upon for Herold, Atzerodt, and Payne. They were found guilty of both charge and specification without debate and sentenced to die by hanging. O'Laughlin was found guilty of the charge in general, but the majority were unwilling to find him guilty of the specification that charged him with lying in wait to assassinate Grant. He was given life imprisonment.

Spangler, the stage hand at Ford's Theater, the only defendant not found guilty of the charge, was given six years' imprisonment.

The three remaining persons, Arnold, Mrs. Surratt, and Mudd, were found guilty of conspiracy, but each received a five to four vote for clemency. This was one vote less than required for the death of each.

The commission stood firm on this 5/4 vote in the case of Arnold, and he was given life imprisonment.

What happened in the case of Mrs. Surratt is a mystery. Somehow the 5/4 vote for clemency was changed to 6/3 for the death penalty with a plea to President Johnson to commute the death sentence on the basis of her sex.

One supposition was that Secretary of War Stanton thought she should receive the extreme penalty and that the judge-advocate pushed for this in spite of the fact she was a woman. "Her boarding house was the nest in which the conspiracy was hatched." Another theory was that her son, John Harrison Surratt, was deeply involved in the plot. He had been a Confederate courier. He had fled the country. She should pay the price for him. No one knows. This was at the end of a long hot day and the meeting adjourned.

On the following day, June 30, the commission reconvened to consider the case of Mudd. This time the members of the commission stood firm on their original 5/4 vote for clemency. Mudd received the following sentence:

COURTROOM, Washington, D.C.
June 30th, 1865, 10 o'clock A.M.
The Commission met, behind closed doors, pursuant to adjournment. All the members present; also the Judge-Advocate and the Assistant Judge-Advocates.
The Commission does, therefore, sentence the said Samuel A. Mudd to be imprisoned at hard labor for life, at such place as the President shall direct.
The Commission thereupon adjourned sine die.
J. Holt   D. Hunter[63]

The findings needed the signature of the president. He was ill in bed and could receive no one. The prisoners continued to swelter under their hoods, and the whole country waited to learn the fate of the seven men and one woman. The 4th of July came and went, but there was still no word.

Finally, on July 5, the president recovered enough to meet with Judge-Advocate Holt.[64] The president was described as pale and weak from his illness. He listened to Holt's presentation, read the document presented, and after discussion, signed it. Whether he actually saw the petition for clemency for Mrs. Surratt is open to question.[65] The president later said he did not see it.

With the findings of the military commission completed and signed by President Johnson, things moved rapidly. The report of the commission had set the date of execution for July 7. That was just two days away. With great haste, the erection of scaffolding was begun in the prison courtyard. Mudd faintly heard the noise of carpenters' hammers in the distance, but did not know the meaning. Under his hood he could not see and his hearing was severely impaired by the hood.

The order signed by President Johnson stated that the prisoners Samuel Arnold, Samuel A. Mudd, Edward Spangler, and Michael O'Laughlin be confined at hard labor in the penitentiary at Albany, New York, during the period designated in their respective sentences.

"This is fine," Ewing told Mudd. "When you get to Albany, we will ask for a writ of habeas corpus in the State of New York. That will bring you into civil court where we should be able to get a fair review of your case before a jury instead of this Military Commission which has just tried you. I did all I could do but a military court-martial is a mighty tough thing. They have their own rules of procedure, evidence and charges which are different from civil law. Thank God you are safe from the gallows in the prison yard. Dwell on that. It was a close call but we made it. Habeas corpus is our next move when the time is right. We will follow things closely and choose the time wisely."

Frances heard the verdict on the evening of the same day it was made and arranged to go to Washington the following morning. She had not seen her husband since the day he was taken from their home. She went to the War Department and secured a pass to visit Mudd at the penitentiary. With this in hand, she was admitted to the Old Arsenal Prison, and shown by messenger to a room on the second floor. As she came through the prison grounds, she noted the construction of scaffolding taking place in the prison yard but did not at first realize its meaning. There were too many things on her mind. The execution of four of the defendants, Atzerodt, Herold, Payne, and Mrs. Surratt, was scheduled for the following day.

Mudd was in his shirt sleeves and wore a pair of carpet slippers without socks, she later wrote.[66] "He had a sore on his ankle and I asked if it was from the chains he had to wear. He paused a few moments as though hesitant to answer in the presence of the guards and said, no." He said one of the guards had told him who was to be hanged and what his sentence was before he heard it from Ewing.

On her way out she met a poor girl weeping bitterly and was told it was Anna Surratt, Mrs. Surratt's daughter, who was trying frantically and vainly to save her mother.

12
Later Information
and Claims

The trial of the eight conspirators, including Mudd, began three and a half weeks after the assassination of Lincoln. This was a very short time in which to round up suspects and get ready for such an important trial. Citizens of the country, especially in the North, were up in arms about the assassination. For this reason, primarily, there was great urgency among those in charge, particularly Secretary of War Stanton, to get on with things and bring the plotters of the assassination to justice. This was true even though the main assassin, Booth, was already dead.

Because of this great haste, some avenues were not explored and involved people not apprehended. A number in the latter category fled the country. Others, although apprehended, were able to remain silent for years until it was safe to talk, after the hysteria following the assassination had died down.

An outstanding example of the latter was Thomas A. Jones, who was incarcerated on two occasions by federal authorities along with his foster brother, Samuel Cox. He succeeded in concealing his involvement with the underground Confederate mail service and with the escape of Booth until many years later. In 1893 he wrote a small monograph about his personal involvement.

The Confederate Mail Service

Thomas A. Jones, age forty-one, owned a five-hundred-acre farm facing the Potomac River that he had purchased a few years before the beginning of the war.[1] This farm overlooked the river from a bluff eighty to one hundred feet high, giving it an excellent view of the river, both north and south. It offered an ideal spot for a clandestine Confederate river-crossing operation. The Potomac River formed the western boundary of Jones's property, while a stream flowing into the Potomac from the east, Pope's

Creek, formed the northern boundary. From the wharf at Pope's Creek it was a two-mile boat trip across the Potomac River to Mathias Point on the Virginia side. This was the narrowest point in the river and served as a main crossing point for traffic between Richmond and Washington in the 1860s.

Jones had a single-story home a short distance from the edge of the cliff with a fireplace built at each end. His neighbor just to the south, Major Roderick G. Watson, lived even closer to the edge of the cliff in a two-story home, which was even more prominent due to its greater height. A loyal Confederate, Ben Grimes, lived near the water on the Virginia side. Jones, Watson, and Grimes worked together for the Confederate cause. A small black shawl in the upstairs window of the Watson house indicated danger. No shawl meant the coast was clear and that packets of Confederate mail could be quietly rowed across in Grimes's "fishing" boat and quickly deposited in the crotch of a fallen tree on Jones' beach.

After war broke out, help was costly and hard to get on Jones's farm. When farming became less profitable, Jones took up ferrying passengers across the river on their way to and from Richmond. He was apprehended on one of these trips and placed in Old Capitol Prison, where he spent six months. This cut off his meager income and he was unable to make his mortgage payments. His wife became ill in his absence and died soon after his return from prison. While in prison he met some interesting, prominent people whose Southern interests were the same as his.

After his stint in federal prison, Jones concentrated more on the mail service at the request of Major William Norris, chief of the Confederate Signal Service.[2] He accepted the post after careful consideration even though it was at great risk to him personally and the fact that he alone was responsible for the care of his family.

Jones was the Confederate mail operator in charge of Lower Maryland from 1861 until the end of the war. He received packets of mail from Grimes that were left in the crotch of the fallen tree on his beach. He then mailed the enclosed letters or had them mailed in U.S. post offices in Maryland, from which points they would be carried to destinations throughout the United States.

Jones had many associates who helped in this clandestine operation so that suspicion was not centered on him or any one person. Especially important matters were entrusted to special agents. Two of his more trusted ones were Dr. Stowten W. Dent, M.D., and his brother-in-law, Thomas H. Harbin.[3]

The boats for the mail were kept on the Virginia side of the river, where they were safer and less of a hazard to Jones. Jones is said to have had a rather doleful appearance, which served as an additional cover to his keen mind.

The northgoing mail had proper U.S. postage on it so that it needed only to be dropped in a U.S. post office to be delivered normally through U.S. channels. Many postmasters in Lower Maryland were disloyal to the Union, especially in the early part of the war.[4] Return mail was received by various people who brought it quietly to Jones to be placed in the "fallen tree" post office for the return trip to Richmond. Northern newspapers were transported in the same manner and were in Richmond the next day.

This operation was not completely unknown to Union authorities and probably was a source of counter-espionage about happenings in Richmond. This may be an important reason why it succeeded as well as it did.

Booth's Second Visit to Charles County

The important issue of Booth's second visit to Charles County in 1864 was never followed up at the trial. John C. Thompson, Dr. Queen's son-in-law, testified on Friday, May 26, that Booth made a second visit to Charles County about the third week of December 1864 and stayed again with Queen. Did Mudd meet Booth again on this second visit? Thompson claimed ignorance of where Booth went after he left Queen's home. Thompson's testimony was definite and was reported in all three versions of the printed trial testimony.[5] A Confederate agent from Bryantown said later that Booth did make a second visit according to newspaper reports.

The Confederate agent was Thomas H. Harbin. Knowledge of him did not exist at the time of the trial before the military commission. He, like Surratt, was out of the country. Thomas Jones referred to him as his brother-in-law and one of his trusted agents in the mail service, along with Dr. Stoughton Dent.

Harbin operated mainly on the Virginia side of the Potomac, but worked closely with Jones and others on the north of the river as well.

In Atzerodt's confession of May 3, he spoke of Harbourn or Halborn when a boat was being purchased in January 1865 by Surratt at Booth's request at Port Tobacco for the kidnap scheme. He stated that Harbourn was in it first; he came with Surratt to get Atzerodt to join in the plot to ferry the kidnapped president across the river. An expensive boat was purchased for this purpose in January 1865 and hidden south of Port Tobacco by Atzerodt for use at the proper time.

It has been postulated with fair certainty that the person referred to by Atzerodt was Harbin, the name having been distorted by Atzerodt's German accent.

Harbin was supposed to make the necessary arrangements to welcome the party when it arrived in Virginia and to lead it once on the south side of the Potomac.

Knowledge of this man, like that of many others, did not come out at the trial of the Lincoln conspirators in 1865. He had a price on his head if his part in the planned kidnapping of Lincoln became known.

Realizing his situation, as soon as possible after the assassination, he secured a parole at Ashland, Virginia, April 28, 1865, and disappeared from the country.[6] He escaped to Cuba and then England, where he remained for five years until things settled down and it was safe to return. He then became a desk clerk at the National Hotel in Washington, D.C., where he worked up to the time of his death in November 1885. He frequently talked about his role as a Confederate agent. George Alfred Townsend, writing under the pen-name GATH, published articles in the *Cincinnati Enquirer* in 1892. In one dated April 18, the results of an interview with Harbin, which had been made a number of years previously, are given. The latter portion, which is in regard to Booth's second visit to Charles County in December 1864, reads as follows:

> Dr. Queen's family heard Booth enquire about the price of land and horses in that neighborhood and say that he was a rich person who had money to put out in the country.
>
> The next day Booth was taken to the Catholic Church and the actor was introduced to Dr. Samuel Mudd, the principal slave holder mentioned who lived five miles north of Bryantown in the direction of Surrattsville. Of course Mr. Booth had been to Montreal and there had participated with the fly by nights such as those who had raided St. Albans and John Y. Beall, aforesaid, and through his unadjusted mind had run the idea of doing some great performance at Washington City then escaping into the South, securing his wardrobe from Canada which he had left there and starring in his father's great parts in "Richard III," "Pescara" etc. throughout the English speaking countries.
>
> Through the men in Canada and some he had met in Washington, he was told about the free intercourse with the South through the lower Potomac ferries.
>
> After church that day, Booth went into Bryantown a mile or two distant and in plain sight was introduced by Dr. Mudd, at the village hotel, to Mr. Thomas Harbin who was the principal signal officer or spy with the lower Maryland Counties.
>
> Toward the close of the war rigorous policing of the lower Maryland country was relaxed or dispensed with, as the enemy had been pushed south of the James River and seldom molested these parts. Harbin, whom I talked to at great lengths just before he died, about 1885, gave me particulars concerning Booth which would now be past discovering. He told me that in Bryantown, at the tavern, Dr. Mudd introduced him to Booth who wanted some private conversation with Mr. Harbin; they took a room on the second floor, where Booth went through The Thespian motions of

Top: Bryantown Hotel, ca. 1864 (courtesy of the Library of Congress); *bottom:* Bryantown Hotel, 1990.

pacing and watching the hallway and escapements. He then outlined a scheme of seizing Abraham Lincoln and delivering him up the same evening in Virginia. He said that he had come down to that country to invite cooperation and partners and intimated that there was not only glory, but profit in the undertaking.

Harbin was a cool man who had seen many liars and rogues go to and fro in that illegal border and he set down Booth as a crazy fellow, but at the same time said that he would give his cooperation. GATH

The above account is second-hand. Mudd had slaves but was not a principal slaveholder as stated. He lived four miles north of Bryantown in the direction of Surrattsville.

The sequence of events differs from testimony given at the trial. In spite of this, Booth was very much interested in meeting Confederate agents for his undertaking. Surratt, whom he would meet a few days later, was in that category. Booth was concerned about the reception of the party in Virginia after crossing the Potomac. Harbin covered that aspect. Harbin is reported as having said he would cooperate with Booth's scheme and if the assumption in Atzerodt's confession that Harbourn and Harbin are the same person is correct, he did according to that account. From a hypothetical standpoint, it is possible and that is about all that can be said.

Facts about Harbin are as follows:

1. He lived about one-half mile south of Bryantown in the 1860s, according to residents living in Bryantown today.

2. He was postmaster at Bryantown, Maryland, from December 27, 1854, until June 21, 1855.

3. Living at the edge of Bryantown and having been postmaster in the village, it seems likely that Mudd would have known Harbin or at least known of him.

4. Harbin was a Confederate agent as told by his brother-in-law Thomas Jones. This is also indicated by Atzerodt's confession of May 3, although the name written in the confession was Harbourn or Halborn.

5. When Jones sent Booth and Herold to Mrs. Quesenberry's house at Machodoc Creek near Mathias Point, Mrs. Quesenberry contacted Thomas Harbin, who came there with Joseph Badden of Prince George's County, Maryland. The two did all they could to assist the fugitives and put them on their way to Dr. Stuart's summer home farther inland and south.[7] This must have been one of Harbin's last Confederate acts. Harbin expected to be arrested by the federal authorities for his Confederate activities and considered his life in danger. On April 28, 1865, he secured a parole at Ashland, Virginia, and disappeared.[8]

6. Booth made a second trip to lower Maryland about the third week of December 1864, according to the testimony of Thompson.

7. The dates of Booth's registrations and departures at the National Hotel in Washington, D.C., are as follows, according to the testimony of G. W. Bunker on May 12, 1865:[9]

No entries for October								
Arr.	Nov.	9	evening		Dep.	Nov.	11, 1864	early train
"	"	14	eve.		"	"	16,	"
Arr.	Dec.	12			Dep.	Dec.	17, "	morning train
"	"	22			"	"	24, "	
"	"	31			"	Jan.	10, 1865	
"	Jan.	12			"	Jan.	28, "	
"	Feb.	22			"	Feb.	28, "	8:15 train
								Closed his acct.
"	Mar.	1			"	Mar.	21, "	7:30 PM train
"	"	25			"	Apr.	1, "	Aft. train
"	Apr.	8				Assassination Apr. 14th.		

These entries do not help much in deciding where Booth might have been at any particular time, however. He was spending some of his time with his lady friends. He apparently had plenty of them.

November 1864

Sun	Mon	Tues	Weds	Thur	Fri	Sat
		1	2	3	4	5
6	7	8	(9)	(10)	11	12
13	(14)	(15)	16	17	18	19
20	21	22	23	24	25	26
27	28	29	30			

December 1864

Sun	Mon	Tues	Weds	Thur	Fri	Sat
				1	2	3
4	5	6	7	8	9	10
11	(12)	(13)	(14)	(15)	(16)	17
18	19	20	21	(22)	(23)	24
25	26	27	28	29	30	31

Nights Booth registered at the National Hotel, November–December 1864.

Booth's time at the National Hotel was brief in November 1864. He registered on the evening of Wednesday, November 9, and left on the early train on Friday, the 11th. He returned the evening of Monday the 14th and checked out on Wednesday the 16th, the time not given.

In December he registered on Monday the 12th and departed on the early train Saturday the 17th—according to testimony, which means according to notations on the hotel register. These are not always accurate. If he did go to Lower Maryland the third full week of December, it could have been the first part of that week. He returned on Thursday the 22nd, so that he would have been there Friday, December 23, when Mudd introduced him to Surratt on 7th Street as testified by Wiechmann. He then could have gone off Saturday the 24th to spend Christmas with his mother, brothers, and sister.

13
The Executions

July 7, 1865, the second day after the ailing president signed the Order for Execution, was a day of misery. The families, ministers, and the counsel for the four sentenced to die tried frantically to stop the inevitable. Herold, Payne, and Atzerodt were doomed, it seemed certain, in spite of efforts for clemency by their immediate families. Herold had accompanied Payne to Seward's home on the night of April 14. He had been Booth's close and active accomplice during the twelve days between the assassination and Booth's capture and death at Garrett's tobacco barn. There seemed to be no hope for him.

Payne had been the vicious assailant of Secretary of State Seward and his son. Payne was doomed on this score, even though his two victims had miraculously survived his dagger. He remained calm throughout the ordeal and made a final statement to General Hancock that the general transmitted to President Johnson on the morning of the execution. It read: "The prisoner Payne has just told me that Mrs. Surratt is entirely innocent of the assassination of President Lincoln, or of any knowledge thereof." At the close of the letter Hancock wrote, "I believe that Payne told the truth in this matter."[1]

Atzerodt, the boatman from Port Tobacco, was to ferry the kidnapped president and kidnap party across the Potomac River to the safe Confederate shore of Virginia in the original capture plan. He did not know his role was changed to assassin of Vice President Johnson until two hours before it was to be done. It is tragic how Booth mercilessly drew others into the scheme of his demented mind. Although Atzerodt did not carry out the attempt, he failed to report the scheme before it was to happen. He was doomed.

Mrs. Surratt had an older son in the Confederate Army. Her young son had been a Confederate courier deeply involved in the plot to kidnap Lincoln. He had now deserted her by fleeing the country. Her daughter Anna struggled to see President Johnson personally without avail. Mrs. Surratt's priest intervened without avail. At ten A.M. a writ of habeas corpus was granted by Judge Wylie of the Supreme Court of the District of

Columbia. This was taken to the president. At half past eleven, Hancock, accompanied by Attorney General Speed, appeared before Judge Wylie and, by order of the president, declined to obey the writ on the ground that it was suspended.[2] The minister of war argued against commuting the death penalty on the basis of the fact she was a woman.

Soldiers were everywhere about the Old Arsenal Prison. Crowds were in the streets. The Potomac was crowded with boats of all descriptions.

The prisoners had been brought from their cells to the scaffolding and had ascended the thirteen steps to the gallows, where they were seated on chairs next to the four nooses that dangled from the overhead cross-bar. The nooses had been previously tested with three-hundred-pound weights to be sure that all worked properly. General Hartranft, the officer in charge, kept glancing in the direction of the prison gates for any sign of a last-minute reprieve for Mrs. Surratt. He read the specifications and sentences to the prisoners. Chaplains administered last rites. The prisoners stood and the nooses were adjusted about their necks. The crowd was silent. Atzerodt said, "Goot bye, Shentlemens."

When all was ready, Hartranft loudly clapped his hands twice. This was the signal. The posts supporting the platforms on which the prisoners were standing were knocked away by guards. This was done by horizontal timbers placed in the gallows for that purpose.[3] The platforms dropped from beneath the feet of the victims. They fell heavily downward until the nooses tightened about their necks with a jerk. They dangled in mid-air, struggling, then became quiet. Thirty minutes later, they were cut down and buried in wooden coffins resembling gun boxes in freshly dug graves adjacent to the gallows.[4] The crowds began to disperse in the heat of the afternoon sun. One group at the prison gates yelled, "Judicial murder."

Murder, yes, that was what the whole story was about. Murder brought on by the depraved brain of an actor.

On following pages:
The executions (courtesy of the Library of Congress).

14
Exile

The prisoners who survived the military trial dropped out of sight temporarily. Mudd, Arnold, O'Laughlin, and Spangler awaited their fate in their cells in silence. The hoods had been taken from their heads during the latter part of the trial on June 10. They were taken into the prison yard daily, near the fresh graves of the recently executed, for short periods of exercise.

At midnight on July 17, 1865, ten days after the executions, a guard came to Mudd's cell with a lantern and awakened the doctor. "Gather up your belongings, you are moving out. You are leaving here now, permanently." There was no mention of the destination.

With his few belongings gathered, Mudd was taken, under heavy guard, to the prison yard. Here he was joined by Arnold, O'Laughlin, and Spangler.

Arnold recalls many things in his personal account written in later life and published after his death in 1906. The uncomfortable canvas hoods were worn from April 23 until June 10. These were exceedingly uncomfortable and, in the hot weather, nearly suffocating. Even worse was the psychological effect of having one's eyes and ears covered constantly and being completely incommunicado. It is a wonder that the victims did not lose their minds. The hoods were very tight about the face and neck. Cotton was placed over the prisoners' eyes and ears. The hoods were worn constantly except while in the courtroom and, during the latter part of the trial, during two-hour periods of exercise in the prison yard. They were not removed for washing or eating. The latter must have been a feat—eating with shackled hands and without vision![1]

At midnight, by lantern light, on July 17, Arnold was also told to gather his things for travel. He was taken by guards to the prison yard and here joined the other three. "We were silently marched, except for the clanking of our irons, to a steamer moored to a wharf in the Potomac River. Each side of the route was lined with armed sentinels and soldiers as we emerged from the prison gates. Our clanking irons in the solemn midnight pierced the vaults of heaven, crying out to God for vengeance on those who had traduced, defamed and victimized us to satiate public revenge."[2]

With the four prisoners aboard, no time was wasted. The steamer took off into the darkness of the night. On the afternoon of July 18, it arrived at Fortress Monroe. Here the party transferred to a tugboat. Under heavy guard it was escorted to the *Florida* lying far out in the harbor. On boarding the *Florida,* the prisoners were given their first bit of information about their destination. They were sailing under sealed order to be opened in two days. Albany was given as the place of incarceration according to the order signed by President Johnson on July 5, but the boat headed south.

The prisoners were quartered deep in the hold—the most secure, inaccessible place, where air, light, and ventilation were minimal. It was already hot, in spite of a sea breeze, and getting hotter.

Arnold speaks of the difficulty getting into the hold in their shackled condition with only eight inches of chain between their ankles. "After leaving the second deck, we were forced to descend upon a ladder whose rounds were so far apart that the chains lacerated the flesh and bruised the bones of our ankles. We remained in this sweltering hole during the night, in an atmosphere pregnant with disagreeable odors. About 8 o'clock next morning, we passed through the same ordeal in our ascent to the upper deck, which was attended with more pain than the descent owing to the raw condition of our wounds."[3]

The prisoners had an armed marine with them at all times and were not allowed to talk to the crew. Food was of the grossest kind, consisting of hardtack and fat salt pork. They were allowed to remain on deck during the day under guard. Finally, after negotiation and consideration, they were allowed to remain on deck during the night. Their commander, Captain George W. Dutton, showed a little mercy. They were allowed to bring some bedding on deck at night and store it below during the day.

The second evening they arrived off Hilton Head, South Carolina, and lay in port at Charleston during the night. Supplies were taken aboard and the prisoners could hear the officers having a party in their quarters. Dutton informed the prisoners that the sealed orders would be opened the next day at sea. He also said that their leg irons would be removed during daylight hours as a reward for good behavior. This was welcome news.

This gave a brief, pleasant interlude which was broken by the announcement next day of their destination by the captain: Dry Tortugas, Fort Jefferson.

This was a stern blow. The prisoners knew little about the place, but accounts of it in the newspapers had described it as "Devils Island." They would be exiles on a small island, a military prison, where military rule prevailed.

On July 24, 1865, Fort Jefferson was sighted. A warning signal shot was fired from the *Florida* and answered by a return shot fired from the fort.

Top: the Dry Tortugas Islands; *bottom:* Fort Jefferson, Dry Tortugas Islands.

In the early 1800s, the U.S. government decided to construct a series of forts around the periphery of the country for coastal defense. Fort Jefferson, built in 1846, was intended to protect the sea lanes to the Gulf of Mexico and to bring law and order to pirate-infested waters.

In 1861 the fort came under command of Union forces. In 1864 it was converted into a maximum security military prison. The commander ruled with an iron hand; state courts had no jurisdiction.

According to Arnold the prisoners were met by Colonel Charles Hamilton, commandant of the post. They were told that rules were to be obeyed and that there was a dungeon for those who did otherwise. He said they would have the same privileges as others confined here. Of course, this was a military prison and that might mean anything. Conditions could change and different commanders could have different ideas. The prisoners would become very aware of that as time went on.

The *Florida* lay in port that night. Some supplies were delivered. Officers from the *Florida* came ashore and visited with the command of the fort. Early the next morning, the gunboat departed to the east and went out of sight. A new feeling of loneliness and despair set in for Mudd. He realized he was exiled on a tropical island military prison for the rest of his life, the sentence said, at hard labor. What had he done except treat Booth? Something that any member of his profession should have done. Where was justice?

The days wore on. One day a newspaper arrived by ship. To Mudd's horror, Captain George Dutton, the army officer who accompanied Mudd to Dry Tortugas, had written a letter to Judge-Advocate General Joseph Holt who had been in charge of the military tribunal that prosecuted Mudd and the others. This letter was printed in the paper.

Camp Fry, Washington, D.C.
August 22, 1865

Brig.-Gen. Joseph Holt
Judge Advocate General U.S.A.

Sir: I am in receipt of your communication of this date, in which you request information as regards the truthfulness of certain statements and confessions reported to have been made by Dr. Mudd while under my charge en route to the Dry Tortugas.

In reply, I have the honor to state that my duties required me to be constantly with the prisoner, and during a conversation with Dr. Mudd on the 22nd of July, he confessed that he knew Booth when he came to his house with Herold, on the morning after the assassination of the President; that he had known Booth some time but was afraid to tell of his having been at his house on the 15th of April fearing that his own and the lives of his family would be endangered thereby. He also confessed that he was with Booth on the evening referred to by Wiechmann in his testimony;

that he came to Washington on that occasion to meet Booth by appointment who wished to be introduced to John Surratt; that when he and
Booth were going to Mrs. Surratt's house to see John Surratt, they met on
Seventh Street, John Surratt was introduced to Booth, and they had a conversation of a private nature; I will here add that Dr. Mudd had with him
a printed copy of the testimony pertaining to his trial, and I had a number
of times referred to the same. I will also state that this confession was
voluntary, and made without solicitation, threat or promise, and was
made after the destination of the prisoners was communicated to them
which communication affected Dr. Mudd more than the rest; and he frequently exclaimed, "Oh, there is now no help for me." "Oh, I cannot live
in such a place."

Please acknowledge receipt of this letter.

I am, General, very respectfully,

Your obedient servant,

George W. Dutton.

Capt. Co. C. 10th Regt. V.R.C.; Com'dg

Guard.

Sworn and acknowledged at Washington, D.C., this 23rd of August
1865 before me,

G.C. Thomas,

Notary Public.

In fact, this letter had been published widely in newspapers across the
country.

Mudd wrote to his wife on September 3, 1865. "This story is a complete fabrication. I made no admissions or confessions as reported by the
various Northern newspapers. I have lost all confidence in the veracity and
honesty of the Northern people. . . . There was never before a more persis-
tent effort to incriminate and to blast one's character and fortune than was
resorted to in my case."

Mudd faithfully wrote home to his wife during the nearly four years
that he was separated from her and their four small children. She saved the
letters and in later years wrote an account of her own that does not adequately describe the great part she personally played in keeping the family
together during that difficult period. The letters describe the conditions
that Mudd endured as a prisoner at Fort Jefferson on the Dry Tortugas
Islands sixty-eight miles west of Key West.

Excerpts from Mudd's letters are given here to show what went on in
his mind during his years of incarceration and to give an intimate picture
of this man.

Mudd considered his conviction as an accomplice in the murder of the
president an astonishing, utter injustice. He knew nothing of Booth's late
change in plans, although he probably did know of the previous plot to capture the president. When he was taken into custody on April 24, 1865, he
thought he was being taken to Washington for interrogation. It was some
time before he realized the true situation.

He was never allowed to take the stand in his own defense. People gave false testimony during the trial, in Mudd's opinion, some of which may have been in the hope of collecting large sums of reward money.

After Frances saw her husband at the Arsenal Prison on July 6, 1865, there was a void of information from him. The public executions of Herold, Payne, Atzerodt, and Mrs. Surratt on the following day had attracted great attention in Washington and in the news media of the day.

When the gunboat *Florida* stopped at Charleston, South Carolina, Mudd was able to write a letter home during that brief stop there. His wife did not receive it for several weeks. This letter was not preserved. In this letter, Mudd did not know his destination. Frances did not learn where he was until the end of the month. There were several weeks of extreme uncertainty and worry. She did not know where her husband was or how to communicate with him.

Frances made a trip to see Stanton and received a cool reception. She asked for permission to communicate with her husband and to send him clothes and other necessities to make him more comfortable. She received a formal communication back in which she was told that necessary clothing was supplied by the government. She could communicate with her husband by unsealed letters that were subject to inspection.

She also paid a visit to President Johnson. She was received more warmly by the president, who sent her to Judge-Advocate General Holt. When she saw him he stated that he was sorry he could do nothing for her husband.

During the time that she did not know where or how to communicate with her husband, Mudd thought that he was completely forgotten.

In the first letter preserved among those written from Fort Jefferson, Mudd says that it had been one month since his arrival. It seemed much longer. Time passed very slowly; days were years. He had received no news from home. Others had received mail, but there was no information about his release. He feared that some misfortune had overtaken his family. It was all-absorbing in his mind. He tells his wife that she and the children are everything to him. Without her and the children, life was void. He pleads for her to write. He writes that he had sent letters with every ship that had left but had received no word from home. He feared that letters had been intercepted.

He had been assigned to the hospital, he says, which was a good thing. At the time he wrote the letter he had very little to do. The only contact with the outside world was ships that docked there every week or so. He was on a small island with two smaller ones adjacent, which were little more than nesting places for birds. There was a larger one visible about two miles to the west and a small one about the same distance to the northeast. Otherwise there was no land in sight on the horizon, just shark-infested waters as far as the eye could see. Ships passed nearly every day on the southern horizon and to the east, but did not stop at this godforsaken place. Apparently they were next to a shipping lane of the high seas that passed on both sides.

The major portion of the sixteen-acre island was taken up by a fort with fifty-foot-high brick walls, outside of which was a moat even wider. There were about 550 prisoners. Rules were strict. There was a dungeon for those who did not obey. The food was abominable. The principal diet was coffee, butter, and bread three times a day. There might be a mess or two of Irish potatoes and onions about once a week. Vegetables did not last many days in the climate before decomposition set in. Pork and beef served in a decomposed state were poisonous. Mudd had severe cramps and diarrhea and would not eat them again. There was molasses when the prisoners were able to buy it, and occasionally fish.

Aside from the heat and humidity the place so far had not been unhealthy but Mudd worried about diseases being brought in aboard ships from infected ports. At present there was a vessel at anchor; all hands aboard were sick with fever of some sort. Several had died and no one was well enough to nurse the sick.

Without warning the four prisoners, Mudd, Arnold, O'Laughlin, and Spangler, were suddenly placed in chains in strict confinement. They were told nothing.

As learned later, the acting assistant secretary of war had received a telegram on August 17, 1865, stating that an attempt to free state prisoners on Dry Tortugas was about to be made. This word came from Brigadier General L. C. Baker, head of what was then the secret service. The group was organizing in New Orleans for that purpose. Baker had the facts from a reliable source, the dispatch said.[4] The word had been passed to the commanding officer at Fort Jefferson. The four prisoners were consequently placed in chains under heavy guard.

Nothing happened while the men were under heavy guard. The facts turned out to be false rumor. The heavy guard lasted for nearly a week, following which the men were able to resume their usual restricted prison activity.

The possibility that diseases could be brought in by ship from other ports existed. Mudd was assigned to the dispensary as ward steward. He worked long hours but the tasks were welcome and in keeping with his training and knowledge. He was very glad for it. It helped take his mind from the thoughts of the terrible problems of his family, from whom he had not heard and about whom he was very worried. He had written several letters to his counsel but had heard nothing. Somehow he hoped at this late date, justice might still prevail. He thought perhaps the mails were intercepted.

Mudd did not know that his wife was far from idle. In addition to all the cares of the children, she bravely made visits to President Johnson and Judge-Advocate Holt, pleading for the release of her husband. Johnson said he would sign a release if the judge-advocate would do so. Holt only scowled and said he was sorry but he could do nothing for her.[5]

About a month later Mudd wrote that he was hopeful that word of his release would arrive with every steamer. A transport was in port and would take off with a hundred prisoners. He felt forgotten. There was no word from his counsel. Mudd lived in despair. He had written thirty to forty letters to various people. He writes that he had an opportunity to escape but, believing that it would show guilt, had decided against it. A transport arrived that day but no release for him. Worse yet, there was word that they were to be placed under guard by a black regiment. Dr. Mudd wrote, "I was told by members of the 161 at NYV Reg., that as soon as they departed, the prisoners would be denied many of their former privileges" (Nettie Mudd p. 123).

Word came from Mudd's counsel that early review of his case was not possible since he had been removed from state jurisdiction. Review had to await the convening of the Supreme Court, which sat in December. He was in exile from his country. Shall I ever see home again, he probably asks himself. Only God knows.

Two months after his arrival at Fort Jefferson, and after the arrival of a black regiment, the situation seemed unbearable. Mudd attempted to escape. He wrote a letter to his brother-in-law stating that he had intended to arrive home ahead of his last letter but that providence was against him. His attempt to gain freedom had failed. He had been in chains for two days in the dungeon. There were ecchymoses and bruises on his ankles and wrists. His arms and legs ached and he was weak from a diet of bread and water and lack of exercise, he says. The experience was extremely humiliating.

He had dressed in his good civilian clothes and was able to get up the gangplank of the U.S. transport *Thomas A. Scott* and on board without difficulty. He would have succeeded if he had not met a party on board that he knew before getting to his hiding place. With the help of a member of the crew he would have made it if he had not been recognized. It seemed to be a reasonable risk at the time. Later he thought he would probably pay dearly. He felt terrible for his family, the ones he had hoped to help, he says. The crew member, Kelly, who helped him on board was placed in jail in a cell with a man named Smith who had been caught stealing. One night the two broke their chains and escaped through an iron-grated window.

They let themselves down with their chains, robbed the sutler of fifty dollars, took clothing and provisions, and stole a boat in which they escaped.

Mudd also writes that the 161st N.Y. Regiment had been very kind and generous to him, which was a further inducement for him to make the attempt. He goes on to say that his object in leaving was to avoid greater degradation. After getting into the jurisdiction of a state he would have turned himself in, hoping to get a review of his case. He thinks the Northern newspapers will probably make a lot of this and that he had probably hurt himself by his indiscretion. The disagreeable situation and prospect of it worsening, led him to it. In retrospect it was not a wise thing. He had been in chains in the dungeon but was now out. He regrets that he had to inform on the young man who helped him. It was all done by a slip of the tongue. He hopes that Kelly, his accomplice, has made good his escape, which he thought he had. He writes that he had been thrown out of his position as chief of dispensary and does not know what degree of degradation they had in store for him.

There had been several cases of a strange disease that he had not seen at home. It presented with high fever, headaches, and extreme pain in the bones. One man the previous week had so much pain in the bones of his legs that Mudd had given him morphine. The severe symptoms passed in three or four days, leaving the victim quite weak. There had been no deaths from it, but it seemed to be a most violent affliction.

His friend Arnold, a clerk in the provost marshal's office, had been ordered to hard labor for no reason at all. He did nothing to bring on this change of treatment and had been told nothing. They were prisoners under guard and slept in the guardhouse. During the day they cleaned bricks.

He writes that the fort was then wholly guarded by black troops with the exception of a few white officers. New rules were then in force and many of their liberties were gone. He was placed in the guardhouse in chains for two days before being put on the brick-cleaning detail. Little did he ever think that he would be required to do such a chore. The order also had him closely confined whenever a ship was in port. He had been transferred to a small damp room with Arnold who had been on the brick-cleaning detail with him. Also in the room with them was Colonel George St. Leger Grenfell, formerly an English officer, then a sheep rancher in Argentina, and more recently an officer in the Confederate States Army. He had many tales of war experiences and vowed that he would escape this hell hole. He was a very determined person, and spoke French, German, and Spanish fluently. They sometimes chatted in French to break the monotony. He had served with Morgan's Raiders in Ohio and Indiana. Grenfell was also one of the leaders in the attempt to free the Confederate prisoners at Camp Douglas in Chicago in 1864.

That daring attempt nearly succeeded and would have let loose ten thousand armed Confederate soldiers on the streets of Chicago. It could have been quite helpful to the South if it had succeeded. The Copperheads were supposed to assist but failed to carry out their part. They talked big but were not there for "roll call." Mudd ends his letter to his brother-in-law hoping that his release will not be long deferred.

Hope, the marvelous beacon that gives courage to go on was all Mudd had. He fortunately did not know that his confinement would last three and a half years more. The dungeon was a low, dark casemate with only one small window.

Much was made of Mudd's attempted escape in publications throughout the country.

Grenfell had a letter smuggled off the island reporting extreme cruelty and torture of a prisoner, James Dunn. Grenfell's letter was published in the *New York Herald.* It caused a great furor at home and had repercussions at the fort. There was much resentment among the command at the fort. Grenfell was treated cruelly in punishment for his deed. He was thrown in the water with a rope tied to him and nearly drowned off the end of the pier by some of the guards. He was a good swimmer and made it back without trouble. They then tied weights on his body and tied his arms, but he swam with his feet and was able to survive. After that he was hung by his thumbs for a period of time and was then made to carry heavy cannon balls.

The guards gave Grenfell the same kind of treatment that he saw being given to Dunn. His thumbs were greatly swollen. Mudd thought for a time that he would lose a portion of one from gangrene but the color was better in the last two days. Grenfell was desperate. Anything could happen. His health was not good. His legs were swollen. This was not helped at all by the bread and water diet he was on.

The mosquitoes attacked in droves. The heat and humidity were nearly unbearable in the damp, squalid room. Water stood in one corner of it and the stench from the moat outside the porthole was sickening. Vermin bit them during the night. Blood stains on the bed clothes in the morning attested to that. They were all helpless.

In a letter home to his wife a month after his escapee attempt, Mudd asks again how the Northern newspapers are reporting his escape attempt. He is naturally quite concerned about it. This was important to him not only because it was a failure but because of the effect it might have on his eligibility for release.

He says that he has learned from a friend that a lengthy account of his escape attempt had been sent in for publication.

He mentions again to Frances how it was bad enough to be a prisoner in the hands of white men, but to be lorded over by black people was more than he could submit to. He had believed that his chances of success were almost certain when he made the escape attempt and that he had dreamed of being home with her and the children. His failed escape attempt apparently bothered him very much. He asks Frances, "Why should I be expected to act more honorable than my persecutors who sent me here?" He would henceforth yield his opinion and bear up under the indignities and hardships they heaped upon him. He would yield to the better judgment of his advisors, to God, and to the justice of his cause. He tells Frances to have no further apprehension regarding his conduct. He says he has never had a cross word with an individual, soldier or prisoner, since being closeted upon this island of woe and misery. He writes that he has striven to the utmost of his ability to visit the sick and make those around him comfortable.[6]

All these things indicate that Mudd was a very gentle man who was very greatly affected by the indignities and humiliating experiences he was experiencing as a prisoner.

Mudd indicates that his counsel might have prepared him more for his ordeal. He says, "No mortal mind can appreciate the feelings of one who has been so foully dealt with, and separated suddenly and violently from family and all near and dear, and banished hundreds of miles away—no opportunities afforded for visits and imperfect and irregular mail service, for no fault and for having done my duty to God and man. I trust my present good resolutions will be supported by grace from above, through the prayerful mediation of you [Frances] and all."

Next, in the long letter, Mudd goes into financial matters with Frances and advises her to prepare for conditions that may not be as favorable as they have been. He sends some unpaid medical accounts from his patients and asks Frances to collect them. He seems to realize after nearly three months on the island that there will not be a quick end to his incarceration there.

On October 12, three more prisoners made good their escape, taking a boat in daylight. Following Mudd's attempt, eleven prisoners had escaped, he writes. He asks Frances again to send him information in the news there about his escape attempt.

Five days later, Mudd writes that orders had been given to look into all correspondence arriving and leaving the post. He wants Frances to be aware of that in her correspondence. He says that he was very well at present and confined to a small damp room with Arnold, O'Laughlin, Spangler, and Grenfell. What led to that he did not know. He tells his wife not to let this trouble her; he had been through worse and was in hopes, through the mercies of God, to live through this and be a consolation to her and his dear little family. They were being guarded by a black regiment. He asks for prayers and sends love to all.[7]

In a later letter to Frances from her brother Jere Dyer in Baltimore, Jere relates having communication with ex–Governor Ford of Ohio. The ex-governor had successfully met with a man by the name of Webster who had been in Congress but had been appointed collector of this port. He was said to be decidedly in favor of Mudd's release and was sanguine about success. This was heartening to Frances and showed that Mudd's case was being kept alive in the government. In spite of this news, Jere cautions his sister not to be too sanguine about early release. He cautions that it is necessary that the folks at home must do their part by sending petitions to Him who is mightier than man. HE may not immediately hear and patience may be necessary. HE will not refuse much longer, he hopefully predicts.

Jere refers to another case of typhoid among Frances' neighbors and urges Frances to bear her troubles with Christian resignation.

Jere also writes that he was showing some of Mudd's letters to R. I. Brent. He was a big man and a warm friend. Keeping Mudd's case on the minds of men of influence in the government would eventually have the desired effect. To cheer Frances up, he tells her that Mudd may carve the turkey at home on Christmas Day. It is doubtful that he really meant this but thought it good psychology for his sister, in those bleak and trying days. Those behind-the-scenes activities did show that much was being done at home that Mudd was not aware of.[8]

On November 11, 1865, Mudd writes to his brother-in-law Jere that four companies of heavy artillery had arrived to relieve the black regiment, which made him hopeful that conditions would improve.[9] They could not get any worse, he writes. When a ship came into port, the prisoners had been put in leg irons and marched down to the wharf, where they were made to clean bricks in plain view where they could be seen by all. This was to show that the prisoners were at work. He writes that they had been closely confined under guard for a fortnight. In spite of being in irons, they were closely guarded and were not allowed to leave the door without having a black guard with musket and bayonet at their side. At night their chains were taken off, but the guardhouse door was locked with a sentry on duty. Mudd believed it was to degrade and lessen them. Every day increased his hatred toward the authors of his ruin, he writes. The expectation of relief he hoped would keep him within bounds. He wishfully writes to his brother-in-law, telling him that if he should obtain his release, to lose no time in forwarding the joyous news! "We all are in chains at this time. Colonel Grenfell and I have not been taken out to work for the last three days."

Mudd's brother-in-law Thomas Dyer made contact with General Sheridan, then in charge of the Gulf, for permission to forward clothing and other articles to Mudd at Fort Jefferson. Prior to that time many of the things sent had not gotten through.

Letters from Mudd became less frequent because of greater censorship being imposed on outgoing mail.

Mudd wrote in November and December 1865 that he was as good as circumstances would permit. He sends love to all members of his family. He tells the children to study their lessons and pray for him. He was afraid to write more, he says. He was still in hopes of a speedy release.

Mudd wrote a letter to Jere. He had received a trunk from Tom from New Orleans. It came through per Sheridan's order with all items of food and clothing present but minus two bottles of whiskey. The black regiment was partially replaced and conditions were better, he writes. He was still in irons and was washing down the bastions each day. He was closely guarded and not allowed to talk to other prisoners. They were allowed to purchase some food items. Tom had sent twenty-five dollars, which was placed in the hands of the commander. Prisoners were allowed only three dollars a month. He writes that he is well and in hopes of speedy release from his chains.

Two weeks later Mudd wrote to Frances. He was getting impatient with the previous expectation of release for Christmas and referred to flimsy pretense. He felt that those at home had been misled and this caused cruel disappointment to visit him in "this ungodly place." He writes that they had not been visited by a priest up to that time and there was no minister of any denomination there and no religious observation on Sundays or holidays. He again cautions his wife to tell Fannie to be more discrete about what she writes in her letters, that all were opened and read before he got them. Her last letter was not delivered to him because of the language she used. She must use caution in the future to allow nothing to be said that might prolong his misery. His spirits were very low. He writes that he had arrived at the point where he would accept any terms for an immediate release—even death—to a much longer protraction. In regard to his son Tommy who had been sick, he writes, "I fear I shall not be home in time to render him any benefit. I hope we shall be spared the loss of one of our dear children." He writes that what he had undergone was beyond his power of expressing and nothing but the consciousness of having done no wrong, but a duty, caused him to bear up against his adverse fortune.

A week later he writes that he was well and things were status quo. The weather was very hot. Mosquitoes and bedbugs were numerous and troublesome. He expresses his disappointment in not being able to be home for Christmas.

He tells Frances not to send any more money to him because she needed it at home. He was worried about finances with no family income during his confinement. "You and the children will need every dime and even then will suffer privations and hardships," he says. He wonders if she had succeeded in hiring any field hands and a cook for the coming year. He advises her to avoid being dependent on others and at the same time try to prevent want for herself and the children. The latter thought troubled him more than any other. Mudd writes that he read nothing in the occasional newspapers that he received that inspired him with hope for himself or restoration of peace and good will among the States. He greatly desired the South to resume a proper relation in the Union. This reference is to the great political differences that were being argued in Congress regarding reconstruction of the Southern states. These were the things that had President Johnson occupied at the time and that were leading to great differences with elements of Congress. Mudd writes that if he were freed at this time, it would be hard to decide where on earth it would be possible to rest happy and content. He would likely be detained longer than anticipated and urges Frances to take care of her health for the sake of the children. "Let not the cares which now press heavily upon you, lead you to unnecessarily expose your health and strength." He closes his letter by regretting that he has nothing good that refutes the bleak present situation.

On December 22, 1865, Frances wrote a strong pleading letter to President Johnson that demonstrated her fortitude.

She says that she hated to address him but love was stronger than fear and that timidity must yield. She tells the president that after many weeks of anxious waiting she had finally received word from her husband and that he was heavily ironed at Fort Jefferson and forced to do hard work. The treatment was evidently in response to a rumor of a New Orleans plot to rescue the prisoners.

In addition, the food was so poor that the doctor was not able to eat it, and his health and strength were failing. She says that when she saw him (the president) on her visit to his office in September, she saw in his face "a kind heart that can sympathize with the sufferings of others." She drew this assumption because "the face is the index of the heart."

She says it struck her that his excellency was ignorant of the order that was bringing suffering to her husband and she pleads for better food and treatment for him and that he be released to her.

She states that setting a leg was no crime that called for forgiveness and she prays for him to interpose his high authority. "By a stroke of your pen you can cause these irons to fall and food to be supplied. By a stroke of that same pen, you can give him liberty." She pleads eloquently: "You were elected Father of this people. Their welfare is your welfare. Then, in the name of God, if you let him die under this treatment, he an American citizen, who has never raised his arm, nor his voice against his country, can these people love you?

"Forgive me, I speak plainly, but my heart is very sore." She then tells of the children who missed their father and the doctor's elderly parents. "In the Doctor's childhood home, there is his father, who is old and infirm. When he hears the name of his boy, his lips tremble, but he thinks it is not manly to yield to tears; besides he has confidence in you."

She continues. "His mother has scarcely left her sick room since his arrest. She waits to see him; then like Holy Simeon, she is willing to die." Frances says that she as a wife was dragging out a life of despondency when previously she had been shielded from every care by he who is "now suffering a living death." She speaks of her four babies, the eldest seven years old, the youngest but one, in a heart-touching appeal to the president to help her husband and to release him.

Mudd's wife was doing everything in her power, but he had no way of fully knowing it and would not realize during the next three and a half years how hard she was working on his behalf.

On Christmas Day, 1865, Mudd wrote to Frances expressing his regret that they were not experiencing a joyous reunion together. He says he was well in spite of their mutual disappointment. Jere had suggested that Frances rent out the farm. Mudd opposed that idea. He asks himself what he has done to bring such trouble on his family and reminds himself that the greatest saints were the most persecuted. This is some consolation to him. He renews his religious vows. He states that his duties were to sweep down the bastions of the fort each day under guard. He thought his attempted escape was the cause of his treatment. When a vessel came into port he was placed in irons in his quarters.

On January 1, 1866, Mudd writes that it being the first day of the New Year, he had no better way at his command of spending time appropriately than writing to his wife to afford her all the consolation in his power. He had had a very much appreciated visit from Bishop Verot of Savannah and Reverend Father O'Hara several days before, and had the happy fortune of "being present for divine service." After the service he had a short conversation with them both. This had been very valuable to him and had lifted his spirits. In the evening Bishop Verot had given a very learned and practical lecture and after the lecture called on him in his quarters. Mudd had received confession from him. Mudd writes, "I have not language at my command, my darling, to express the joy and delight I received on the occasion of this unexpected visit."

Mudd then repeats that he had but one affliction: uneasiness of mind regarding her, Frances, and the precious children. This preyed on his mind. He mentioned it over and over. He says that his worry about his family was the hardest thing for him. Imprisonment, chains, and the humiliation of prison life were small in comparison to that worry.

He also was worried about the stories in the newspapers about the large numbers of crimes being committed.

He asks Frances what disposition was made of the farm, horses, cows, and sheep, and whether Old John would remain with her. He urges her to try to remain comfortable and free from dependent position. "Tell me all you can with propriety in your next letter remembering that all letters are inspected. Disappointment produces more pain than the pleasure of hope so my darling say nothing illusive and advise Henry and Fannie the same. Life and everything in it is uncertain and changeable. We do not know what other trials lay ahead."

A letter from Fannie had been sent to the War Department according to the provost marshal. Mudd asks Frances to be very careful about writing imprudent things that might dissuade the president from listening to appeals on his behalf.

Soon after Mudd wrote a three and a half page letter to his sister in which he tactfully and gently reminds her that all mail was censored and that she should not write anything that could be misconstrued by those who wished to attach adverse meanings to what was said. It was a long and very friendly letter. Mudd states that he thought he would have to remain "there" some time yet to keep up appearances. An early release would be a virtual acknowledgment of the injustice of the court-martial.

In the latter part of January 1866, Mudd wrote that he was beginning to understand the meaning of the words of the psalmist, "I have grown old in my youth." He goes on to describe the conditions of his confinement. He was loaded with heavy chains, locked up in a dark, damp room twelve hours out of every twenty-four and all day Sundays and holidays. No outside exercise was allowed, only that in the limited space of the room with the irons on. He writes that the air was heavy with hydrogen sulfide gas, which was disagreeable and injurious to health. The gas came from sinks that emptied into the sea enclosed in the breakwall immediately under a small porthole that was the only entrance they had for air and light. The odor was that of rotten eggs. He writes that his legs and ankles were swollen and sore and that he frequently had pains in his shoulders and back. He was losing his hair and his eyesight was getting bad. When he was outside during the day the overpowering bright sunlight made his eyes painful and irritated. "With all this imagine my gait with a bucket and broom, and a guard, walking from one corner of the fort to another, sweeping and sanding down the bastions." He writes that he had been doing that for the past three months, since his attempted escape the previous September.

He then, in a lighter vein, writes of the subtropical weather, which in mid-winter back home was like mid-summer there. Inhabitants were in their bare feet and shirtsleeves. It was strange to read in the papers of people freezing to death in heavy snows. He was worried that Frances might not have enough fuel to keep warm. With the picture he had painted, he tells Frances not to think that he has no pleasures. His principal consolation was having no responsibilities other than the salvation of his own soul. He tells her he had done all in his power toward that end. He mentions again the religious services he recently had with the bishop from Savannah and Father O'Hara. It apparently meant very much to him. Father O'Hara was then stationed at Key West and Mudd hoped to see him every four or five weeks. He was a very fine preacher, he writes.

In January near the end of the month Mudd writes that he had been relieved of his horrible chains. He was greatly relieved to learn that their little boy was recovering. He writes that he had sent twelve to fifteen letters home since Christmas.

In February Mudd wrote a letter to Jere stating that Jere's letter of the 26th had been received. They evidently were in frequent communication. Mudd writes that he had hoped that he would be bounding the billows of the ocean on the way home but supposed that it was decreed otherwise. He must be resigned. He complains again about the bright sunlight and heat. The meals were a little better, probably because of Frances's letter to President Johnson.

Mudd continued to write faithfully to his wife once or twice a week. Her return letters meant much to him; he felt close to her when he read them. At times he was impatient that he was not being released but was making himself realize that the folks at home were doing all they could. He felt that his incarceration was a great injustice and that this would be recognized and that he would be set free. When it did not happen he became depressed and irritated and thought he was forgotten and was critical of his family and friends who actually were doing everything in their power to secure his release. He had no one else he could express himself to.

In a letter later in the month Mudd was again impatient. His wife and other members of the family tried to cheer him up by saying that he would soon be released. They were making every effort possible to bring this to pass but from his letters he sounded as though he did not think so.

He says he received two letters from Frances but they brought him nothing definite. He was happy that she and the children were in good health. He expresses impatience and asks Frances what she meant when she said it would be a short time until his release. He says he is tired of those references and wonders if three years was a short time. "It takes twelve to fifteen days for a letter to get here from home so you can judge how long it would take me to come once I am released," he wrote. "Our chains are now removed and we have been moved to healthier quarters where it is not so damp. Water sometimes lay on the floor in our first floor location."

About this same time Jere wrote to Frances. Jere writes that on his way up he had stopped at Washington and had a conference with ex-Governor Ford regarding Mudd. Ford said that he had had a long conference with President Johnson the previous day. He said that the president gave every assurance that he would release Mudd at the earliest possible time that he could do so. The president said Mudd was a mere creature of accident and ought not to have been put there. In the present state of political excitement, with the radical republicans trying to impeach him, he did not think it prudent to take action at this time. It would give the radicals something more to use against him. The issue with the radicals would be made in a few days. If they persisted in their extreme measures he would take a decided stand against them. Jere was of the opinion that the president would release Mudd as soon as he could so with propriety. It was Jere's opinion that the time would not be long.

In the third week of February there was a letter to Mrs. Mudd from Thomas Ewing, who had defended Mudd. He writes that he did not think it was the right time to move on her husband's case. The Supreme Court was going to consider the jurisdiction of a military commission on a case in Indiana. This was also in regard to the right of a civilian to a trial in civil court when the civil court was intact. He writes that it was best to wait for the decision on this case before anything was done.

Mudd learned of the impending case of Milligan in Indiana and how closely it resembled his own from a legal standpoint. He was cheered by the thought that the question of civil rights was being brought before the Supreme Court. This Milligan case, however, did not involve the assassination of the commander-in-chief or the reaction of an irate populace in response to the deed. [The case was finally decided, after a great deal of delay, in favor of Milligan.]

The end of February 1866, Mudd wrote to Frances about letters being animated with hope of his early release. He did not think it was so in view of the vindictive hate that had followed him. [Mudd referred to the letter of Captain George Dutton to Judge-Advocate Holt, in which he had claimed that Mudd had made confessions to him during the voyage to Fort Jefferson on the gunboat *Florida*.]

He writes, "I can't divine the motive of the author or the prosecution in appending these affairs and unjust fabrications after my trial, because they do not give me a chance for refutation. To hold me responsible for such, would be equivalent to the denial of all justice, and all that would be necessary to condemn a man would be first to bind and gag him, then allow his enemies to come forward and make their accusations. This was the exact proceeding in my case. In the letter to Jere I wrote in relation to this, fearing he might not receive, I again make mention, and request you to confer with General Ewing or Stone in that regard, and let me know what, if any, bearing it has upon my case. It is not my wish to agitate the matter, knowing it will have no tendency to benefit me. All I wish you to do is speak to my counsel, and act under their wise instructions."

During the next three months Mudd became very impatient about his release. Frances and Jere Dyer were meeting with people in Washington and Baltimore. On March 3, 1866, Mudd wrote to Frances that two mails had arrived without mention of his release. He admonishes her that she knows of his anxiety and disappointment with each incoming mail. After all, she is his main contact with the outside world. He expresses his impatience to her when she and Jere were doing all they could for him.

Jere had made repeated contact with persons who had access to the president. The truth was that President Johnson had his hands full with a radical majority in Congress who were accusing him of being too lenient on the Southern states.

Father O'Hara came to Fort Jefferson and visited the sick without "affording us an opportunity for confession."

On March 13, 1866, Mudd was encouraged by reading that President Johnson had indicated that Congress had had enough time to know what the people wanted and had decided to take the initiative. Mudd hoped that the president's plan would be accepted and acted upon throughout the land.

In regard to Dutton's letter to Holt falsely stating that Mudd had made a confession to Dutton that he had recognized Booth at the time he treated him, this was a complete falsehood, Mudd said. It was a complete fabrication. He told Frances to have Jere contact Colonel or Judge Turner of the War Department to determine any statements that he had made on the way to Fort Jefferson. He was often in Turner's company, he says. Mudd hoped the mystery would soon be cleared up and that an honorable release would be his.

On March 17 in a letter to Frances, Mudd speaks of the unfairness of the detectives of the court. He writes that many of the witnesses made false and injurious statements about him after the trial when they knew that he had no way of rebuttal. The only pleasure Mudd had was to write to Frances and receive her letters.

Mudd had seen an account in a Baltimore paper stating that Judge Crain was chairman of a committee there. He told Frances that Crain would lend his aid.

On March 22 Mudd wrote that he was well but entirely without other news. He knew that his letters were being censored and that he could not write anything objectionable to the administration of the fort. He was brief, he writes, because the main subjects of conversation were thus denied him. Criticism was objected to. He writes how much he would like to write something that would cheer and console and free her from her many anxieties and hardships but such was unhappily not in his power. Gloom and monotony were the main things there. "Even the little birds who stray away from more congenial climes, migrating birds, when they stop here do not sing. That shows that they also are affected by the gloom of this place."

Mail arrived about once every ten to fifteen days and the papers brought only stale news that served to occupy Mudd for only a few hours. He repeats how he longed to be with her and the little ones. His worry was about having the little ones trained and educated. He reassures Frances that she was in his thoughts constantly and prayed that God would speed the time when he could say adieu to this land of exile.

About a week later Mudd sent home a photo of Fort Jefferson with the location of his cell just above and to the left of the sally port marked. The picture showed the original lighthouse of the fort and also Logger Head Key in the background. Mudd said that turtles weighing up to 300 pounds were still caught in the area. He expresses less resentment in this letter.

Owing to the excitement and influence prevailing at the time of his trial he could excuse much but since that was past now and things were more sober he was vexed at his protracted exile. He was sorry to learn of his mother's bad health. He expresses some concern with advisors for his case but leaves things up to Frances for further action. He cautions his wife to use care in writing to him, but to let him hear further about "these" incendiaries.

A week later, Mudd writes that he was very well and that the island continued healthy. Yellow Fever and cholera were reported in Key West. Precautions had been taken to prevent introduction of the diseases to the fort. He did not mention what those precautions were. Did he say this to comfort Frances?

A few days later there was a letter from Jere to Frances. Jere writes that he has had a conference with Judge Crain, the person Mudd had suggested a few weeks earlier, and that he would get the decision of the Supreme Court on the Milligan case. He thinks that the Court decided that there is no law governing the trial of civilians by a military court. The report on the Milligan case had not yet been made public. The judge would go to Washington in a few days and ask Reverdy Johnson to go to the president to have Mudd released. The judge thought that the president might not want to release Mudd on his own under his present circumstances with Congress. In that case Mudd could be gotten out through the courts. He would write and give any information he got.

Mudd avidly read all the newspapers that belatedly arrived and in that way kept up with current events as best he could under the circumstances. He did not miss much.

In the middle of April, Mudd wrote to Frances that he was pleased that President Johnson had vetoed the Civil Rights Bill and the Proclamation of Peace. He thought that that would restore equal rights to all states in the South and suspend military proceedings in civil cases. He was awaiting the good news of his release.

The end of April he received a derogatory newspaper article that had troubled his wife. He told her he was sorry she was troubled by it. It seemed to be the intention of prejudiced parties not to let the effect of one slander die without breeding another. He was under guard at all times. His health was good, but his strength was not good due to lack of exercise. He was sweeping bastions once a day, which was not strenuous.

In May he described the weather as quite warm. Two people were overcome with the heat but no deaths had occurred. It was best to stay out of the direct sunlight at mid-day if possible. He had sent some pressed moss cards and wondered if they were received.

A few weeks later Thomas Dyer wrote from New Orleans that he was sending a box containing canned fruits and other foods. He was also forwarding thirty dollars under separate cover. Tom says that Mudd should let him know if he needs anything and he will get it for him. Tom was a man of action rather than words.

Near the end of May another box of canned fruit and some books came from a cousin. Mudd had some relief, even though there was no release. This cheered him up a bit, but he was constantly thinking of release and hoped that the arrival of each boat that docked would bring word of it.

In mid–June 1866 Mudd told Frances once again how her letters were his only consolation in view of his disappointment in regard to his release. President Johnson was having extreme difficulty with the so-called radical element of Congress, which was accusing him of being too lenient with the Southern states. He could not free Mudd at that time. Mudd writes that it had been two months since the decision of the Supreme Court in the Milligan case, but the decision had not been made public. He had lost his patience. "Stone and Ewing seem to be doing nothing!" he tells Frances. He had received not a word from them. He told his wife one good thing. He had received a box of food and thirty dollars from her brother Tom.

Also in mid–June, a letter came from Jere. He had been to Washington and while there saw William P. Wood, the keeper of Old Capitol Prison, who gave his word that he would do all in his power to help Mudd and promised to write a letter to that effect. John T. Ford of Ford's Theater had engaged Reverdy Johnson to represent Spangler. This was a fine gesture on the part of Ford for his old friendless stage hand. Johnson would take action as soon as Congress adjourned. It was considered useless to do anything before the adjournment of Congress due to the radical element there. It might do harm. He writes that he was very sure that after the adjournment of Congress, probably in July, Mudd's release might be possible.

In a long letter written in the middle of June in response to the truth of the complex situation in Washington, Mudd is more realistic. He says Frances's last letter was less optimistic about his release. This had made him disappointed and depressed at first, but he felt better later. He realizes that immediate release was probably not possible. He writes that he is grateful that providence had bestowed so much ambition and cheerfulness in his wife so that she was able to bear up against their sudden change in fortune. He says that he was proud of her success in farming and regretted the inability of language to express his praise. He writes further that the long close confinement that he has endured may have rendered him less capable to contend actively with the pursuits that the farm and his profession demanded.

Mudd acknowledges that Frances had freedom of action and could probably run the farm better than he, if it were necessary. He expresses this confidence in her by telling her that perhaps she should no longer use the advice of counsel but her own judgment in regard to further action on his part. Being in no situation to advise, however, he leaves it up to her and her friends to judge what steps were necessary. He says he was well but weak and nervous from the long confinement.

Later in June Mudd writes that the weather was almost suffocating and mosquitoes, fleas, and bed bugs infested the island. They could not rest day or night because of them. Half of the garrison was composed of black troops. There were about 170 prisoners on the island, and of this number there were only about thirty whites.

 Mudd's letters to Frances became longer. He realized that he was not to be released soon and tried to reconcile himself to his fate but found it very difficult.

 In July Mudd's father reached Major General Phil Sheridan through a friend. The general wrote that he would contact General Foster to see that Mudd was subjected to only such punishment as was warranted by his sentence. Soon after that there was improvement in the food and living quarters.

In August 1866 Mudd writes of newspaper accounts of proceedings in Washington. He was pleased with President Johnson's proclamation restoring all former privileges to all the states. He writes of getting a dry plank floor for sleeping quarters to do away with some of the dampness that had bothered them.

Near the end of the month, Mudd writes that he could not believe that those in authority would much longer disregard every principle of justice and fair dealing to satisfy vulgar thirst for vengeance. He says he was very tired of his present life.

 In the latter part of 1866 he took up pressing moss as a hobby and making artistic objects with it. In early 1867 they had a garden in front of the fort with soil that was brought from the mainland. Many vegetables were maturing, which would improve their limited diet.

In the third week of August 1866, Mudd wrote that his main pastime was writing to his family. In this letter he refers to the report of the Judiciary Committee, which favored the trial of Jefferson Davis on the false and frivolous charges that were adduced upon their trial in connection with the assassination. He writes, "With equal justice might every distiller of whiskey be arraigned and tried for all the crimes committed by its abuse, and every man be at the mercy of an enemy capable of writing him a fictitious letter." Arnold's letter, upon which they built the conspiracy, shows conclusively that up to a late period in March 1865, Booth had no connection with the Richmond authorities or their Canadian agents.

The following day Mudd wrote another long letter to his wife, saying that he was sorry that her visit to Washington was not more fruitful. Four recently arrived prisoners from Charleston were being transferred to Fort Delaware, placing them under the operation of the writ of habeas corpus. This was what Mudd was hoping for.

He writes that he is subsisting by making little work boxes and picture frames that he inlayed with different colors of wood. These commanded a ready sale to visitors and soldiers of the garrison. On August 31 he asks to be remembered to Mr. Best, his faithful helper who made the crutch for Booth. On September 3, Mudd writes that he was truly glad to hear that Frances is all right. The newspapers had told of a riot. He writes again of receiving the box of food from Tom Dyer in New Orleans. In an October 14 letter Mudd comforts Frances about an article in the newspaper about him which he says was completely false.

On October 28 Mudd wrote the time was growing short until the assembling of the next Congress and the indications were that there would be a stormy time between the president and the majority. "If matters are prolonged until that is clarified, I give up hope," he writes. "*Neither the President nor Congress* will assume the responsibility to release and I shall be here a living sacrifice to the damnable ends of party."

Mudd had it right. Here was where the problem lay. President Johnson was under extreme attack by a so-called radical majority in Congress, accusing him of leniency toward the South. His enemies were looking for every thread of evidence to bring against him. Some even went so far as to accuse him of complicity in the assassination for which there was no evidence whatsoever. These enemies of the president soon after would muster enough strength to bring impeachment charges against him.

Two days later, Mudd took out his wrath on his wife, who was doing everything possible in her power to get him free. He writes, "I am fast losing all forbearance under the cruel and unwarranted oppression to which I am subjected, the result of a tyrannical and unjustified usurpation. I have for over eighteen months been languishing in prison for no crime against God or man that I am cognizant of, and I think it high time the friends of humanity and law, particularly my own personal friends and relations, were coming to the rescue." The poor man was suffering severely. Frances was suffering severely also. She was well aware of her husband's condition. Still it threw a terrible additional strain on her.

President Johnson had told Frances that he would release her husband but could not do it "now." Why? Because of the conflict with Congress and the charges being made against him. Was the "radical" majority in Congress responsible for Mudd's continued incarceration? Yes, most of all. This element was preventing the president from taking action.

Did they want revenge against the South? Did they want what Sir Walter Scott describes as "That last sweet morsel of satisfaction cooked in the furnace of hell"? Apparently so.

President Johnson was trying to carry out a lenient course of action as Lincoln had suggested in his second inaugural address and in his last talk from the White House on April 11.

During the next months things were pretty much at a standstill. Mudd continued to write voluminous letters to Frances expressing dissatisfaction with his situation. Frances and Jere kept very busy in Mudd's behalf. The Supreme Court decision was rendered in the case of Milligan who also was a civilian tried before a military court. In the decision civilians were found entitled to trial before a civil court when civil courts were in operation. This gave much impetus to Frances and Jere. Jere saw Reverdy Johnson in Washington in an effort to get a writ of habeas corpus for Mudd. Attorney Johnson turned the case over to his son-in-law, Ridgely, to draw up the papers. Many specific questions had to be answered: the date Mudd was arrested, the name of the arresting officer, to which prison he was taken, the specific charges, and the complete name of the commanding officer at Fort Jefferson. With all this finally accomplished, the cost of drawing up the request for the writ was $250. If it had to be argued before Judge Chase it was $250 more. These were not small amounts of money required of a family already severely depleted and with the breadwinner incarcerated in jail for nearly two years.

On December 30, Mudd wrote to Frances that they had received a box from O'Laughlin's friends and would enjoy it for New Year's 1867.

Mudd, Arnold, O'Laughlin, and Spangler had become quite close friends. Colonel Grenfell was now added to their group.

The writ of habeas corpus before Judge Chase was denied. Mudd was vexed that the Milligan decision did not apply to him. He wrote to his wife that Milligan was tried during the existence of active war and his trial was at the end of the war. If the trial of Milligan before a military court during war was wrong, his was even more so, in his opinion.

Several letters later Mudd spoke of spending time in the carpenter shop, which proved to be a great outlet for him. He constructed fine furniture during his stay. Keeping busy took his thoughts away from his problems.

An item of much interest came on the scene and was described in the belated newspapers that Mudd received. John H. Surratt, the youngest son of Mrs. Mary E. Surratt, was apprehended in Egypt and was being returned to the United States. His ship left Alexandria, Egypt, December 21, and was expected to arrive in Washington on February 21, 1867. This excited

Mudd. Would Surratt be given the benefit of a civil trial, the thing that his counsel had tried in vain to get for him and a review of which he had been denied?

If Surratt had been tried before the military commission in 1865, he would likely have had the fate of his mother. His mother might have been spared. In a January 15 letter to his wife, Mudd writes that they had a garden in the center of the parade grounds inside the fort. Soil had been brought from the mainland. They were growing tomatoes, beets, peas, and radishes. They were anticipating these pleasant additions to their diet. They also had two caged song birds that sing for them.

Frances received a letter from Andrew Ridgley in Washington who represented Mudd in quest of a writ of habeas corpus. He had not given up hope of freeing Mudd and suggested that they try again in a while by making application to the judges of the District of Columbia. On January 23 Mudd wrote that he was held by armed hand in spite of the law. On February 6 he wrote that the weather was becoming quite warm. Matters had assumed a complicated nature. "I am in hope that the sober thought of the people will not sustain the ultra and unconstitutional legislation of Congress." In the next letter, on February 14, he writes, "Judging from papers, the old ship of state is adrift, floating without a rudder, without a captain, and they threaten to throw overboard the chief engineer, the President."

He writes that they are yet under close guard. He fears he would become accustomed to this life and would look for a guard to accompany him on all occasions. He had not lost his sense of humor. On February 20, 1867, he writes that he had had his occupation changed to the carpenter shop. It afforded more exercise and a greater diversion of his thoughts.

On April 16, 1867, in a letter to Jere, Mudd writes that Grenfell was in close confinement under guard. A few days before he was not well and applied to the doctor for medical attention. It was refused and he was ordered to work. When he refused he was ordered to carry a heavy iron ball, which he also refused. He was tied up for a half-day but still refused. He was taken to the wharf and thrown overboard with a rope attached to him. He kept himself up, following which a heavy weight was attached to his feet. They tried to break his spirit but could not conquer him.

On April 25, Major Stone took over command of the fort from General Hill. The number of prisoners there was about forty-five.

The dull, hot, monotonous days of prison life wore on at Fort Jefferson. Newspapers arrived with articles on Surratt. These were of much interest to Mudd. Surratt was finally caught in Egypt and had been brought back to Washington and was going to stand trial there. He was lucky. This was two years after Lincoln's assassination. The furor of an enraged nation had died down. The war was definitely over. There had been much discussion and debate regarding the rights of private citizens to trial before a civil jury.

Surratt was much more deeply involved in the kidnap plot than was Mudd, yet he was going to be tried in a civil court instead of before a harsh military commission.

15
The Belated Trial
of John Surratt

Why was John Surratt allowed to go free? Why was he allowed to live out his life of seventy-two years when so many others suffered and his mother was hanged? Mudd and his family suffered tremendously during his four years on Dry Tortugas. He never regained his health and died at the age of forty-nine. His involvement was minimal in comparison to that of Surratt.

Surratt was deeply involved in the plot to kidnap Lincoln and take him to Richmond from its very early stages. He was the third person recruited (after Arnold and O'Laughlin, the two boyhood acquaintances of Booth who were recruited in August 1864). Surratt met Booth in December 1864, according to Wiechmann.

Prior to meeting Booth, Surratt had been an active Confederate courier between Richmond, Washington, and Montreal. Surratt's father operated a tavern at a cross-roads in Maryland about fourteen miles south of Washington. He was also postmaster there. When war broke out in 1861, many if not the majority of the people in the area were pro–Confederate in their political beliefs and the Surrattsville tavern and post office became a clearinghouse for Confederate information.

When Surratt's father died in 1862, he took over the task of postmaster as well as helping his mother with her many new duties. Surratt left school in order to do this. He had little difficulty doing this as his interests were with the Confederacy. His older brother was already in the Confederate Army. Very exciting things were happening because of the war, especially the transmission of secret dispatches between Richmond and Washington, and across the Canadian border. These activities were not only exciting but lucrative and he was soon deeply involved with them. On suspicion of opening mail, the postmastership was taken from young Surratt, giving him even more time for clandestine activity.[1] His trips to Richmond, Washington, and Montreal increased in frequency. On these trips to Richmond, he used the services of a boatman named George Atzerodt in Port

Tobacco to cross the Potomac River into Virginia. From here it was easy
sailing through Port Royal and Bowling Green to the Confederate capital.
The return journey was just the reverse.

In October 1864, Surratt's mother gave up operating the tavern and
moved her family from Surrattsville to a house at 541 H Street in Washington, D.C., which she also owned. The tavern in Surrattsville was losing
money and was too much work for her. She rented it to John Lloyd, who
turned out to be one of his own best customers at his bar. Mrs. Surratt was
of the opinion that she could more easily operate a rooming house in
Washington than the tavern. Little did she know what she was getting into.
On the other hand, since it was her son's activity that got her into trouble,
it probably would have happened even if she had remained at the Surrattsville tavern.

Undoubtedly it was Surratt's courier activity, especially his knowledge
of crossing the Potomac into Virginia, that attracted Booth to him. Booth
needed precisely this kind of help to carry out his scheme of kidnapping
Lincoln. After Surratt's introduction to Booth in December 1864, Surratt
not only joined Booth's plot to kidnap Lincoln, but enlisted the services of
George Atzerodt and David Herold. Herold, being well acquainted with
the many roads from Washington to Port Tobacco, was to help particularly
on the Maryland portion of the journey. Atzerodt was to ferry the kidnap
party across the Potomac River, an enterprise in which he had expertise.
This was very important. Once in Virginia, within the Confederate lines,
they would be safe.

The plans to kidnap incubated in Booth's mind. Tentative plans to
kidnap Lincoln on his way to an afternoon performance at the Soldier's
Home at the outskirts of the city were made. He at times visited there by
carriage unattended. This seemed to offer an excellent opportunity. The
actual planning of the effort could only be tentative since the visits of the
president were sporadic.

During the delay, according to Arnold,[2] the one and only meeting of
all the participants of the capture scheme was held at Gautier's Restaurant
in Washington on March 15, 1865. (The date of this meeting varies in
different accounts. Arnold was present at the meeting and his date is
taken.) This is the only time that Booth invited all of his accomplices to
meet as a group. Several had never met all of the other participants. It was
an elaborate meeting held in a private dining room. Good food, liquor,
wine, and cigars were served in abundance at Booth's expense. He dazzled
his accomplices with his extravagance.

During this meeting, however, in view of the uncertainty of the president making a visit to the Soldier's Home, Booth presented the idea of capturing the president at the theater instead. Arnold objected strenuously that
the idea was unsound and that it could not be successfully carried out. A

heated argument ensued in which Booth threatened to shoot Arnold. It finally was settled without bloodshed when Arnold stated that his involvement was only as originally planned and that the plan would need to be carried out within the next week. He feared that federal authorities would learn of the idea. The party lasted until 5:00 A.M.

The day following the all-night party, word came that the president was, finally, making a visit to the Soldier's Home. This was probably March 17. Hastily the six armed participants mounted their horses and rode casually in pairs to a restaurant near the home: Arnold-O'Laughlin, Atzerodt-Payne, and Booth-Surratt. On arrival it was learned that the president had changed plans and was not making a visit that day. This was a great disappointment after all their preparation and waiting. They had their courage up, ready for the long-awaited event, and were foiled.

Following this aborted attempt, many of the group had misgivings. Arnold and O'Laughlin withdrew and returned to Baltimore. Arnold was suspicious that the authorities had word of the plan and wanted nothing to do with any scheme at the theater. Surratt left on an extended courier trip to Richmond. He returned to Washington, briefly passing through, on his way to Montreal on the night of April 3. That is the last he was in Washington according to DeWitt.[3] Three people testified at Surratt's trial in 1867 that they saw Surratt in Washington on April 14 and two swore that he was the tall, slender, mysterious, well-dressed man with a mustache that called out the times at the entrance of Ford's Theater on the night of the assassination, the last being 10:10.

It was sometime during the next three weeks that Booth changed his plans in his own mind but did not notify the others. What started as a scheme for kidnapping the president in exchange for prisoners became in his mind a plot to assassinate. It may have come to his feverish, zealous mind in desperation with the fall of Richmond. The crafty Booth kept this plan to himself until the day of the assassination, April 14. Atzerodt said he did not know until late afternoon on that day that he was to assassinate Vice President Johnson. This late change in plans was something Atzerodt wanted nothing of and made no attempt to carry out.

The conflicting testimony that Surratt was in Washington the night of the assassination was not established. There is well confirmed evidence that when he left Washington on the night of April 3, he went to Montreal, arriving there on April 6. He remained there until the 12th. He was then sent on a mission by Confederate General Edwin C. Lee, whom he met in Montreal, to reconnoiter and gain information about a military prison in Elmira, New York, which housed Confederate prisoners.

He registered at the Brainard House Hotel in Elmira on April 13 as "John Harrison." The following day, April 14, he carried out his mission in regard to the prison and returned to his hotel. Next morning, he awakened to news of Lincoln's assassination. Evidence was presented that Surratt sent a telegram to Booth in New York City, where Surratt presumed Booth was, and then learned afterward that Booth was the assassin in Washington. On Saturday the 15th he went by train to Canandaigua, New York, arriving there the same evening and registering under the same assumed name.

On Monday, April 17, he saw his name listed in the local newspaper as the attempted assassin of Secretary of State Seward. Realizing his danger, he lost no time crossing the border into Canada and returning to Montreal. From there he vanished.

Colonel Conger of the U.S. Secret Service, accompanied by Louis Wiechmann, Surratt's former roommate, was not able to locate him. Conger had been instrumental in finding and capturing Booth and Herold after their twelve-day evasion of justice in southern Maryland.

From later testimony at the Surratt trial in 1867 it came out that he was in hiding at this time and during his mother's trial, in the home of a priest in a country parish nearly fifty miles from Montreal. Supposedly he heard no news from Washington until it was too late to save his mother from the gallows on July 7, 1865.

About two months after his mother's death, he went in disguise by boat to Quebec City, where he embarked for Liverpool, England. There was at this time a $25,000 reward for his capture offered by the U.S. government, making him a worthy prize for whoever would recognize him.

During his ocean voyage to Liverpool he confided his identity to the ship's surgeon, Dr. McMillan. Arriving in Liverpool, McMillan, contrary to his Hippocratic oath, notified the U.S. vice consul in the expectation of receiving reward.

What transpired next is amazing. The authorities in Washington were not interested, or at least from their reactions, appeared not to be interested in Surratt's capture.

The employment of a military tribunal to try civilians and the hanging of Mrs. Surratt had backfired on Secretary of War Stanton and Judge-Advocate Holt. The public reaction had been severe and they did not want another Surratt trial to rehash the subject. Furthermore, there was severe difficulty between Congress and President Johnson over methods of procedure for reconstruction of the Southern states.

As a result of all these things, no action was taken. Instead of taking action to apprehend Surratt, the reward for Surratt's arrest was cancelled.

Somehow, Surratt was able to raise funds and travel to Rome, Italy, where he enrolled in an English college. In the spring of 1866, he enlisted under the name of "Watson" in the Papal Zouaves, serving under the pope.[4] He went on garrison duty. After a time another unusual thing occurred. He was recognized by a former friend, Henry St. Marie, who was also serving there. This man was a friend of his roommate Louis Wiechmann, whom he had met at his mother's house in Washington in 1865.

Henry St. Marie needed money and reported his knowledge of Surratt to the American minister in Rome, Rufus King. King reported to Washington. The response was similar to that received by the vice consul in Liverpool, in spite of the fact that St. Marie was urging haste.

Things were even worse in Washington in 1866. President Johnson was in conflict with Congress, which now had a two-thirds majority in both houses against him. Events were leading up to possible impeachment, which he survived by only one vote. Secretary of War Stanton and Judge-Advocate Holt were little interested. They referred the case back to the State Department. Things dragged on all summer. Finally in October, the American minister was instructed to proceed. The arrest of Surratt was ordered on November 2, 1866. On the way back to Rome with six guards, "Zouave Watson" plunged down a ravine one hundred feet deep and escaped. He somehow made his way to Naples, where his trail was again picked up when he sailed for Alexandria, Egypt. When he arrived there on November 27, he was intercepted by the American consul. This was more than a year after the government was first notified of his whereabouts.

Some back home in Congress ("radicals") were of the opinion that President Johnson did not want any further investigation into the circumstances of Lincoln's death. The House of Representatives ordered an investigation. According to DeWitt,[5] the delay was not on the part of President Johnson, but on the part of Stanton and the judge-advocate who had been responsible for the execution of Mrs. Surratt and who did not want the case reviewed once again in a civil court in Washington. The trial of Mrs. Surratt's son would raise her ghost once again above their heads.

John Harrison Surratt was returned to the United States on a slow steam vessel. He left Alexandria on December 21, 1866, and arrived at the Washington navy yard on February 21, 1867. By order of the secretary of state, he was given over to civil authorities. The War Department made no objection. Actually, a grand jury in the District of Columbia had made an indictment for murder and the district attorney had begun preparation for trial.

There were no allegations in the indictment regarding Confederate complicity. This allowed former Confederate detectives and spies to act as witnesses.

The trial began on June 10, 1867, two years after the court-martial that convicted Mudd. A diary kept by Booth during his twelve fugitive days was produced. It had come to light only after the court-martial trial of 1865. It was claimed by some that Stanton was responsible for it being withheld. There is no evidence to support this. The *New York Times* of April 27 and the *New York World* of April 28 had each referred to it being found on Booth's body at the time of his death. It was probably in the War Department Archives all the while, where it was found in 1867.[6] The defense somehow overlooked this bit of evidence. It referred to the plot to kidnap Lincoln during a six-month period before assassination was considered. The fact that this plot existed would have helped the defense of Mudd. The nature of this gentle man was such that he might have listened sympathetically to a capture plot to return Confederate prisoners, but would have abhorred any plot for assassination. At the military trial, Mudd and the others were accused of conspiring to assassinate. There was no other consideration for them.

Now, two years later, in a civil court, Surratt, who was much more involved than Mudd, was only implicated in a plot to capture. He was not implicated in a plot to kill as were the defendants in 1865 before the military commission.[7]

Wiechmann was called again to the stand. In his testimony he placed the collapse of the plot to capture about three weeks prior to the assassination. This verifies the account of Arnold, which placed it after the meeting at the restaurant on March 17, 1865.[8]

The question of whether Surratt returned to Washington surreptitiously on the night of the assassination was dealt with by much testimony and finally given up. The evidence that he was in Elmira, New York, stood. (Confederate) General Edwin C. Lee was placed on the stand and testified that Surratt was in Elmira. This testimony and the hotel records from Elmira and Canandaigua made his presence there quite certain.

The last testimony, that of rebuttal, was heard on July 26. District Attorney Carrington addressed the jury.

There were eighty witnesses sworn by the government, half of which did not testify at the conspiracy trial of 1865, and ninety for the defense.[9] Judge George P. Fisher gave his charge to the jury on August 7, 1867, and the jury retired at noon the same day.

On August 10, 1867, at 1:00 P.M., after three days of deliberation, the jury returned to the courtroom and the foreman announced that the jury was divided and a verdict could not be reached.

The jury was discharged. The defendant was returned to his cell. Another jury was to be called in six months.

In February 1868 the House of Representatives was busy impeaching President Johnson. This overshadowed the necessity—and the desirability in the minds of certain important people—to have another civil trial for Surratt. Also the possibility of changing the outcome was not great.

Finally, on June 22, 1868, the prisoner was released on bail and three months later went free.[10]

Surratt lived until 1916. He harbored a deep hatred for Wiechmann, his former schoolmate and later roommate at his mother's boarding house. He conveniently blamed Wiechmann for the death of his mother. On two occasions Wiechmann reported near-miss gunshots in his vicinity, the origin of which was suspicious.

Surratt had the audacity to schedule public lectures in the 1870s about his experiences as a Confederate courier. Most people stayed away but some were interested. Interest in a man who had forsaken his mother on trial for her life was small.[11]

Surratt saved his own life by fleeing the country in 1865, but he sacrificed the life of his mother in so doing. This should have bothered his conscience and undoubtedly did unless he had none.

He escaped the public hysteria of Lincoln's assassination and the military court-martial by fleeing the country. He benefited from the Supreme Court decision in the Milligan case of April 1866, which held that civilians should be tried in civil courts when they were intact rather than by military tribunals.[12] He also benefited from the arguments of Ewing and Johnson given at the court-martial. Ewing's arguments were particularly significant. He was a man of high caliber and a Union general who commanded respect before the military court. The ideas that Ewing and Johnson presented regarding the trial of civilians before a military court when the civil courts are intact were very influential in bringing Surratt's trial before a civil court.

16
Yellow Fever

On May 25 in a letter to Frances, Mudd wrote that the papers mentioned the release of Jefferson Davis under bail without trial. This seemed strange. Possibly they would not try Surratt. "Our government seems to be a complete mobocracy instead of a Government of law and order. . . . I remarked to Judge Turner on the way to Fort Jefferson that the Government had not the slightest direct evidence against me." He remarked that someone had to suffer. Mudd urged Frances to take action on the part of those trusted with his care. Booth's diary had been brought into the news. Mudd sees no reason why it was withheld from the court that convicted him. "The diary shows clearly that I could have had no knowledge of the deed. It would have tended to show my innocence if it had been produced in court."

In mid–June 1867, the Surratt trial started in Washington. There had been heavy rainstorms at Dry Tortugas and the bedding of the prisoners was wet. Mudd was working in the quartermaster's carpenter shop. He had more annoyance from conflicting orders than from the work that he had to perform. His health was good. On June 30 he wrote that the commanding officer was Major Andrews. He was glad to see the Surratt trial progressing. There was very little sickness on the island.

In August Mudd wrote that his health was better than it had been. His diet was principally salt pork, bread, and coffee. There was fresh beef two or three times every ten days. They had been issued a peck of Irish potatoes—the first vegetables of any kind since January. Mudd wrote that he thought he looked about the same but his hair was thinner and his bald area larger. On August 12 he wrote that they were still having heavy storms.

In August 1867, just a little over two years after Dr. Mudd arrived at Fort Jefferson, a new severe disease began to occur on the island. The first case was on August 18th. These patients had some of the symptoms of the milder "Break Bone Fever," that he had been seeing. The new cases were much sicker. The fever was very high with severe headache and sensitivity to light. As the disease progressed the patient's skin became yellow (jaundice from liver involvement) and many of them died. Pain in the bones was

174

not as prominent a symptom as had been seen previously in the cases with "Break Bone Fever." Examination was negative except for the things mentioned. Tenderness sometimes occurred in the right upper abdomen due to involvement of the liver as the disease progressed. Dr. Mudd recognized the symptoms as those of the Yellow Fever. He had seen cases of that disease in Baltimore many years before. "Yes, it seems like an eternity. I was young then, thirteen years ago, an eager medical student anxious to help humanity," he said to himself.

Dr. Mudd wrote that a strange man came by boat the morning of August 18 and visited with them soon after he landed. He represented himself as Doyle, a correspondent from the *New York Herald*. He was anxious to quiz them about many subjects but they were suspicious of him and told him little. Dr. Mudd cautioned to be slow to credit anything written by him.

Late in August Mudd wrote that the long trial of Surratt was over, at least for the present. Surratt's jury had not been able to reach a verdict on August 10. The expectation was that another jury would be called in six months. This never occurred. Mudd makes reference to an article by the *New York Herald*, which he says had bitterly denounced anything Southern or Democratic. It had now turned around and was advocating principles and advice on action by President Johnson that had been scorned a few months ago. He does not mention if the reporter was Doyle.

Dr. J. Sim Smith, the attending physician at the post, was related to the William B. Hill family. He seemed like a very nice person. Major Stone, the commander of the post, had relieved many grievances. They had been allowed to purchase potatoes from Key West.

On August 28 Dr. Mudd wrote that another case of high fever, severe headache with sudden onset occurred. He also was from Company K. He complained of more pain in his back and legs but Mudd noted, in general, he thought this man had the same disease as the young man seen ten days ago. They were both isolated and on complete bed rest.

On August 30 he wrote that still another case of severe headache and high fever occurred. This man was also from Company K. That made three from that same company. Mudd looked into that matter. The unit was quartered in the casemates on the south side of the Fort immediately over the unfinished moat, which at low tide gives rise to offensive odors. The first young man died on this day. He was jaundiced at the end. Mudd was sure this was Yellow Fever and suggested three things to Dr. Smith:

1. As much of the garrison as possible from the island should be removed.

2. Until this can be done, Company K should be moved from its present location in the south casemates of the fort and the port holes above the unfinished moat on the south side closed tightly.

3. These sick men should be kept isolated on the post at complete rest in darkened rooms so that they can use every ounce of their energy to combat the poisons of this dread disease. Taking these sick men in open boats to another island two miles away should be discontinued. They were too sick and could not stand the trip.

"Having the honor at this time of being a member of the carpenter's shop, it fell to my lot to aid in the work of barricading against this unseen foe."

Later that day Mudd noted a fourth case was received at the dispensary.

On September 1 Mrs. Mudd received a letter from Tom Dyer, her brother in New Orleans, which stated that Attorney Merrick and Governor Black of Pennsylvania would do what they could in Mudd's case. They would need one thousand dollars for Black. He had written to Jere telling him that he had five hundred dollars that was at his disposal. Jere should let him know if the family or any of his "praying friends" could raise the balance.

On September 1 Mudd wrote that Dr. J. Sim Smith was ill in his barracks. He did not yet know the exact nature of his illness but was suspicious that it was Yellow Fever.

Looking at the location of the beds of the four soldiers admitted so far Mudd felt it was significant that they were all contiguous. The fort was hexagonal with a bastion at each corner. Company K after its removal was placed on the east side, the bastion forming the center with several casemates above and below boarded up separating it from Company L on the north and the prisoners on the south. (Mudd thought that should help. The prevalence of the wind up to this period had been from the southeast.)

Three more fatal cases of Yellow Fever occurred on September 2. A number of new cases had been admitted. A soldier who was too ill to walk was taken from Company K on a stretcher. The fever had spread rapidly and had reached Company L, which was adjacent to the wooden barrier that had been erected. The disease had also spread to the south, to the prisoner's quarters. The first two cases that occurred in Company L and the first two cases among the prisoners were immediately next to the boarded petition that separated them from Company K, where the fever was raging. It passed through the open spaces between the planks that were loosely nailed together.

On September 3 more new cases of Yellow Fever had been admitted. To prevent spread of the disease, one company of soldiers was removed to an adjacent island. A hospital was erected on Sand Island, about two miles northeast, where patients were taken as soon as they were diagnosed. An officer was ill and was not expected to recover. Quite a panic existed among soldiers and officers. No one knew who would be the next victim.

By September 4 Dr. Smith, the post physician, was quite ill. His fever had been very high; he had delirium and had been unmanageable. This created further complications.

On September 5 Dr. Smith took a sudden turn for the worse and become uncontrollable. That left the post officially without an acting physician. Things were in turmoil. The disease was deadly and no one understood it or had specific treatment for it. Everyone knew this and was frightened that he would be the next victim. Mudd volunteered to fill the post of physician until Smith improved or until a replacement could be found. Major Stone was very pleased to accept his offer. Mudd was then the physician in charge.

Mudd recorded on September 7 that Dr. Sim Smith died. He left a wife and child. Two rooms were set apart at the northern end of the barracks as additional hospital space. These were about thirty feet square each.

On September 8 Mudd wrote to his brother-in-law Jere. He told him about the illness of Smith, the post physician, and that he had volunteered to the commanding officer, Major Stone, to take his place. The doctor had died that morning. Mrs. Smith also had the disease but was recovering. Things were in chaos. Everyone expected to be the next victim. Dr. Whitehurst had arrived from Key West the night before.

Mudd was called to Company I early the morning of September 9 and found Sergeant Sheridan and a private who slept in the next bed ill with the fever; another instance of contiguous cases. The hospital supply of beds and bedding gave out. They were compelled to bring a bed along with each patient into the hospital. There had been five deaths due to the fever. Convulsions were a very bad sign. They made every effort to keep the patients quiet in a darkened room. These measures had been quite helpful.

Another very bad sign, even worse than convulsions, was black vomitus. This had been an almost sure sign of death within a short period. The disease somehow interfered with blood clotting and the patient bled into his stomach. Dr. Whitehurst, the new post physician, was congenial and the two doctors worked well together.

On September 10 Mudd wrote that two days after they began bringing beds into the hospital area from the barracks because of a bed shortage, nurses became ill. Mudd did not want to bring beds from the dormitory but had no other choice. He wrote, "Now our nurses are coming down with the fever and I think it is due to these infected beds. We have had a total of sixteen deaths to date. The disease has spread right and left until it reached Company L. The first two cases in Company L and the first two cases among the prisoners, were immediately next to the boarded partition that separated them from Company K where the fever was raging. This shows that the germs, or cause, spreads by continuity and that it spread through the open spaces between the planks which were loosely nailed." Mudd thought his method of treatment by isolation and complete rest was largely responsible for the low mortality.

The epidemic seemed to be increasing in fury. It was hard to get adequate nurses. They had to enlarge the hospital area again. There were scarcely enough well to attend the sick and bury the dead. Whitehurst was an incessant laborer. He was an elderly physician from Key West who was expelled from the island at the beginning of the war because of the sympathies of his wife.

Mudd remained up every night until eleven or twelve or later. Whitehurst had arrived several days after the duties of the post fell on him. They agreed on medical treatment. Every officer was down with the disease except Lieutenant Gordon. Mrs. Stone, the wife of the commanding officer, was quite ill with the fever.

On September 16 Mudd recorded that the three-year-old son of Dr. Smith, the former post physician, was very ill. On his visit that day, Mudd found him worse with black vomitus. He did not expect him to live many hours. They had saved only one so far after the appearance of black vomitus. The little boy was sweet. He reminded Mudd of his own children at home. Mudd wondered if he would ever see them again. Fortunately, Mrs. Smith had recovered quite well. The little daughter, about seven, was still well.

The three-year-old son of Dr. Smith was no better by the next day. They then had over a hundred cases in the hospital. Arnold had had the disease and was well. O'Laughlin was sick.

On September 18 there were three deaths, including the little three-year-old son of Dr. Smith. Mrs. Smith had recovered from the fever but this was a terrible blow. She had lost not only her husband, but now her son. Her little daughter was all she had left.

On September 19 Mudd noted O'Laughlin had come down with the fever but seemed a little better. They tried to keep him quiet in their room. His fever was down some. Spangler and Arnold had been giving him close attention under Mudd's supervision. O'Laughlin and Mudd were very close. Mudd felt he could speak with him probably more freely than with any of the others.

Arnold was the first of the four prisoners to come down with the disease. Among the patients taken to Sand Key Hospital, more than half had died. Mudd deserved credit for breaking that procedure up. "We had cases of Yellow Fever at the Baltimore Infirmary from the epidemic in Norfolk in 1855. I became acquainted with the pathology of the disease then," he wrote. Because of Mudd's great efforts and success, Major Stone had kindly promised to make known his service during the epidemic to the authorities in Washington.

The Sand Hospital was consolidated with the post hospital at Mudd's direction. It was much better in that the very sick men did not have to be subjected to the strenuous trip of two and one half miles over open sea in small boats. This was especially so since they frequently had a long waiting period on the hot pier until the boats were available. These same boats frequently hauled caskets of dead soldiers along with them, which was not conducive to high spirits. Two more nurses had recently been struck with the fever. This was hard to understand. They were taking care of the sickest patients over at Sand Hospital and escaped the disease. (Hindsight tells us that probably there were fewer mosquitoes on Sand Key.)

O'Laughlin was still quite ill on September 21. He had a convulsion, which they were able to control with cold compresses to his head. An imprudent visitor had given an account of recent deaths, which caused him to become excited. This brought on the convulsions. It was very serious. Mudd thought he was dying. "These sick people must be kept quiet during their acute phase," he had said firmly.

There had been three deaths. Mrs. Stone, the commander's wife, the little son of Dr. Smith, and Lieutenant Orr. Arnold had it and recovered.

Mudd noted on September 22 there had been no case of the disease among the two companies of the garrison taken to Sand Island.

On September 23 O'Laughlin died. He had been feeling better and against advice was up and about looking for reading material when he collapsed. Mudd was up with him most of the night. Mudd knew the end was near when O'Laughlin exclaimed, "Doctor, Doctor, you must tell my mother all!" O'Laughlin called then to Spangler and said, extending his hand, "Good-by, Ned." These were his last words. He fell back instantly into a profound stupor and for several minutes seemed lifeless. Mudd wrote that "by gently changing his position from side to side, and the use of stimulating and cold applications, we succeeded in restoring him to partial strength and recollection. I never met with one more kind and forbearing, possessing a warm friendly disposition and a fine comprehensive intellect. I am not feeling so well today. My head aches and I am tired. It may be from being up so much at night but I fear it is the premonitory symptoms of the prevailing epidemic."

On September 24 five were buried, including O'Laughlin. The hospital was still full and there were scarcely enough nurses to attend the sick. Mudd had been acting physician and nurse for a considerable time until he was nearly exhausted. He wrote, "My heart sickens at the prospect which is before me. Were an enemy throwing shot and shell in here a more horrible picture could not be presented."

Mudd wrote to Dr. Dent on September 25 and gave him the mode of treatment by isolation in a darkened room for complete mental and physical rest. Critically ill victims were not able to tolerate exertion or excitement. He thought the low death rate indicated that these things were significant, especially in comparison to the statistics of other epidemics.

He wrote, "Sometimes the poor creatures are struck with delirium from the beginning and are wild and unmanageable; some die the same day they are taken ill but most live to the third day. More die for want of proper nursing care than lack of medicine. I am up all day until twelve o'clock at night. Dr. Whitehurst comes around between that time and sunrise."

Whitehurst treated Mudd with professional respect and courtesy at a time when this had been severely lacking. The two became good friends. Mudd slept until five or six o'clock in the morning and returned at seven. The number of patients in the hospital had diminished, but only for want of victims. Nearly everyone in the garrison had had the disease. The cases that came in at that time were of the most malignant form. Colonel Grenfell was quite sick. He had been helping faithfully as a nurse with the officers.

Major Stone, the commanding officer, became so worried after the death of Mrs. Stone that he did not go to see her buried (although he idolized her), but bundled up immediately and started north, taking his little son, a child of about two years.

The burial method was described by Mudd as follows: "The burial party are allowed a drink of whiskey both before and after the burying. They move quickly, and in half an hour after a patient dies, he or she is put in a coffin, nailed down, carried to a boat, rowed a mile to an adjacent island, the grave dug, covered up, and the party returned, in the best humor, for their drinks."[2]

Major Stone, before reaching the mainland, was seized with fever and died at Key West. This was particularly upsetting to Mudd, not only because he was a friend but because the major had told the doctor before he left that he would take word to Washington of his devoted and laborious efforts at the fort. Now there was no one to do that and his hopes were shattered. The doctor could expect no one to take any interest in his behalf. Lieutenant Gordon of Baltimore was swept away by the disease. He was always kind and courteous. The disease thus far had destroyed one family, Major Stone and his wife, and made desolate three young wives, Mrs. Orr, Mrs. Smith, and Mrs. Gordon. The doctor had attended Mrs. Smith through the active stage of her disease, and a nobler woman he had never met, he wrote.

Whitehurst was to be relieved by a new post physician by the name of Thomas who was expected to arrive next day. Whitehurst had been very cooperative. The two had worked hard together through the worst of the epidemic.

On September 30 Mudd had been indisposed. Spangler and Arnold had been looking after him faithfully. His headache was gone but he was very weak. His fever was down. He had experienced the epidemic from the viewpoint of the patient. He thought that he was recovering, thanks to his good and loyal friends. The new post physician, Dr. Thomas, had not come to see him. Arnold said that he had stayed in his quarters and had not ventured out. Perhaps it was better that way. Mudd wrote, "His men know my methods and none could have carried them out better. I am grateful." Grenfell was quite sick.

On October 1 Mudd's strength was better but he was still weak. He had lost much weight but gave thanks for his survival. By the hand of providence his fetters were broken, he wrote, yet he would run not, preferring to share the fate of those around him and to lend what aid was in his power to break down the burning fever, overcome the agonizing delirium, and give all the hope and encouragement possible to the death-stricken victims of the pestilence. They had, up to that time, lost by fever at the post thirty-three in all, counting men, women, and children. That was a low mortality considering the number attacked with the disease and the inadequate facilities for treatment.

By October 11 Mudd had recovered from the fever but did not have his strength back. Since being sick he had the greatest craving for fruits, especially apples and peaches. Such thoughts were pure fantasy there. Occasionally a few oranges, bananas, and pineapples came on the boats but the prices were astronomical.

One of the officers came to Mudd and said that he wanted to make known Mudd's services to the government. Mudd wrote he was very pleased with the suggestion.

On October 14 Mudd wrote that he had answered a previous letter on October 11 sitting up in bed. That was why the letter was very short. From this it can be assumed that his illness could have lasted from September 23, the day O'Laughlin died, when he first reported his headache, until about October 12 or 13. He was now fully recovered from the fever "with some exception of strength and flesh which will take some time to restore in this climate and under the circumstances we are placed." This would have meant the illness lasted about twenty days. In a summary of his illness,[3] however, he states that he became ill on October 4, forty-seven days after the beginning of the epidemic. In that case, the acute phase of his illness lasted about nine days.

He wrote that John Ford, the owner of Ford's Theater, had sent Spangler a barrel of potatoes and that an unknown donor had sent a ham. Apparently the four prisoners were able to prepare some of their own food.

On October 18 Mudd wrote a formal petition to the government, with a preamble enumerating the services rendered the garrison, was drawn up and signed by every noncommissioned officer of the post. The two officers expressed themselves favorably toward the idea but feared it might offend Dr. Thomas, the post physician, if they signed it. Thomas stayed in his quarters and did not come to visit Mudd when he was ill. The officers were confident the petition would be attended with success.

No one afflicted with Yellow Fever had died in the last twelve days. Only two cases were in the hospital at that time.

On October 19 there were three cases of fever in the hospital. Dr. Thomas was down with it.

By October 22 Mudd wrote Dr. Thomas was quite sick with the fever. Medical duties had again devolved upon Mudd. He was feeling fairly well with the exception of strength, which was returning slowly. Fortunately, his duties were lighter. He was able to get along fairly well. There was no news stirring. Things had quieted down. He wrote that everything was lifeless and inactive. He sent a copy of the petition for clemency to his wife Frances.

In December they were back in chains! There was a change of administration and what had gone before was not a consideration. Prisoners were to be treated indifferently, the new command thought.

The prisoners were to wash down the bastions of the fort each day. These bastions housed the concrete stairways at the corners of the fort that gave access to the gun rooms being used to house prisoners. Their treatment could only have been in retribution for the exposure of cruelty that Grenfell had made. The truth had hurt the command and they were making the prisoners suffer. They had the upper hand and could do as they wished with the prisoners, who had no rights. Arnold had had severe dysentery and was very thin and weak.

In the latter part of December 1867, while in chains, Mudd heard from his wife that his petition for clemency had not arrived in Washington. She had been told this by Montgomery Blair, who had access to the administration. This was a severe blow to the doctor. He had been pinning his hopes on that petition to win his freedom. Mrs. Mudd was told by Blair that this petition would carry much weight with the president in winning the release of her husband if it could be gotten to him.

The present commander, Major G. B. Andrews, had Mudd in chains but he was the only person through whom to appeal. Grasping at straws, Mudd wrote him a letter. He appealed to Andrews to think not only of his own ease and comfort but of the anguish and distress of his wife and four small children. He said that he solicited his kind office in their behalf.

He referred the major to the hospital report, but knowing how little attention is frequently paid to past reports, reiterated the events of the Yellow Fever outbreak for his benefit. This letter never received an answer. Mudd thought that the major may have destroyed it.

About the middle of December, a letter was received from Dr. Whitehurst in Key West, asking specific questions regarding the Yellow Fever outbreak for a report to the surgeon general.

Mudd responded that the first case had occurred on August 18, 1867.

It was not possible to state where the first case came from. It seemed to arise locally although there had been sick people arriving on ships that docked there. Mudd stated that he took charge on September 6, the day after Dr. Smith became ill. Captain Crabb was of the opinion that he had the disease when he came from Havana about the first of August. About the middle of August the steamer *Matchless* landed from Tampa with two sick men aboard who were taken to the hospital. Mudd stated that he had been placed in charge two or three days before Whitehurst's arrival and that about twenty cases were sick in the hospital at that time.[4]

On New Year's Day 1868, Mudd wrote a long letter to Frances, speaking of the children and wondering if she had enough wood for heating the house. He said he was fine and hoped that he would soon be released. He hoped it would be before planting time in the spring. He said that they were all suffering for a crime that never entered their heads. If this was justice he would like it visited on those who had brought on the wrong. He was glad to hear that the local medical society had taken action on his behalf. He referred to an expected return visit of a representative of Congress looking for further affidavits regarding the assassination. He wrote that he would not make a statement until placed right before the law. He had heard that the post would once again be guarded by black soldiers. Two companies of soldiers had been ordered to leave for New Orleans on the first steamer. He was making a small inlaid mahogany work box for Lilly Pop. The inlay would be three leaves of a branch in each corner and her initials in the center with German letters. He also wrote of sending small crabwood crosses to be distributed. A box and barrel of potatoes had been received. Andrews had given permission for the prisoners to receive anything that might be sent. This was a marked change in the attitude of the commanding officer, who had ordered leg irons only a month before. A jug of whiskey had been received as a real treat and had been consumed very sparingly for a week.[5]

Mudd wrote on March 1 things were going from bad to worse. Major George Andrews had been replaced by Brevet Major C. C. McConnell as post commander. The latter was the officer who was presiding when James Dunn was tortured. McConnell lost his post over that episode. "We will now suffer more in all probability. Grenfell's letter exposed him and he will likely seek revenge. All mail is censored. I shall stop using it. Lt. Frank Thorpe is Provost Marshal. He picks the most contemptible men of the garrison who abuse, curse, strike and maltreat the prisoners in every conceivable manner."

A letter on March 6 tells that Grenfell had made an escape with four others. They made off in a small sailboat at night during a storm. The sea was so rough that no one dreamed that an escape attempt would be made. It would be a miracle if they did not drown. The steamer *Bib* was in port but no one on that ship saw them. The *Bib* had made a ten-hour search but had returned without sighting them. McConnell is reporting them drowned which is probably correct.

Dr. Mudd described that Grenfell had a very nice garden in the fort grounds and was supplying them with vegetables. He also recalled the fact that Grenfell had been a dedicated nurse during the Yellow Fever epidemic. In spite of this McConnell relieved him of his garden duties almost at once and put him at hard labor. The fact that he had been a dedicated nurse during the Yellow Fever epidemic was not considered. Grenfell told Dr. Mudd: "I might as well have a go at escape. A watery grave is better than these indignities." Dr. Mudd wrote "God bless him. I hope he made it to freedom."

As for his own fate Dr. Mudd wrote that he would stick it out here hoping against hope that some good fortune will occur. His good wife Frances had been to see President Andrew Johnson and he promised to do what he could. Mudd noted the president was having severe troubles himself and just barely survived impeachment.

Who was Grenfell? This fabulous British subject, who spoke four languages, had fought for France in Morocco, then under Abd-el-Kader led an unsuccessful revolt against the French. He was a man who fought the Riffe pirates off the coast of Morocco, served with Garibaldi in South America, then fought in the Crimean War and India during the Sepoy Rebellion—all this before entering the ranks of the Confederate Army, serving valiantly with Morgan's Raiders, then on the staff of J. E. B. Stuart and back with John Hunt Morgan. Finally, he was a man who made a final agonal effort for the Confederacy, with Thomas Henry Hines in the North West Conspiracy, as the fortunes of the Confederacy fell.

Mudd found him a most interesting cellmate at Fort Jefferson on the Dry Tortugas Islands along with Arnold, O'Laughlin, and Spangler in 1865. They spoke French together frequently to break the monotony of the hot humid days and damp nights of confinement.

George St. Leger Grenfell had had a very checkered career, which he embellished with tales of strange places and doings to the delight of his listeners. He had actually been to many of the places and done many of the things he claimed. The life of this unusual character is well portrayed by Starr in *Colonel Grenfell's Wars.*

Grenfell was born in 1808 in Cornwall, England, to wealthy parents. He demonstrated great independence at an early age and was sent to Holland for his education. Here he remained with only one visit home in four years. He settled in Paris in the late 1820s after working in the London office of his father's firm where extravagance and financial irresponsibility were problems. In Paris he also worked in a branch of his father's firm.

In 1833 he married Hortense Louise Wyatt, and three daughters were born to them. Financial problems again occurred, this time involving forgery, and he took flight to avoid prosecution.

He entered the French cavalry and was sent to Algeria during the French conquest of that territory, where he remained several years until his affairs in Paris settled down. During this time he sometimes bragged that he had a harem of four wives. Following this he leased land in Morocco near the city of Tangiers with the idea of settling there. It was confiscated during one of the many political uprisings, several of which he took part in. He was acting British vice consul in Morocco for a time.

Later his legal wife came to Gibraltar, where she started a school for girls. He went off to Crimea and India, becoming a British officer. The level of his rank is not known with certainty.

After more than twenty years, his wife gave up on him and returned to Paris, successfully transferring her school for young ladies there. They were not divorced and he frequently corresponded with at least one of his daughters.

After his fighting experiences in India, according to his account, he settled in South America to raise sheep. This apparently soon turned out to be too dull for his restless soul. He longed for adventure.

The War Between the States was in progress. This attracted him. He traveled by way of England, where he obtained a letter of introduction to General Robert E. Lee. He then ran the blockade to Charleston, and arrived in Richmond in April 1862. Lee was impressed with his credentials and pleased to have so prominent a foreign volunteer. He sent him to the Western front. On his way Grenfell met John Hunt Morgan. They immediately became close friends and Morgan soon made him his adjutant. Discipline was very lax among Morgan's Raiders, most of whom were either kinfolk, friends, or neighbors from Lexington. Grenfell was to spruce things up a bit in this regard, but found his efforts not well received.

When they went into battle, however, Grenfell showed them some impressive tricks. Wearing a bright scarlet cap from his Moroccan uniform, with the bullets flying, he charged ahead of the others into the thick of the fighting with his saber flashing. The Kentucky boys were impressed with his courage and bravery. They called him "Old St. Leger." Morgan was very pleased and gave much credit to Grenfell. He was given the rank of lieutenant-colonel in the Confederate Army on May 17, 1863.

Later Grenfell was on the staff of Stuart, but did not strike the same chord there. They did not get on well and he returned to Richmond, helping there with Morgan's unsuccessful reorganization in early 1864.

Things were not going well for the Confederacy at this stage. Grenfell, after nearly two years of Confederate service, was considering a return to England.

He met an old friend, Thomas Henry Hines, of Morgan's Raiders days who had just escaped from the Union prison at Columbus, Ohio, and who had a grandiose scheme to free and arm Confederate prisoners of war at Camp Douglas and burn the city of Chicago. This fantastic scheme, known later as the North West Conspiracy, with the aid of Copperheads, proved to be Grenfell's undoing. Hines wanted his help. Grenfell was undoubtedly flattered by this. He was at loose ends. It was a risky enough task to appeal to him. He agreed to help.

This involved becoming a free British subject in the North so that he could move about. He renounced his Confederate ties, and took passage on a blockade runner to Nassau and then to New York City.

Courage and nerve he had plenty of. On his arrival in New York, he called on the military governor, John A. Dix, requesting permission as a British subject to remain in the North. Dix sent him to Washington, where he was interviewed by Colonel Wishwell and Colonel Hardie. He wound up with an interview with Secretary of War Stanton himself. He told Stanton that he had renounced the Confederacy and wished to remain in the North to observe the Union before returning to England.

He gave Stanton reams of information about the strength of Confederate forces in the field. Stanton had this all recorded without Grenfell's knowledge. The information was mostly false, Stanton soon learned. Grenfell was given permission to travel in the North as a British national. He passed freely between the United States and Canada on hunting trips, frequently traveling with hunting dogs on leash.

Hines's scheme was to have the uprising staged on the day of the Democratic primary convention in Chicago so that the presence of strangers on the streets would not be as noticeable. This was July 4, 1864. Copperheads, Southern sympathizers, were to come by the thousands to take part. Arms were cached at the home of a rabid Irish Copperhead named Charles Walsh. This prosperous Chicago contractor was prominent in politics and had been an unsuccessful candidate for sheriff of Cook County. The Copperhead organization was known as the Sons of Liberty.

Grenfell's role was never spelled out completely. Supposedly he was to lead the charge against Camp Douglas from the outside. Camp Douglas was named for Stephen A. Douglas, the statesman. On his death in 1861, his estate, located near the University of Chicago, was donated for public usage. Due to wartime necessity a prisoner of war camp was constructed there, housing ten to eighteen thousand Confederate prisoners in 1864. The prisoners were to revolt at a certain signal in the predawn hours so that the attack would occur internally and externally simultaneously.

All seemed well. On the day before the convention, however, only a few Copperheads showed up. They had been strong supporters verbally but were not there when the bugle blew. The attack was delayed until August. When this date neared, it was delayed again until election day, November 8. This was too much delay and it involved too many people to be kept secret.

The commander of the camp, Colonel Benjamin Sweet, was an astute combat veteran with a disabled arm due to a battle wound. He was aware of the plan of the conspirators from several sources and put out his own men to spy on their groups. He was quite aware of what they were up to. The night before the attack, groups of conspirators were rounded up and arrested. Walsh's home was raided and a large cache of arms taken. Grenfell was taken prisoner at the Richmond House Hotel, where he was found in front of his fireplace with his hunting dogs beside him. This was the end of his freedom.

Hines escaped. Eight conspirators were brought before a military commission of nine Army officers in Cincinnati, Ohio. The trial began on January 9, 1865, and lasted until April 10.

The charges were: conspiring in violation of the laws of war to release rebel prisoners of war at Camp Douglas by suddenly attacking the camp on or about November 8, 1864; and conspiring in violation of the laws of war to lay waste and destroy the city of Chicago by capturing the arsenal, cutting telegraph lines, and setting fires. The defendants were: Judge Bruckner S. Morris, Charles Walsh, and George St. Leger Grenfell.

Originally there were five others. Charles T. Daniel escaped. Benjamin M. Anderson committed suicide. Vincent Marmaduke was acquitted and released. R. T. Semmes was found guilty without argument and given five years' imprisonment. George E. Cantrill was granted a separate trial because of illness.

Attorneys for the defense gave their closing arguments for their clients on April 13, 1865. Then followed a recess of four days to allow the adjutant-general, Lieutenant Colonel Henry Lawrence Burnett, time to prepare his closing arguments for the prosecution.

The assassination of Abraham Lincoln intervened. The effects of the assassination were far-reaching. They colored the adjutant-general's 119-page closing arguments on April 18 against the defendants in this trial, particularly against Grenfell. The military commission retired and later that evening reached a verdict. Grenfell and Walsh were found guilty. Judge Morris was acquitted. On April 27 Walsh was sentenced to five years' imprisonment and Grenfell was sentenced to be hanged.

Burnett received a summons from Secretary of War Stanton in Washington to report to that city for the trial of the Lincoln conspirators.

Grenfell was convicted largely on the testimony of one man, John T. Shanks. Grenfell's counsel, Robert Hervey, objected due to the fact that this man was an incompetent witness. He had been convicted of forgery in a court in Texas. Testimony had been given to this effect. The court overruled his objection.

On July 22, 1865, President Johnson commuted Grenfell's sentence to life imprisonment on Dry Tortugas Islands. In September of that year he arrived there. The tale has been told of his austere experience there; how in reporting the torture of James Dunn he brought torture upon himself under the cruel autonomous rule of a military prison.

His companionship brought some comfort to Mudd and his three associates. Grenfell worked heroically as a nurse during the Yellow Fever epidemic at great personal risk. He raised vegetables in a parade ground garden, which helped raise morale until stopped by a vindictive commanding officer. His attempted escape during a tropical storm led to a watery grave.

17
Pardon and Release

In 1868, Mudd's relatives and friends were doing all in their power to gain his freedom. The president, who alone had the power to do this, was occupied with his own personal Congressional problems. Mrs. Mudd had visited President Johnson and he had promised her that he would free her husband before he left office. The waiting was extremely difficult, and Mudd became depressed.

Action was taken through the local courts at Key West but no word came for a long interval. Finally, through the fort commander, General B. H. Hill, word came that the request for a writ of habeas corpus was denied.

Frances wrote that he should remain patient. President Johnson had told her that he would make the release before leaving office. If that failed, she was sure that President Grant would do so. Time wore on.

In December 1868 wooden barricades were built in front of the quarters of the prisoners. Mudd wrote to Hill asking for an investigation as to what led to this. There was no response from the commander.

In January 1869 word came that Mudd's mother had died. This was one more sad shock.

On January 30 Frances wrote stating that she thought this would be the last letter she would need to write to "this terrible" island. She tried to cheer him up. "I feel sanguine of seeing you before the last of March. I will send you a paper with the last petition from the Maryland members of Congress, and Mr. Merrick's and Mr. Stone's appeals in your behalf. May our Lord protect us from another disappointment for I am in no disposition to bear it." She was bravely trying to cheer her husband after the long, trying ordeal. She was also wearing down from the strain of it.

At home, pressures for Mudd's release were building from many sources. The Medical Society of Hartford County had petitioned the president, as well as the Maryland members of Congress. A friend and consultant attorney, Mr. Merrick, had petitioned and Mudd's personal attorney, Mr. Stone, had never stopped petitioning. [The records of this portion of the happenings have been lost. A reasonable reconstruction follows.]

One afternoon there was a knock at the door of the Mudd farmhouse. It was not a particularly loud knock but it was firm and regular. Frances was not expecting any one at that hour. She saw a horse in front of the house with its reins hanging down loose from the bridle.

On opening the door a young man inquired, "Mrs. Samuel A. Mudd?" When she nodded, he handed her an envelope, saying, "From the President of the United States. Please sign this receipt to certify that I have delivered it to you. If you have a reply, I shall return it for you."

She asked him to come inside as she quickly opened the neatly addressed envelope. The message was on White House stationery. It read as follows:

> Dear Mrs. Mudd:
> As promised, I have drawn up a pardon for your husband, Dr. Samuel A. Mudd. Please come to my office at your earliest convenience. I wish to sign it in your presence and give it to you personally.
> Sincerely,
>
> ANDREW JOHNSON
> President of the United States
> of America

Mrs. Mudd just stared at the letter. She slowly sat down at her hall desk and took out a sheet of her best stationery and wrote the following message:

> Mr. President: I shall come to your office tomorrow morning. Thank you greatly. You have answered my prayers. God bless you.
> (Signed) Frances Dyer Mudd

Mrs. Mudd then folded the letter neatly and placed it in an envelope. She then handed it to the waiting courier, saying, "You have made me very happy. Thank you very much." The young man took the letter, went out the door, mounted his horse, and rode out the driveway.

Frances went to the White House the next morning with Mudd's brother-in-law, Dr. J. H. Blandford. They were soon shown into the executive office. There the president signed and affixed the seal of the United States and delivered to her the papers for the release of Mudd. [The pardon was several handwritten papers.] When she asked if the pardon could be sent to Mudd through the mails, the president replied as follows: "Mrs. Mudd, I have signed and put the president's seal on it and I have fulfilled my promise to release your husband before I leave the White House. I no longer hold myself responsible. Should these papers go amiss you may never hear from them again, as they may be put away in some pigeon-hole or corner. You may think I am tardy in carrying out the promise I made to you two years ago but the situation was such that I could not act as I wished."

Mrs. Mudd took the papers, thanked him graciously, and left the room. It was almost unbelievable. She had her husband's pardon in her own hand after almost four years of hardship, worry, and waiting.

THE PARDON OF SAMUEL ALEXANDER MUDD
February 8, 1869

ANDREW JOHNSON, President of the United States of America
To all to Whom these Presents shall come, Greeting:

Whereas, on the twenty ninth day of June in the year 1865, Dr. Samuel A. Mudd was by the judgment of a Military Commission, convened and holden at the City of Washington, in part convicted, and in part acquitted, of the specification wherein he was inculpated in the charge for the trial of which said Military Commission was so convened and held, and which specification in its principal allegation against him, was and is in the words and figures following, to wit: "And in further prosecution of said conspiracy, the said Samuel A. Mudd did, at Washington City and within the Military Department and military lines aforesaid, on or before the sixth day of March, A.D. 1865, and on divers other days and times between that day and the twentieth day of April A.D. 1865, advise, encourage, receive, entertain, harbor and conceal, aid and assist, the said John Wilkes Booth, David E. Herold, Lewis Payne, John H. Surratt, Michael O'Laughlin, George A. Atzerodt, Mary E. Surratt and Samuel Arnold and their confederates, with knowledge of the murderous and traitorous conspiracy aforesaid, and with intent to aid, abet, and assist them in the execution thereof, and in escaping from justice after the murder of the said Abraham Lincoln, in pursuance of said conspiracy in manner aforesaid:

And whereas, upon a consideration and examination of the record of said trial and conviction and of the evidence given at said trial, I am satisfied that the guilt found by the said judgement against the said Samuel A. Mudd was of receiving, entertaining, harboring, and concealing John Wilkes Booth and David E. Herold, with the intent to aid, abet and assist them in escaping from justice after the assassination of the late President of the United States, and not of any other or greater participation or complicity in said abominable crime;

And whereas, it is represented to me by intelligent and respectable members of the medical profession, that the circumstances of the surgical aid to the escaping assassin and the imputed concealment of his flight are deserving of a lenient construction as within the obligations of professional duty, and thus inadequate evidence of a guilty sympathy with the crime or the criminal;

And whereas, in other respects the evidence, imputing such guilty sympathy or purpose of aid in defeat of justice, leaves room for uncertainty as to the true measure and nature of the complicity of the said Samuel A. Mudd, in the attempted escape of said assassins;

And whereas, the sentence imposed by said Military Commission upon the said Samuel A. Mudd was that he be imprisoned at hard labor for life, and the confinement under such sentence was directed to be had in the military prison at Dry Tortugas, Florida, and the said prisoner has been hitherto, and now is, suffering the infliction of such sentence;

And whereas, upon occasion of the prevalence of the Yellow Fever at that military station, and the death by that pestilence of the medical officer of the Post, the said Samuel A. Mudd devoted himself to the care and cure of the sick, and interposed his courage and his skill to protect the garrison, otherwise without adequate medical aid, from peril and alarm, and thus, as the officers and men unite in testifying, saved many valuable lives and earned the admiration and the gratitude of all who observed or experienced his generous and faithful service to humanity;

And whereas, the surviving families and friends of the Surgeon and other officers who were the victims of the pestilence earnestly present their dying testimony to the conspicuous merit of Dr. Mudd's conduct, and their own sense of obligation to him and Lieut. Zabriskie and two hundred and ninety nine noncommissioned officers and privates stationed at the Dry Tortugas have united in presenting to my attention the praiseworthy action of the prisoner and in petitioning for his pardon; And whereas the Medical Society of Hartford County, Maryland, of which he was an associate, have petitioned for his pardon, and thirty nine members of the Senate and House of Representatives of the Congress of the United States have also requested his pardon;

Now, therefore, be it known that I, Andrew Johnson, President of the United States of America, in consideration of the premises, divers other good and sufficient reasons me there unto moving, do hereby grant to the said Dr. Samuel A. Mudd a full and unconditional pardon.

In testimony thereof, I have hereunto signed my name and caused the Seal of the United States to be affixed.

Done at the City of Washington, this Eighth day of February, A.D. [Seal] 1869, and the Independence of the United States the ninety third.
                                          ANDREW JOHNSON
By the President
    WILLIAM H. SEWARD
    SECRETARY OF STATE

In keeping with her character Frances decided to take the pardon to Tortugas herself! Ships left from Baltimore for Tortugas and according to a schedule she had, one was leaving next day. So off she went. But when she arrived at the port the vessel had departed! The next ship was to leave in three weeks.

Back home, a family conference was held. Frances knew from correspondence with her brother in New Orleans that ships went to the Tortugas from that city. This was another possibility.

We do not know the details. Possibly telegraph messages were exchanged in making the arrangements. There were no telephones at that time. Finally the pardon was sent by express to Thomas in New Orleans, who in turn hired a Mr. Loutrel to take it to Tortugas by special boat. The sum of $300 was paid for this service. Dr. Richard Mudd remembers the sum as $500, according to family legend.[1]

Orders were going through military channels as well.

WAR DEPARTMENT, Adjutant-General's office
Washington, February 13, 1869

Commanding Officer,
    Fort Jefferson,
        Dry Tortugas, Fla.
Sir: The Secretary of War directs that immediately on receipt of the official pardon, just issued by the President of the United States, in favor of Dr. Samuel A. Mudd, a prisoner now confined at Dry Tortugas, you release the said prisoner from confinement and permit him to go at large where he will.

You will please report the execution of this order and the date of departure of Dr. Mudd from the Dry Tortugas.

I am, sir, very respectfully your obdt. servant.

E. D. TOWNSEND,
Assistant Adjutant-General

Headquarters, Fort Jefferson, Fla.
March 8, 1869

Special Order No. 42:
    In obedience to communication from War Department A.G. Office, Washington, D.C., dated February 13, 1869, Dr. Samuel A. Mudd (prisoner) is hereby released from confinement and permitted to go at large where he will.
By order Brevt. Major General Hunt.

J. M. Lancaster
Brevt. Capt. U.S.A., 1st Lieut.,
3rd Artillery, Adjutant.

Records have been lost but the pardon arrived and Mudd was released from prison on March 8, 1869. He left Fort Jefferson three days later on March 11, 1869. How he traveled home is not known.

He could have returned to New Orleans on the boat that brought the pardon to him, but that is not where he wanted to go after three years, ten months, and twelve days away from his wife and family.

It is presumed that he was able to book passage directly to a port on the East Coast such as Baltimore or Washington. At any rate, he arrived home on March 20, 1869.[2]

After Mudd's death in 1883 a reporter for the *New York Tribune* interviewed Frederick Stone, Mudd's friend and personal attorney, from Port Tobacco. He is reported as having said, "The court very nearly hanged Dr. Mudd. His prevarications were painful. He had given his whole case away by not trusting even his counsel or neighbors or kinfolks. It was a terrible thing to extricate him from the toils he had woven about himself. He had denied knowing Booth when he knew him well. He was undoubtedly accessory to the abduction plot, though he may have supposed it would never come to anything. He had denied knowing Booth when he came to his house when that was preposterous. He had been intimate with Booth."[3]

Thomas Ewing, who fought so hard for Mudd as chief counsel, like the champion he was, never made a statement.

It comes down to the delicate, complicated question of mixed loyalties being put to a test unexpectedly. Both Booth's visit and his deed were a complete surprise to Mudd on the early morning of April 15—if indeed Booth did tell him what he had done on the previous night. Sometimes truth and loyalty are not miscible, especially when there is little time to consider. What mothers teach their children is right but in this situation painful decision was required and Mudd had little or no time to reflect. The Confederate cause was lost but he was not a turncoat. He did not make Booth sleep in the woods, although he probably wished later that he had. This worked against him. Hindsight is brilliant but not immediately helpful.

Mudd was acquitted of some of the charges against him but convicted of others. The words "advise," "encourage," "receive," "entertain," "harbor," "conceal," "aid and assist," are used in the pardon as the charges of which he was pardoned and hence must have been convicted. The military commission evidently thought he recognized Booth or it could not have found him guilty of these charges.

Mudd never admitted that he recognized Booth at the time he treated him. He denied it over and over again. Mrs. Mudd also maintained this view. It seems strange, but that is how it remains years later. Allowing Booth to sleep upstairs in his own home and stabling his horses in his barn made the charge of harboring the criminal possible. Mixed loyalties of Union, Confederacy, and family were staggering.

★★★

Summary of the Yellow Fever Outbreak
August 18–October 22, 1867

The total number of cases	270
Deaths	38
Death rate	1
	4%

This mortality rate of Dr. Mudd's is exceedingly good in comparison to other outbreaks of this terrible disease. This is also true in view of the fact that nearly one half of his patients that were being transported to Sand Key after the onset of their disease were dying, a practice he put a stop to. He had full right to be very proud of his results.

18
Life after Exile

When Mudd arrived home after being away from his wife and family for nearly four years, he was weak, tired, and frail. He never regained robust health. The farm was in a shambles. The fences were down. The buildings were in very bad repair. The barn had been practically destroyed by a storm and help was scarce with wages extremely high. His practice was gone and people were so poor they could not pay.

The first thing was to get some plants in the ground. Gradually some of Mudd's former patients began to call on him, but many of them had no money. They brought him produce instead, which at the time had more value.

In the fall there were enough crops to make things brighter. Ned Spangler appeared one day at the farm. A strong attachment had developed between the two during those long, hard times at Tortugas. Mudd gave him five acres of land, with a spring and a place to build a house.

Spangler and Samuel Bland Arnold were released together from Tortugas on March 29, 1869. They were taken by ship to Key West and there given liberty without funds or means to return home.

Arnold contacted his father, who came to Key West for him. He returned home and had, as far as is known, a fairly normal life lasting until 1906. In 1904 he wrote his memoirs, which were published in 1943. These, although written with hyperbole, constitute a first-hand account written by a participant and survivor of the Lincoln conspiracy. They are very interesting in that light and give the closest view of John Wilkes Booth from his prep school days until his final act against Lincoln.

Spangler apparently had no one to turn to when released in Key West. He found odd jobs for cash and slowly worked his way back North. When he arrived in Washington, he found Ford's Theater closed. He then hitchhiked to the home of his best friend, Dr. Samuel Mudd. They had been through the valley of death together and appreciated each other. He was looking for a place to start over in life and Mudd's farm needed a lot of repair work. At Mudd's farm he was welcomed warmly and he stayed. Mudd gave him five acres of land near a spring where he could build a house.

Grave marker of Edmund (Ned) Spangler.

The land would not have been necessary to induce Spangler to stay, but it was a very kind offering and sincerely appreciated. He never got around to building the house but did build a small dwelling next to the spring. His health was not robust and about a year and a half later he developed a respiratory problem and died. It may have been pneumonia or possibly tuberculosis. Conditions in the prison certainly made him a candidate for the latter. Mudd buried his friend in what is now the cemetery at St. Peter's Church at the corner of Poplar Hill and Gardiner Roads, about five and a half miles north of Bryantown.

Mudd is said to have had an offer from the U.S. Public Health Service, soon after his return to civilian life, to travel about the country investigating outbreaks of Yellow Fever. This was a subject in which he had had extensive clinical experience and was very interested. He is said to have suspected the mosquito as a vector of the disease. The job involved travel away from home and he either turned it down or worked at it for only a short while before settling down on his farm and returning to his former medical practice. He was elected to the Maryland legislature in 1876, but was not a strong supporter of the Republican party.

After Mudd's return to civilian life, he and Frances continued adding to their family. Henry was born in January 1870, but died at the age of eight months of unknown cause. Stella Marie was born in the summer of 1871. Edward Joseph arrived two years later in the summer of 1873. Rose De Lima was born in October 1875, and Mary Eleanor (better known as Nettie) came in January 1878.

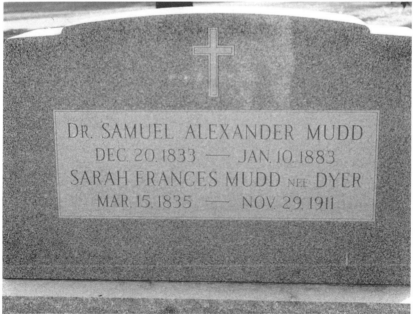

Grave marker of Dr. and Mrs. Mudd.

In January 1883 Mudd is said to have had a heavy schedule with many sick patients and was exposed to the elements on his calls during the cold winter. He contracted a severe cold and died nine days later of what was thought to have been pneumonia. He was forty-nine years old. Burial was in the cemetery of St. Mary's Church near the very place where he had first met Booth nineteen years earlier.

So ended the life of Doctor Samuel Alexander Mudd who by chance became involved in the most horrible crime of the nineteenth century.

If Booth had not injured himself and had not required medical attention, Dr. Mudd would have lived a normal life without his terrible troubles which were brought on my mixed loyalties and the element of surprise.

How well the doctor knew Booth before the assassination is still an open question. Some of the claims made later by others from the area, although plausible, are not proven.

The attitudes and differences of opinion between the people of the North and those of Lower Maryland where Dr. Mudd resided in the early 1860s were strong. The country was sharply divided on a sectional basis. In spite of this Maryland did not secede.

The Declaration of Independence written eighty-five years earlier had stated that "Governments instituted among Men, deriving their just powers from the consent of the governed." On this basis the people of the South in 1861 thought they had a just reason for leaving the Union. The Constitution on the other hand (including the first ten amendments to it, commonly referred to as the Bill of Rights) gave no provision for legal separation from the Union. This was the dilemma of 1861 into which young Mudd and his countrymen around him found themselves. He was a slave owner at the beginning of the war as was his father and as his earlier ancestors had been. His way of life and the tobacco industry, upon which he partially depended, were built around slavery. He probably wanted to continue with the then current economic structure.

Although his sentiments were with the South at the beginning of the War Between the States, Mudd took an oath of allegiance to the Federal government and voted for a Union candidate in 1864.

The extreme nature of Booth's crime and the reaction to it at the close of the war led to the trial being carried out as it was. It was most unfortunate that Dr. Mudd was tried with seven others and that the real culprit was not there to take the responsibility for what he had done.

The first victim of Booth's bullet was President Lincoln, commander-in-chief of the armed forces of the United States. As things turned out, the next victims were the people of the South and those with Confederate sympathies.

It has been a satisfaction for me to write about the life of Dr. Mudd and about the political conditions and attitudes of many people in Maryland about him at that time. I learned a great deal in my investigations. This gentle man lived his life well, marred only by some enthusiasms of early adulthood and finally by a sudden unexpected entanglement with an egotistical zealot who had committed a horrendous crime.

Mudd was caught up in the events of his day and the many mixed loyalties that existed as the Confederacy fell. The evidence indicates that he had no direct connection with the assassination though he was aware of the previous plot, during the latter part of the war, to kidnap the president for an exchange of Confederate prisoners.

Whenever I now gaze over the Gulf of Mexico in the direction of Tortugas, I think of Dr. Mudd with better understanding. I hope that is also true for you.

19
Follow-up

Mrs. Sarah Frances Mudd continued to live at Rock Hill Farm after the death of Mudd in 1883. She reared nine children, and remained on the family farm until just a few days before her death. She died on December 29, 1911, at the home of her daughter Rose on the Gardiner farm.

When Frances died, her son Samuel A. Mudd II bought the farm and continued to operate it. When he died, his son, Joseph Burch Mudd, bought out the heirs and continued to farm the land. His son, J. Allan Mudd, farms the land at present. It was Joseph Burch Mudd who sold ten acres of land and the home of Dr. Samuel to the Dr. Samuel A. Mudd Society in 1983.

This society has brought the home into splendid repair and maintains it beautifully. Granddaughter Louise Mudd-Arehart, sister of Joseph Burch Mudd, is the able president of the society today.

Richard Dyer Mudd, M.D., grandson of Dr. Samuel Mudd, has practiced in Saginaw, Michigan, since 1931 after surgical training at Henry Ford Hospital in Detroit. He has studied the ancestry and descendants of his grandfather and written monumental works on the Mudd family in the United States. This has been published in four editions. He also, in 1989, compiled and published the sixth edition of *The Descendants of Dr. Samuel A. Mudd.* At that time he listed 466 direct descendants in order of descent.

In addition, he has updated and added to the book originally published by Mudd's youngest daughter, Nettie. This book contains the letters written home by Mudd during his incarceration at Fort Jefferson in the Dry Tortugas Islands. The most recent edition of *The Life of Dr. Samuel A. Mudd* was published in 1983. It has additional letters that have come to light in recent years as well as an added chapter on the descendants of Mudd. This book is a tremendous source of information and should be read by all those interested in the life of Mudd. This work has been of great value in the preparation of this manuscript and the author is deeply indebted to Dr. Richard Dyer Mudd for it.

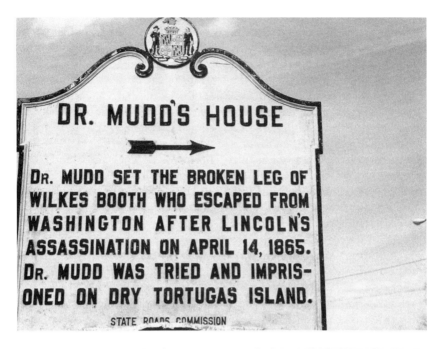

Home of Dr. Mudd as it appears today.

Dr. Richard has worked indefatigably during nearly all of his adult life, since 1918, to completely clear his grandfather of any complicity in the assassination of President Lincoln. He has contacted all presidents of the United States since and including President Dwight Eisenhower in an effort to gain an annulment of the findings of the military commission of 1865. These efforts to gain an annulment have not been successful. Congress authorized a bronze plaque for Dr. Samuel A. Mudd in recognition of his heroic work during the severe Yellow Fever epidemic of 1867 at Fort Jefferson. President Eisenhower signed this authorization in 1959. The plaque now hangs in a cell at Fort Jefferson, Dry Tortugas Islands, once occupied by Mudd. President Carter thought that Mudd was improperly tried before a military commission. President Reagan thought he was innocent but could do no more than President Johnson had already done with his presidential pardon of February 8, 1869.

Dr. Richard Mudd and his wife Rose have been married more than sixty-one years and maintain a lovely home in Saginaw. It is hoped that they continue to enjoy good health for many more years.

President Andrew Johnson left the White House on March 4, 1869, a very disheartened and embittered person. He did not confer personally with his successor, President Grant, to hand over the reins of government. He left amidst turmoil just as he had arrived.

At home in Tennessee, after several unsuccessful attempts, he became the only ex-president to return to the U.S. Senate. His Tennessee constituents returned him to that body in 1875, but his time there was brief. He died in July of that year. He asked to have his head cradled on the Constitution of the United States.

John Wilkes Booth's body was exhumed on President Johnson's order in February 1869. Due to the emotional state of the nation after President Lincoln's assassination it had been secretly buried at the Washington Arsenal in the floor of a cell there following an autopsy.

It was delivered to the Booth family at a funeral home in Baltimore, where it was received by Edwin Booth and buried eventually at Greenmount Cemetery in that city.

Samuel Bland Arnold, the school friend of Booth who with *Michael O'Laughlin* was the earliest recruit for the kidnap scheme of President Lincoln, lived to be seventy-two years of age. In 1904, two years before his death, he wrote his memoirs, which were published posthumously in 1943. This is the only first-hand account written by a participant of the kidnap attempt of March 17, 1865. DeWitt includes a letter which Arnold had written to him on October 12, 1904. It was written from Ward D of Johns

Dr. and Mrs. Richard Dyer Mudd.

Hopkins Hospital, Baltimore, where he was scheduled for surgery the following day. He tells there once again that he and O'Laughlin were recruited in August 1864 for the kidnapping of President Lincoln. In this letter Arnold says that the only meeting of the whole kidnap group was at Gautier's Saloon on March 17 and that the attempt to capture the president near the Soldier's Home was soon after. During his confinement with Mudd at Dry Tortugas, the doctor denied any connection with Booth.[1] Arnold died in Johns Hopkins Hospital in 1906, two years after his operation. O'Laughlin died of Yellow Fever on Tortugas in September 1867.

Edwin McMasters Stanton, Lincoln's secretary of war, continued in that office under President Johnson. He and Johnson clashed on many issues, including the use of martial law in the Southern states as well as the fourteenth amendment to the Constitution. Johnson opposed this "Reconstruction Amendment," which guaranteed citizens' rights and representation in Congress, with the exclusion of certain people from representative government who had taken part in the rebellion. It also disallowed U.S. responsibility for the debts of the Confederacy. It was passed by Congress over a presidential veto.

Johnson finally suspended Stanton from office in August 1867, allegedly in violation of the recently passed Tenure of Office Act. This was one of the last straws leading to Johnson's impeachment by Congress, which he survived in the Senate by only one vote. Congress ordered Stanton returned to his post in January 1868, following which he served out his term of appointment.

President Grant nominated Stanton to the Supreme Court in early December 1869, a post which Stanton greatly wanted and which he looked forward to filling. A severe acute attack of chronic asthma put a sudden end to his life on the day before Christmas of that year. Rumors that he took his own life in remorse for the death of Mrs. Mary Surratt are very unlikely.[2]

Corporal Thomas P. Corbett, better known as "Boston" Corbett, the man who shot Booth in Garrett's barn, became an enthusiastic evangelist. It is said that he gained his religious fervor at a revival meeting in Boston. Due to his military record, he became sergeant of arms of the House of Representatives of the Kansas legislature. One morning he appeared with two pistols, shooting and gesticulating wildly, which led to an immediate adjournment of the House without a dissenting vote.[3] He was committed to a mental institution in Topeka, from which he escaped. He was later a traveling salesman for patent medicine and lived in Enid, Oklahoma.[4]

Mary Todd Lincoln never recovered from the loss of her husband. She spent forty days in bed following the assassination before giving up the White House to Andrew Johnson. The last seventeen years of her life were spent in black mourning garments.[5]

Following the assassination, her oldest son, Robert, practiced law in Chicago. She and Thomas (Tad), age eleven, lived with him there for a time and then in a hotel. When Robert married, Mrs. Lincoln put Tad in school in Frankfurt, Germany. He was having difficulty learning and the German schools enjoyed a very good reputation at that time. She also lived there for several years, where she felt more at ease. In 1870 war broke out, causing their return to Chicago.

Tad died in 1871 at age eighteen of a pulmonary problem. Following this Mrs. Lincoln's eccentricities became worse. She made unusual shopping sprees to downtown Chicago, where she made strange purchases such as ten pairs of gloves and three watches for her son Robert. She argued with the salespeople about price and time of delivery.

Robert promptly returned the watches sent him. In 1875 he arranged to have her committed to a mental institution but in less than four months she was able to free herself and a second jury declared her competent. She never forgave Robert.

After traveling abroad and living in France for several years, she returned home when her health deteriorated. She lived with her sister, Elizabeth Todd-Edwards, in Springfield, Illinois. She died there following a stroke in July 1882 and is buried near her husband.

Robert Todd Lincoln became secretary of war under President Garfield in 1881 and continued in office during the Arthur administration. He died in 1926 at age eighty-three.

John Harrison Surratt, after going free in 1868, gave lectures on the part he played in the Lincoln conspiracy. Many people stayed away. They were not interested in hearing a man who had abandoned his mother, allowing her to be hanged in 1865. His lecture, given in the courthouse at Rockville, Maryland, December 6, 1870, was well attended. Surratt was teaching school in Rockville at that time and had decided to give lectures to raise money. In his Rockville lecture he said that Mudd did not introduce him to Booth two days before Christmas; he had met Booth in the fall. He told how he carried dispatches from Richmond to Montreal. He told about the capture plot and stated that assassination was never mentioned. He told of the attempted kidnap attempt in mid–March. He says that word of his mother's danger did not reach him until the day of her execution. He did not refer to his mother's innocence, but denounced Wiechmann in the most extreme way. He said that Wiechmann knew of the kidnap plot and wanted to join. He was denounced as a perjurer and a murderer of the meanest hue. Surratt outlived all the other conspirators. He died in 1916.

Louis J. Wiechmann, the former schoolmate and later roommate of John Surratt at 541 H Street, moved to the Surrat house in November 1864 when the kidnap plot was developing. He saw what he thought were strange goings on there but probably did not know the magnitude of what was happening. When the truth about the strange actions became known after the assassination he gave himself up to the authorities. His testimony at the trial was disastrous for Mrs. Surratt and also revealed a closer relationship between Booth and Mudd than had been known previously. The mixed loyalties of the time had wide ramifications. Wiechmann was a federal employee with friends who had Southern sympathies. When he became a government witness, he was considered a turncoat by his Southern friends and castigated by them.

After the trial, Wiechmann spent twenty years working in the customs house at Philadelphia. This was another government post that he evidently carried out well.

After twenty years in Philadelphia, Wiechmann moved to Anderson, Indiana, where he taught school and later started a business school. He operated this until his death in 1902.

Surratt relentlessly pursued Wiechmann verbally by open statements and in the press. He castigated Wiechmann severely during his lecture series. On April 2, 1898, the *Washington Post* published an interview with Surratt by a reporter named Hanson Hiss. In this article Surratt again castigated Wiechmann as a liar and a perjurer.

Wiechmann answered these charges in a letter to the editor of the *Washington Post* on April 18, 1898. In his answer he included letters of support from Judge Holt and a number of other people prominent in the trial of 1865. A. C. Richards, the former chief of police in Washington on the night of the assassination, wrote directly to the editor of the *Washington Post* in his support.

He was accused of perjury by Surratt but his testimony has stood up well over time. Surratt conveniently blamed Wiechmann for the death of his mother. He did not have the courage to blame himself.

Wiechmann died of cardiac asthma at the home of a sister in Anderson, Indiana, on June 5, 1902, thirty-seven years after Lincoln's assassination. He was buried in a Catholic cemetery there.

On his death bed he made the statement: "I told the truth and the whole truth at the assassination trial."

Wiechmann wrote a manuscript about the plot to capture Lincoln and the trial of 1865. He included important information gathered from many sources as they became available. His intention was to publish this in book form to clear his name. This he did not accomplish in his lifetime. The extensive manuscript was preserved. It was eventually edited and published in 1975.

Major Henry Rathbone and Clara Harris, who were in the theater box with the Lincolns the night of the assassination, were later married in Albany, New York, and had a family. The major shot his wife to death some years later and was committed to a mental hospital.[6]

Colonel Samuel Cox and Thomas A. Jones, who harbored Booth and Herold in a pine thicket for nearly a week and furnished a boat for their crossing of the Potomac River, were never prosecuted. Jones was very wise. He did not talk until it was safe to do so. In 1893 he wrote a small book on the part he played. He speaks of another clever undercover operator by the name of Harbin. Thomas H. Harbin lived a half-mile south of Bryantown and was postmaster there the first six months of 1855. He left the country as the war was ending and was abroad for about five years. After his return to the United States, he became a desk clerk at the National Hotel in Washington. He continued in this capacity until the time of his death about 1885. During this time he often spoke of his days as a Confederate agent. He said that he was introduced to Booth by Mudd in the fall of 1864.

Constable John F. Parker, who neglected his post outside the door of Lincoln's theater box, was never prosecuted.

John Lloyd, who rented the Surratt Tavern at Surrattsville from Mrs. Surratt, turned state witness and was never prosecuted. He is said to have succumbed to alcoholism.

Appendices

Appendix 1: President Lincoln's Proclamation

The declaration of martial law and suspension of the writ of habeas corpus
September 24, 1862

By the President of the United States of America.

A PROCLAMATION

Whereas it has become necessary to call into service not only volunteers, but also portions of the militia of the States by draft, in order to suppress the insurrection existing in the United States, and disloyal persons are not adequately retrained by ordinary processes of law from hindering this measure, and from giving aid and comfort in various ways to the insurrection: —

Now, therefore, be it ordered, —

First. That during the existing insurrection, and as a necessary measure for suppressing the same, all rebels and insurgents, their aiders and abetters, within the United States, and all other persons discouraging volunteer enlistments, resisting militia drafts, or guilty of any disloyal practice, affording aid and comfort to rebels against the authority of the United States, shall be subject to martial law, and liable to trial and punishment by court-martial commissions.

Second. That the writ of habeas corpus is suspended in respect to all persons arrested, or who are now, or hereafter during the Rebellion shall be, imprisoned in any fort, camp, arsenal, military prison, or other place of confinement, by any military authority, or by the sentence of any court-martial or military commission.

In witness whereof, I have hereunto set my hand, and caused the seal of the United States to be affixed.

Done at the city of Washington, this twenty fourth day of September, in the year of our Lord one thousand eight hundred and sixty two, and of the independence of the United States the eighty seventh.

ABRAHAM LINCOLN

By the President:
  William H. Seward, Secretary of State.
By order of the Secretary of War:
  L. Thomas, Adjutant-General America

Appendix 2: Statement of Dr. S. A. Mudd

In the matter of the murder of the president
April 21, 1865

Bryantown, Md.

Dr. S. A. Mudd, residing four miles north of Bryantown, Maryland, being duly sworn deposes and says:

Last Saturday morning, April 15th, about four o'clock, two men called at my house and knocked very loudly. I was aroused by the noise, and as it was such an unusual thing for persons to knock so loudly, I took the precaution of asking who were there before opening the door. After they had knocked twice more, I opened the door, but before doing so they told me they were two strangers on their way to Washington, that one of their horses had fallen by which one of the men had broken his leg.

On opening the door, I found two men, one on a horse led by the other man who had tied his horse to a tree near by. I aided the man in getting off his horse and into the house, and laid him on a sofa in my parlor. After getting a light, I assisted him in getting upstairs where there were two beds, one of which he took. He seemed to be very much injured in the back, and complained very much of it. I did not see his face at all. He seemed to be tremulous and not inclined to talk, and had his cloak thrown around his head and seemed inclined to sleep, as I thought in order to ease himself, and every now and then he would groan pretty heavily.

I had no proper paste-board for making splints, and went and got an old band-box and made one of it; and as he wanted it done hastily, I hurried more than I otherwise would. He wanted me to fix it up any way, as he said he wanted to get back, or get home and have it done by a regular physician. I then took a piece of the band-box and split it in half, doubled it at right angles, and took some paste and pasted it into a splint.

On examination, I found there was a straight fracture of the tibia about two inches above the ankle. My examination was quite short, and I did not find the adjoining bone fractured in any way. I do not regard it a particularly painful or dangerous wound; there was nothing resembling a compound fracture. I do not suppose I was more than three-quarters of an hour in making the examination of the wound and applying the splint. [Mrs. Mudd made the bandages by tearing cloth into strands, a practice widely used then and until proprietary bandages became available in the 1920s and 1930s.] He continued still to suffer, and complained of severe pain in the back, especially when he moved. In my opinion, pain in the back may originate from riding. I judge that in this case it originated from his fall and also from riding, as he seemed so prostrated. He sometimes breathed very shortly and as if exhausted. He was a man, I suppose about five feet ten inches high, and appeared to be pretty well made, but he had a heavy shawl on all the time. I suppose he would weigh 150 or 160 pounds. His hair was black and seemed to be somewhat inclined to curl; it was worn long. He had a pretty full forehead and his skin was fair. He was very pale when I saw him, and appeared as if accustomed to in-door rather than out-door life. I do not know how to describe his skin exactly but I should think he might be classed as dark, and his paleness might be attributed to receiving the injury. I did not observe his hand to see whether it was small or large. I have been shown the photograph of J. Wilkes Booth and I should not think that this was the man from any resemblance to the photograph, but from other causes I have every reason to believe that he is the man whose leg I dressed as stated above.

In order to examine and operate upon his leg, I had occasion to cut his boot longitudinally in front of the instep. It seems that when he left my house, this boot was left behind. Yesterday morning my attention was called to this boot which is a long and top-boot. On making an examination of it, I find written on the inside in apparently a German hand, what I take to be "Henry Luz, maker 445 Broadway, J. Wilkes." I did not notice the writing in this boot until my attention was called to it by Lieutenant Lovett. [Boot produced and identified by deponent as the one taken from the leg of the wounded man.]

I have seen J. Wilkes Booth. I was introduced to him by Mr. J. C. Thompson, a son-in-law of Dr. William Queen, in November or December last. Mr. Thompson resides with his father-in-law, and his place is about five miles southwesterly from Bryantown, near the edge of what is known as Zechiah Swamp. Mr. Thompson told me at the time that Booth was looking out for lands in this neighborhood or in this county. He said he was not very particular where, if he could get such a lot as he wanted, whether it was in Charles, Prince George, or Saint Mary's county; and Booth inquired if I knew any parties in this neighborhood who had any fine horses for sale. I told him there was a neighbor of mine who had some very fine traveling horses, and he said he thought if he could purchase one reasonable he would do so, and would ride up to Washington on him instead of riding in the stage. The next evening he rode to my house and stayed with me that night, and the next morning he purchased a rather old horse, but a very fine mover of Mr. George Gardiner, Sr., who resides but a short distance from my house. I would know the horse if I should see him again. He is a darkish-bay horse, not bright bay, with a tolerably large head and had a defect in one eye. Booth gave eighty dollars for the horse. I have never seen Booth since that time to my knowledge until the last Saturday night.

When I assisted the wounded man into my house on Saturday morning last, the other party with him who appeared to be very youthful, took charge of the horse and said he would keep it and the other one until they could be put in the stable. As soon as I could I woke my colored man Frank Washington, and sent him to put the horses in the stable, and the young man came into the house.

After setting the wounded man's leg the best I could for the time, I think I walked around to my farm-yard and gave some directions. When I returned breakfast was ready; and this young man was up knocking about. I asked him to come to breakfast. He did so, but the other man remained upstairs in bed. I did not know who this young man was, but he remarked that he had seen me. He appeared to be a very fast young man and was very talkative. He was about five feet two or three inches high. I would not be positive as to his height. He had a smooth face and appeared as if he had never shaved, his hair was black; and I should consider his complexion dark. I did not notice his eyes particularly. He wore a dark colored business coat. I have seen the photograph of Herold, but I do not recognize it as that of the young man. He seemed well acquainted throughout the whole country, and I asked his name; he gave it as Henson, and that of the wounded man as Tyser or Tyson. I did not hear either of them address the other by the first name.

The only thing that excited my suspicions on reflecting upon these circumstances was that after breakfast, when I was about to leave for my farm work, this young man asked me if I had a razor about the house, that his friend desired to shave, as perhaps he would feel better. I had noticed that the wounded man had whiskers and a mustache when he came into the house. After dinner, I went to see the patient and although he kept his face partially turned away from me I noticed that he had lost his mustache, but still retained his whiskers. I did not pay sufficient attention to his beard to determine whether it was false or natural.

This young man asked me if I could fix up clumsily a crutch for his friend to hobble along with, and I went down to the old Englishman I had had there who had a saw and auger and he and I made a crude crutch out of a piece of plank for him. This young man mentioned the names of several parties in this neighborhood whom he knew; among others, several here in Bryantown. He mentioned being in the store of William Moore; he did not say when. I think he said he knew Bean, who kept store here; and he knew very well Len Roby, Rufus Roby, & Major Thomas Sr. He inquired the way from my house to Bryantown, although he represented in the morning that they had come from Bryantown. He said he knew Parson Wilmer, who lives at a place called Piney Church. He said also that they had met two persons, a lady and gentleman, walking somewhere near Bryantown that morning, and inquired of them the way to my house, and that they also met a negro, but did not state where and that they also inquired of him the way to my place.

I saw only one of the horses which these men rode to my house. She was a bay mare, moderately long tail, dark mane and tail. I won't be certain whether she had a star in the forehead or not. She appeared to be a nettlesome, high spirited animal. I saw her after dinner, between twelve and one o'clock, when this young man and I rode over to my father's place in order to see if we could get a carriage for the wounded man; but I found that the carriages were all out of repair except one and we could not get that one. He then concluded to go to Bryantown for a conveyance to get his friend over as far as his friend's Mr. Wilmer's.

I then went down to Mr. Hardy's and was in conversation with him fully an hour when I returned home leisurely, and found the two men were just in the act of leaving. The young man inquired of me the nearest way to Mr. Wilmer's. I told them there were two ways; one was the public road leading by Beantown; the other led across the swamp directly across from me by which they could save a mile. Both are easterly. This road from my house is directly across in a straight line; it is not a public way, but by taking down a fence you can get through. They concluded to take this latter route, and I gave them the necessary directions. I did not see them leave my house. The man on crutches had left the house when I got back, and he was some fifty to seventy yards from me when this young man came to me and began to inquire of me the direction. I do not know how or where Booth got a conveyance away from my house; he did not go in a carriage, but he undoubtedly went on horseback.

When they came there in the morning this young man said that one of the horses would not stand without tying and asked that both of them should be put in the stable. He held one of the horses until I returned into the house with the wounded man, when I called a colored boy named Frank Washington and sent him around to take the horses to the stable. I also have a white man named Thomas Davis, who has charge of my horses, and I judge that he saw the horses which were in the stable during Saturday.

I judge that between four and five o'clock on Saturday afternoon they left my house. I do not know where they went. I have not been spoken to by any one for professional advice in their behalf since that time, and have not seen either of them since.

It is about four miles across from my house to Parson Wilmer's and by the public road it is about five miles. I suppose they could go in an hour or an hour and a half by walking their horses.

I suppose in a day or two swelling would take place in the wounded man's leg; there was very little tumefaction in the wound, and I could discover crepitation very distinctly. It would be necessary to dress it again in two or three days if it were left in a recumbent posture, but if moved at a moderate rate, I do not know as it would aggravate it very much less unless it was struck by something. I do not know much about wounds of that sort; a military surgeon would know more about those things.

Samuel A. Mudd

Subscribed and sworn before me this
22nd day of April 1865   H. H. Wells, Colonel
and P. M. Genl. Def. S. of P.

[From a typed copy supplied the Surratt Society dated November 1980. From the National Archives, M-599, reel 5, frames 226 through 0239.]

Appendix 3: Extract from the Opinion of Attorney General James Speed

Re: Constitutional Power of the Military

Attorney General's Office
Washington, July 1865

Sir: You ask me whether the persons charged with the offense of having assassinated the President can be tried before a military tribunal or must they be tried before a civil court.

The President was assassinated at a theater in the city of Washington. At the time of the assassination a civil war was flagrant, the city of Washington was defended by fortifications regularly and constantly manned, the principal police of the city was Federal soldiers, the public offices and property in the city were all guarded by soldiers, and the President's House and person were, or should have been, under the guard of soldiers. Martial law had been declared in the District of Columbia, but the civil courts were open and held their regular sessions, and transacted business as in times of peace.

Such being the facts, the question is one of great importance—important, because it involves the constitutional guarantees thrown about the rights of the citizen, and because the security of the army and the government in time of war is involved; important, as it involves a seeming conflict between the laws of peace and of war.

Having given the question propounded the patient and earnest consideration its magnitude and importance require, I will proceed to give the reasons why I am of the opinion that the conspirators not only may but ought to be tried by a military tribunal.

[Seven pages of reasoning follow, constituting more than five thousand words.]

My conclusion, therefore, is, that if the persons who are charged with the assassination of the President committed the deed as public enemies, as I believe they did, and whether they did or not is a question to be decided by the tribunal before which they are tried, they not only can, but ought to be tried before a military tribunal. If the persons charged have offended against the laws of war, it would be as palpably wrong for the military to hand them over to the civil courts, as it would be wrong in a civil court to convict a man of murder who had, in time of war killed another in battle.

I am, sir, most respectfully, your obedient servant,

JAMES SPEED
Attorney General

To the President

Appendix 4: Booth's Diary

Although the contents of Booth's pockets at the time of his death were reported in the newspapers, the diary was not produced at the court-martial trial in May 1865. This remains a mystery. Reference to a plot to kidnap President Lincoln rather than assassinate him is made, a plot the inquiry chose to ignore. It would have been beneficial to Mudd to have this considered. But it was overlooked or deliberately pushed aside. The government at that time was considering a grand conspiracy involving Confederate leaders. The diary did not come to light until the trial of John Surratt in 1867. When it did appear, some eighteen pages of it were missing. The following is a transcript of the remaining portion.

"Te amo"
April 13, 14 The Ides
Until today nothing was ever thought of sacrificing to our country's wrongs. For six months we had worked to capture. But our cause being almost lost, something decisive and great must be done. But its failure was owing to others who did not strike for their country with a heart. I struck boldly, and not as the papers say. I walked with a firm step through a thousand of his friends; was stopped, but pushed on. A Colonel was at his side. I shouted sic semper before I fired. In jumping, broke my leg. I passed all his pickets. Rode sixty miles last night, with the bone of my leg tearing the flesh at every jump.

I can never repent it though we hated to kill. Our country owed all our troubles to him, and God simply made me the instrument of his punishment. The country is not what it was. This Forced Union is not what I have loved.

April 1865

I care not what becomes of me. I have no desire to out live my country. This night (before the deed) I wrote a long article and left it for one of the editors of the National Intelligencer, in which I fully set forth our reasons for our proceeding. He or the gov'r—

Friday 21

After being hunted like a dog through swamps, woods, and last night being chased by gunboats till I was forced to return wet, cold, and starving, with everyman's hand against me, I am here in despair. And why? For doing what Brutus was honored for—what made Tell a hero. And yet I, for striking down a greater tyrant than they ever knew, am looked upon as a common cut-throat. My action was purer than either of theirs. One hoped to be great. The other had not only his country's, but his own wrongs to avenge. I hoped for no gain. I knew no private wrong. I struck for my country and that alone. A country that groaned beneath this tyranny, and prayed for this end, and yet now behold the cold hand they extend to me. God cannot pardon me if I have done wrong, except in serving a degenerate people. The little, the very little, I left behind to clear my name, the government will not allow to be printed. So ends all. For my country I have given up all that makes life sweet and holy, brought misery upon my family, and am sure there is no pardon in the Heaven for me, since man condemns me so. I have only heard of what has been done (except what I did myself) and it fills me with horror. God try and forgive me, and bless my mother. Tonight I will once more try the river with the intent to cross. Though I have a great desire and almost a mind to return to Washington, and in a measure clear my name—which I feel I can do. I do not repent the blow I struck. I may before my God, but not to man. I think I have done well. Though I am abandoned with the curse of Cain upon me, when, if the world knew my heart, that one blow would have made me great, though I did desire no greatness.

Tonight I try to escape these blood-hounds once more. Who can read his fate? God's will be done. I have too great a soul to die like a criminal. Oh may He, may He spare me that, and let me die bravely. I bless the entire world. Have never hated or wronged anyone.

This was not a wrong, unless God deems it so, and it's with Him to damn or bless me. And for this brave boy with me, who often prays (yes, before and since) with a true and sincere heart—was it a crime in him? If so, why can he pray the same?

I do not wish to shed a drop of blood, but "I must fight the course!" 'Tis all that's left me.

Appendix 5: Testimony of Major Henry R. Rathbone

Major Rathbone was in President Lincoln's theater box as a guest with his fiancée, Miss Harris, at the time of the assassination. He struggled with Booth after the shot was fired and was deeply slashed on his left arm as he fended off a knife blow by Booth. His struggling with Booth was probably a major factor in making Booth catch his right spur in the draped flag as he jumped from the president's box, landing off balance.

By the Judge-Advocate:

Q. Will you state to the Court whether or not you were in the box of the President on the night of his assassination at Ford's Theater?

A. I was.

Q. State all the circumstances that came under your observation in connection with the crime.

A. On the evening of the 14th of April last, at about twenty minutes past eight o'clock, I, in company with Miss Harris, left my residence at the corner of Fifteenth and H Streets, and joined the President and Mrs. Lincoln, and went with them, in their carriage, to Ford's Theater in Tenth Street. On reaching the theater, when the presence of the President became known, the actors stopped playing; the band struck up "Hail to the Chief!"; the audience rose and received him with vociferous cheering. The party proceeded along in the rear of the dress circle, and entered the box that had been set apart for their reception. On entering the box, there was a large arm-chair that was placed nearest the audience, farthest from the stage, which the President took, and occupied during the whole of the evening, with one exception, when he got up and put on his coat, and returned and sat down again. When the second scene of the third act was being performed, and while I was intently observing the proceedings upon the stage, with my back toward the door, I heard the discharge of a pistol behind me, and, looking round, saw, through the smoke, a man between the door and the President. At that same time, I heard him shout some word, which I thought was "Freedom!" I instantly sprang toward him and seized him. He wrested himself from my grasp, and made a violent thrust at my breast with a large knife. I parried the blow by striking it up, and received a wound several inches deep in my left arm, between the elbow and the shoulder. The orifice of the wound was about an inch and a half in length, and extended upwards toward the shoulder several inches. The man rushed to the front of the box and I endeavored to seize him again, but only caught his clothes as he was leaping over the railing of the box. The clothes, as I believe, were torn in the attempt to seize him. As he went over upon the stage, I cried out with a loud voice, "Stop that man!" I then turned to the President. His position was not changed: his head was slightly bent forward, and his eyes were closed. I saw that he was unconscious, and, supposing him mortally wounded, rushed to the door for the purpose of calling medical aid. On reaching the outer door of the passage-way, I found it barred by a heavy piece of plank, one end of which was secured in the wall and the other resting against the door. It had been so securely fastened, that it required considerable force to remove it. The wedge or bar was about four feet from the floor. Persons upon the outside were beating against the door for the purpose of entering. I removed the bar, and the door was opened. Several persons who represented themselves as surgeons were allowed to enter. I saw Colonel Crawford, and requested him to prevent other persons from entering the box. I then returned to the box, and found the surgeons examining the President's person. They had not yet discovered the wound. As soon as it was discovered, it was determined to remove him from the theater. He was carried out; and I then proceeded to assist Mrs. Lincoln, who was intensely excited, to leave the theater. On reaching the head of the stairs, I requested Major Potter to aid me in assisting Mrs. Lincoln across the street to the house where the President was being conveyed. The wound which I had received had been bleeding very profusely; and on reaching the house, feeling very faint from the loss of blood, I seated myself in the hall and soon after fainted away, and was laid on the floor. Upon my return of consciousness, I was taken to my residence. In a review of the transactions, it is my confident belief that the time which elapsed between the discharge of a pistol and the time when the assassin leaped from the box did not exceed thirty seconds. Neither Mrs. Lincoln nor Miss Harris had left their seats.

Q. You did not know Booth yourself, did you?

A. No, sir.

Q. Do you think you would recognize him from a photograph?

A. I should be unable to do so as being the man in that box. I myself have seen him on stage some time since.

By the Court:

Q. What distance was the assassin from the President when you first saw him after hearing the report?

A. The distance from the door to where the President was sitting, to the best of my recollection, was about four or five feet; and this man was standing between the door and the President.

By the Judge-Advocate:

Will you look at that knife [exhibiting a knife to the witness], and say if it appears to you to be such a one as he used? I believe the blood is still on the blade.

A. I think this knife might have made a wound similar to the one I received. I could not recognize the knife. I merely saw the gleam. [The knife was offered in evidence without objection, and is marked Exhibit No. 28.]

Q. Did you notice how the blade was held in the hand of the assassin when he held it?

A. The blade was held in a horizontal position, I should think; and the nature of the wound would indicate it. It came with a sweeping blow down from above.

Appendix 6: Extract from the Argument in Defense of Lewis Payne by W. E. Doster, Esq., His Counsel.

I can not allow my duties as counsel to interfere with my convictions as a man so far as to make me blind to the worth of the life of a distinguished citizen, and the awful consequences of an attempt to take it away. If, indeed, such an attempt be allowed to go without rebuke, then it seems to me the office is but a perilous exposure to violence. . . .

That we may accurately, and as fully as the occasion demands, understand the convictions of the prisoner, I invite your attention to a sketch of his life, the customs under which he was reared, and the education which he received. . . .

Let us pause in this narrative and consider what, in the eyes of this Florida boy, was the meaning of war, and what the thoughts that drove him from a pleasant home to the field of arms. At another time I might picture to you the scene, but too familiar, of his taking leave; a mother, like the mothers of Northern boys shedding tears, less bitter, because she was dedicating a son to her country; a sister, whose sorrow, like the sorrow of the sisters of Northern boys, was alleviated with pride that they had a brother in the field.

It was a custom of this State for masters to whip their slaves, sell them and receive the constant homage which the oppressed offer to the powerful. It was the custom to defend this institution in meeting-houses, at political gatherings, in family prayers. It was the custom to hunt fugitives with bloodhounds—even those who tried to help them to freedom.

In this custom the prisoner was bred; education made it a second nature; politicians had taught him to find it in the Constitution; preachers had taught him to find it in the Bible; the laws taught him to regard it as property; habit had made it a very part of his being. In the eyes of the lad, the war meant to abolish this custom and upheave society from its foundations. His inheritance was to be dissipated, his vassals equals, his laws invaded, his religion confounded, his policies a heresy, his habits criminal. Hereafter, to strike a slave was to be an assault, to sell one a felony, to kill one murder. For this, then, the lad was going to fight—the defense of a social system.

It was a traditional political precept of the State in which the prisoner lived, that the State, like its elder sisters, had reserved the right of divorcing itself at pleasure from the Union, and that great as the duty of a citizen might be to the Union, his first duty was to Florida. Schoolmasters taught that the relative rights of State and Nation had been left unsettled; politicians taught that the local power was greater than the central; in support of it men were sent to Washington. The war in the eyes of the boy, meant to reverse this, to subordinate the State to the Nation, the Governor to the President, Tallahassee to Washington City. And therefore, he was going to fight—to defend State rights. That was the second reason.

It was a deep seated conviction of the people in this State that their blood and breeding were better than the blood and breeding of Norterners; that they had more courage, more military prowess, and were by nature superiors. This conviction the war threatened to overthrow, this boast the war was to vindicate, this superiority was, by the war, intended to be proved. And this was the third reason he was going to fight—to show that he was a better man than Northerners.

There was a frantic delusion among these people that Northern men were usurping the Government, were coveting their plantations, were longing to pillage their houses, ravage their fields and reduce them to subjection. The war was to defend mother, sister, home, soil, and honor, and beat back an insolent invader. This was the fourth reason—to repel invasion. . . .

Appendix 7: Sam Arnold's Incriminating Letter to Booth

This letter was written by Arnold to Booth from his brother's home near Baltimore after he had gone there following the failed kidnap attempt of mid–March 1865. It is the letter found in Booth's trunk at the National Hotel, Washington, D.C., after the assassination that drew him back into the "conspiracy."

Hookstown, Maryland Balt. Co.
March 27, 1865

Dear John:

Was business so important that you could not remain in Balto. till I saw you? I came in as soon as I could, but found you had gone to W———n. I called also to see Mike, but learned from his mother he had gone out with you, and had not returned. I concluded, therefore, he had gone with you. How inconsiderate you have been! When I left you, you stated we would not meet in a month or so. Therefore, I made application for employment, an answer to which I shall receive during the week. I told my parents I had ceased with you. Can I, then, under existing circumstances, come as you request? You know full well that the G——t suspects something is going on there; therefore, the undertaking is becoming more complicated. Why not for the present, desist, for various reasons, which, if you look into, you can readily see, without my making mention thereof. You nor any one, can censure me for my present course. You have been its course, for how can I now come after telling them I had left you? Suspicion rests upon me now from my whole family, and even parties in the county. I will be impelled to leave home anyhow and how soon I care not. None, no not one, were more in favor of the enterprise than myself, and to-day would be there, had you not done as you have—by this I mean, manner of proceeding. I am as you well know, in need. I am, you may say in rags, whereas today I ought to be well clothed. I do not feel right stalking about without means with the appearance of a beggar. I feel my dependence; but even all this would and was forgotten, for I was one with you. Time more propitious will arrive yet. Do not act rashly or in haste. I would prefer your first query, "Go and see how it will be taken at R———d," and ere long I shall be better prepared to again be with you. I dislike writing; would sooner verbally make known my views; yet your non-writing causes me thus to proceed.

Do not in anger peruse this. Weigh all I have said, and, as a rational man and a friend, you can not censure or upbraid my conduct. I sincerely trust this, nor aught else that shall or may occur, will ever be an obstacle to obliterate our former friendship and attachment. Write me to Balto., as I expect to be in about Wednesday or Thursday, or, if you can possibly come on, I will Tuesday meet you in Balto., at B———. Ever I subscribe myself.

Your friend,
Sam

Appendix 8: The Petition for Clemency for Mudd

As a result of the heroic efforts of Mudd during the Yellow Fever epidemic at Fort Jefferson from August 18 to October 22, 1867, a petition for clemency was drawn up by the enlisted men and noncommissioned officers of Fort Jefferson and submitted to the government in October 1867. This petition was signed by all noncommissioned officers of the fort. The men were very grateful for his heroic service given with no thought for his own safety during the epidemic. The post physician, commanding officer, and the commanding officer's wife died in this epidemic, which caused 38 deaths among 270 cases.

This was at a time when all members of the post were fearful of being stricken with the deadly disease, which no one understood and for which there was no cure at that time. The commissioned officers withheld their signatures, not wishing to offend a recently appointed new post physician, Dr. Thomas.

A bronze plaque authorized by President Eisenhower in 1959 now commemorates the services of Mudd on the wall of the dungeon cell once occupied by Mudd at Fort Jefferson.

It is not know when the petition reached President Andrew Johnson who, as we know, was having very serious troubles of his own with members of Congress who opposed lenient measures of Reconstruction in the South and who brought impeachment proceedings against him in the spring of 1868. The petition did play a role eventually in Mudd's favor. It was probably an important factor in the pardon of Mudd in February 1869, one of President Johnson's final official actions before leaving office.

It is with sincere pleasure that we acknowledge the great services rendered by Dr. S. A. Mudd (prisoner) during the prevalence of Yellow Fever at the Fort.

When the very worthy surgeon of the Post, Dr. J. Sim Smith, fell one of the first victims of the fatal epidemic, and the greatest dismay and alarm naturally prevailed on all sides, deprived as the garrison was of the assistance of any medical officer, Dr. Mudd, influenced by the most praiseworthy and humane motives, spontaneously and unsolicited came forward to devote all his energies and professional knowledge to the aid of the sick and dying.

He inspired the hopeless with courage, and by his constant presence in the midst of danger and infection, regardless of his own life, tranquillized the fearful and desponding.

By his prudence and foresight, the hospital upon an adjacent island, to which at first the sick were removed in an open boat, was discontinued. Those attacked with the malady were on the spot put under vigorous treatment. A protracted exposure on the open sea was avoided, and many now strong doubtless owe their lives to the care and treatment they received at his hands. He properly considered the nature and character of the infection and concluded that it could not be eradicated by the mere removal of the sick, entailing, as it did the loss of valuable time necessary for the application of the proper remedies, exposure of those attacked and adding to the general fear and despondency.

The entire different system of treatment and hospital arrangement was resorted to with the happiest effect. Dr. Mudd's treatment and the change which he recommended met with the hearty approval and warm commendation of the regularly appointed surgeons, with whom, in a later stage of the epidemic, he was associated. Many here who have experienced his kind and judicious treatment, can never repay him the debt of obligation they owe him. We do, therefore, in consideration of the invaluable services rendered by him during this calamitous and fatal epidemic, earnestly recommend him to the well-merited clemency of the Government, and solicit his immediate release from here, and restoration to liberty and the bosom of his family.

Appendix 9: Samuel A. Mudd's Pardon

ANDREW JOHNSON, President of the United States of America
To all to Whom these Presents shall come, Greeting:

Whereas, on the twenty-ninth day of June in the year 1865, Dr. Samuel A. Mudd was by the judgement of a Military Commission, convened and holden at the City of Washington, in part convicted, and in part acquitted, of the specification wherein he was inculpated in the charge for the trial of which said Military Commission was so convened and held, and which specification in its principal allegation against him, was and is in the words and figures following, to wit: "And in further prosecution of said conspiracy, the said Samuel A. Mudd did, at Washington City and within the Military Department and military lines aforesaid, on or before the sixth day of March, A.D. 1865, and on divers other days and times between that day and the twentieth day of April A.D. 1865, advise, encourage, receive, entertain, harbor and conceal, aid and assist, the said John Wilkes Booth, David E. Herold, Lewis Payne, John H. Surratt, Michael O'Laughlin, George A. Atzerodt, Mary E. Surratt and Samuel Arnold and their confederates, with knowledge of the murderous and traitorous conspiracy aforesaid, and with intent to aid, abet, and assist them in the execution thereof, and in escaping from justice after the murder of the said Abraham Lincoln, in pursuance of said conspiracy in manner aforesaid:

And whereas, upon a consideration and examination of the record of said trial and conviction and of the evidence given at said trial, I am satisfied that the guilt found by the said judgement against the said Samuel A. Mudd was of receiving, entertaining, harboring, and concealing John Wilkes Booth and David E. Herold, with the intent to aid, abet and assist them in escaping from justice after the assassination of the late President of the United States, and not of any other or greater participation or complicity in said abominable crime;

And whereas, it is represented to me by intelligent and respectable members of the medical profession, that the circumstances of the surgical aid to the escaping assassin and the imputed concealment of his flight are deserving of a lenient construction as within the obligations of professional duty, and thus inadequate evidence of a guilty sympathy with the crime or the criminal;

And whereas, in other respects the evidence, imputing such guilty sympathy or purpose of aid in defeat of justice, leaves room for uncertainty as to the true measure and nature of the complicity of the said Samuel A. Mudd, in the attempted escape of said assassins;

And whereas, the sentence imposed by said Military Commission upon the said Samuel A. Mudd was that he be imprisoned at hard labor for life, and the confinement under such sentence was directed to be had in the military prison at Dry Tortugas, Florida, and the said prisoner has been hitherto, and now is, suffering the infliction of such sentence;

And whereas, upon occasion of the prevalence of the Yellow Fever at that military station, and the death by that pestilence of the medical officer of the Post, the said Samuel A. Mudd devoted himself to the care and cure of the sick, and interposed his courage and his skill to protect the garrison, otherwise without adequate medical aid, from peril and alarm, and thus, as the officers and men unite in testifying, saved many valuable lives and earned the admiration and the gratitude of all who observed or experienced his generous and faithful service to humanity;

And whereas, the surviving families and friends of the Surgeon and other officers who were the victims of the pestilence earnestly present their dying testimony to the conspicuous merit of Dr. Mudd's conduct, and their own sense of obligation to him and Lieut. Zabriskie and two hundred and ninety nine noncommissioned officers and privates stationed at the Dry Tortugas have united in presenting to my attention the praiseworthy action of the prisoner and in petitioning for his pardon;

And whereas the Medical Society of Hartford County, Maryland, of which he was an associate, have petitioned for his pardon, and thirty nine members of the Senate and House of Representatives of the Congress of the United States have also requested his pardon; Now, therefore, be it known that I, Andrew Johnson, President of the United States of America, in consideration of the premises, divers other good and sufficient reasons me there unto moving, do hereby grant to the said Dr. Samuel A. Mudd a full and unconditional pardon.

In testimony thereof, I have hereunto signed my name and caused the Seal of the United States to be affixed.

Done at the City of Washington, this Eighth day of February, A.D. [Seal] 1869, and the Independence of the United States the ninety third.

ANDREW JOHNSON

By the President
WILLIAM H. SEWARD
SECRETARY OF STATE

Appendix 10: Samuel B. Arnold's Pardon

ANDREW JOHNSON
President of the United States of America

Whereas, on the 30th day of June in the year of 1865; one Samuel B. Arnold was, by the judgement of a Military Commission convened and holden in the City of Washington, declared guilty of the specification wherein he was charged in the words and figures following to wit:

And in further prosecution of said conspiracy, the said Samuel Arnold did, within the Military department and the Military lines aforesaid, on or before the 6th day of March, A.D. 1865, and on divers other days and times between that day and the fifteenth day of April, A.D. 1865, did combine, conspire with and aid, counsel, abet, comfort and support the said John Wilkes Booth, Lewis Payne, George A. Atzerodt, Michael O'Laughlin and their confederates in said unlawful, murderous and traitorous conspiracy and in the execution thereof as aforesaid;

And whereas the sentence imposed by said Military Commission upon the said Samuel Arnold was, that he is imprisoned at hard labor for life, and the confinement under such sentence was directed to be had in the Military prison at Dry Tortugas, Florida, and the said Arnold has been for more than three years and six months, and now is suffering the infliction of such sentence;

And whereas the evidence adduced against said Arnold before the Military Commission leaves room for uncertainty as to the true measure and nature of the complicity of the said Arnold in said murderous and traitorous conspiracy, and it is apparent that the said Arnold rendered no active assistance to the said Booth and his confederates in the actual execution of said abominable crime; And whereas the pardon of said Arnold is strongly recommended by the City Council and more than two hundred other citizens of Baltimore and vicinity; Now, therefore be it known, that I, Andrew Johnson, President of the United States of America, in consideration of the premises, divers other and sufficient reasons me thereunto moving, do hereby grant to the said, Samuel B. Arnold, a full and unconditional pardon.

In testimony whereof I have hereunto signed my name and caused the Seal of the United States to be affixed.

Done at the City of Washington this first day of March, A.D. 1869, and in the Independence of the United States, the Ninety-Third.

(SEAL)

(Signed)   Andrew Johnson

William H. Seward
Secretary of State.

Appendix 11: Chronology of the Life of Dr. Samuel Alexander Mudd

b. Dec. 20, 1833, Charles County, Maryland, Oak Hill Farm
d. Jan. 10, 1883, age 49 yrs. and 3 wks., Charles County, Maryland

Age 7—Public school—2 yrs.
  " 9—Home tutoring—5 yrs.
  " 14—St. Johns College, Frederick, Maryland—2 yrs.
        Georgetown College, Washington, D.C.—2 yrs.

Apprenticeship with Dr. George Mudd of Bryantown, Maryland
Baltimore Medical College (University of Maryland)—M.D. 1856
Postgraduate hospital practice—certificate of merit

Marriage to Sarah Frances Dyer, Nov. 25, 1857
1858—Birth of Andrew Jerome
1859—Farm of their own
1860—Birth of Lillian Augusta
1862—Birth of Thomas Dyer
1864—Birth of Samuel Alexander II

1864—Nov. Mudd meets John Wilkes Booth at St. Mary's Church; purchase of one-eyed horse arranged with neighbor George Gardiner.
1864—Dec. Booth and Mudd meet again.
1865—Apr. 15, 1865, 4:00 A.M.—Loud knock at Mudd's door. Booth treated by Mudd. Boot cut from left leg. Fracture of tibia splinted. Much pain in

leg and back. Put to bed upstairs. 4:00 P.M. Booth and Herold leave Mudd's house the back way, into Zekiah Swamp.

Apr. 16, Sunday—Mudd confers with cousin, Dr. George, at church.

Apr. 17, Monday—Dr. George reports to Lt. Dana in Bryantown that strangers had visited Mudd.

Apr. 18, Tuesday—Detectives first come to question Mudd.

Apr. 20, Wednesday—Rewards posted for fugitives.

Apr. 21, Friday—Detectives return with cavalry. Razor and boot given to them. Mudd taken to Bryantown for 5 hrs. questioning. Written statement made. Allowed to return home.

Apr. 22, Saturday—Further extensive questioning by Col. Wells. Allowed to return home.

Apr. 23, Sunday—To church. Took Col. Wells to Zekiah Swamp. Allowed to return home.

Apr. 23—Chains, irons, and hoods added to the prisoners on the two Monitors.

Apr. 24, Monday—Mudd taken to Carroll Annex of Old Capitol Prison, Washington, D.C.

May 1—Transfer to Old Arsenal Prison, chains and hood to Dr. Mudd.

May 7—Hood temporarily removed. Charges read to Mudd at night. Trial to be with seven others.

May 9—First meeting of court. Defendants request counsel. Adjournment.

May 11—Time allowed for defense counsel.

May 12—First witness for prosecution heard.

May 23—Testimony of prosecution closed.

May 26—Testimony for defense of Mudd begins.

June 14—Final appeal of Ewing begins.

June 30—Sentence of Mudd: 5/4 life, one short of death.

July 5—Signature of President Johnson.

July 6—Frances visits Mudd.

July 7—Execution of four in courtyard of prison.

July 17—Left Arsenal Prison. Gun Boat, Florida. Charleston, S.C. harbor.

July 24, 1865—Arrival Fort Jefferson.

Sept. 1865—Escape attempt.

Jan. 1867—Writ of habeas corpus denied.

Feb. 1867—Assigned to carpenter shop.

June 10–Aug. 7, 1867—Civil trial of John Surratt. Hung jury.

Aug. 1867—Yellow Fever epidemic at fort.

Sept. 5—Mudd volunteers services with illness of post physician, who dies Sept. 7.

Sept. 23—Death of O'Laughlin from Yellow Fever.

Sept. 24—Mudd himself a victim of Yellow Fever.

Oct. 14—He survives acute illness.

Oct. 23—Epidemic ends.

Dec. 1867—Back in irons! (change of command.)

Mar. 6, 1868—Grenfell escape and probable death.

May 16, 1868—President Johnson escapes impeachment in Senate by one vote, 35/19.

Feb. 8, 1869—Mudd pardoned by President Johnson.

Mar. 8, 1869—Mudd released at Fort Jefferson.

Mar. 11, 1869—Dr. Mudd leaves Fort Jefferson.

Mar. 20, 1869—Mudd arrives home.

Jan. 1870—Another son, Henry born. Dies at age 8 mo.
" 1871—A daughter, Stella Marie born. Spangler arrived. Given five acres of land.
Oct. 1875—Another daughter Rose de Lima born.
" 1875—Spangler died. Buried St. Peter's Cemetery.
Jan. 1878—The youngest daughter, ninth child, Mary Eleanor (Nettie) born.
Jan. 10, 1883—Mudd died of pneumonia. Buried St. Mary's Cemetery.
Dec. 29, 1911—Sarah Frances Dyer Mudd died at home of daughter Rose de Lima
    Mudd-Gardiner, at the adjacent farm where Booth bought the one-
    eyed horse in 1864. Buried beside Mudd at St. Mary's Cemetery,
    Bryantown, Maryland.

Appendix 12: Prosecution of the Conspirators

Name	Involvement	Age	Personal	Custody	Penalty Date Death
Booth, J. W.	Shot Lincoln Apr. 14, 1865, Ford's Theater	27	Tragedy actor	Apr. 26	Shot Apr. 26, 1865, Garrett's barn
Arnold, S. B.	Original capture plot. Recruited Aug. 1864	30	Schoolmate of Booth	Apr. 17	4 yr. Dry Tortugas 1906
Atzerodt, G. A.	Assass. V.P. Johnson, planned 2-hr. notice	30	Boatman, Port Tobacco	Apr. 20	Hanged July 7, 1865
Herold, David	Escorted Payne and Booth	23	Knew roads	Apr. 26	Hanged July 7, 1865
Mudd, Dr. S. A.	Treated Booth 10 hrs.	31	M.D., tobacco farmer. Voted Union. Knew Booth	Apr. 24	4 yr. Dry Tortugas Pneumonia 1883
O'Laughlin, Michael	Original capture plot. Recruited Aug. 1864	28	Boyhood friend of Booth	Apr. 24	Died Yellow Fever, Dry Tortugas Sept. 1867
Payne (Powell), Lewis T.	Stabbing of Seward and son	20	Conf. soldier Worshipped Booth	Apr. 17	Hanged July 7, 1865
Spangler, Edw. (Ned)	Stage hand, Ford's Theater	43	Carpenter	Apr. 19	4 yr. Dry Tortugas Pneumonia 1875

Name	Involvement	Age	Personal	Custody	Penalty Date Death
Surratt, Mrs. Mary E.	Boarding house 541 H St. Mother of John	45	Owner, 541 H St. and Surratt Tavern	Apr. 17	Hanged July 7, 1865

Others, amazingly not prosecuted, were Louis Wiechmann, John Lloyd, Samuel Cox, and Thomas Jones. Some of these people were more involved than those prosecuted. Wiechmann, a school friend of John Surratt who lived at the Surratt boarding house, became a government witness and was thus spared. He gave very damaging testimony against Mrs. Surratt and Mudd. Lloyd's testimony was also very damaging for Mrs. Surratt. Cox and Jones were involved in aiding and harboring Booth and Herold in Zekiah Swamp for six days and then helping them cross the Potomac River. They were never prosecuted. John Surratt, a Confederate courier, was deeply involved in the original plot to capture President Lincoln. He escaped the military court that convicted and hanged his mother by fleeing the country. He was finally captured in Egypt and brought back and tried before a civil court in Washington in 1867. The jury could not reach a verdict. He finally went free in 1868 and lived until 1916.

Notes

Chapter 1

1. Nettie Mudd, *The Life of Dr. Samuel A. Mudd* (New York: Neale, 1906), p. 30.
2. Ibid.
3. Ibid.

Chapter 2

1. Jim Bishop, *The Day Lincoln Was Shot* (New York: Harper and Brothers, 1955), p. 37.
2. *Encyclopaedia Britannica*, 14:139.
3. Leroy Hayman, *The Death of Lincoln* (New York: Scholastic Book Services, 1968), p. 28.
4. Bishop, *Day Lincoln Was Shot*, p. 127.

Chapter 3

1. Benn Pitman, *The Assassination of President Lincoln and the Trial of the Conspirators* (New York: Moore, Wilstach and Baldwin, 1865), p. 100.
2. Ibid.
3. Ibid., p. 72.
4. David Miller DeWitt, *The Assassination of Abraham Lincoln and Its Expiation* (New York: Macmillan, 1907), p. 42.
5. Pitman, *The Assassination*, p. 70.
6. Ibid., p. 113.
7. Ibid., p. 85.
8. Ibid., p. 307.
9. Ibid.
10. Ibid., pp. 228–29.
11. Ibid., p. 72.
12. Ibid.
13. Ibid., p. 78.
14. Ibid.
15. Louis J. Wiechmann, *A True History of the Assassination of Abraham Lincoln and the Conspiracy of 1865* (New York: Knopf, 1975), p. 48.

Chapter 4

1. DeWitt, *The Assassination of Abraham Lincoln,* p. 10.
2. Louis J. Wiechmann, *True History,* p. 434.
3. William A. Tidwell, James O. Hall, and David W. Gaddy, *Come Retribution* (London: University Press, 1988), p. 21.
4. Wiechmann, *True History,* p. 42.
5. Ibid., p. 43.
6. Ibid.
7. Ibid., pp. 49–52.
8. Tidwell, et al., *Come Retribution,* p. 328.
9. Ibid., p. 332.
10. Ibid.
11. Wiechmann, *True History,* p. 45.
12. Ben P. Poore, *The Conspiracy Trial for the Murder of the President, and the Attempt to Overthrow the Government by the Assassination of Its Principal Officers* (Boston: J. E. Tilton, 1865), pp. 269–72.
13. Pitman, *The Assassination,* p. 178.
14. *Philadelphia Inquirer* account of trial (Philadelphia: T. B. Peterson and Bros., 1865), pp. 97–98.
15. Wiechmann, *True History,* p. 48.
16. Ibid.
17. Tidwell, et al., *Come Retribution,* p. 338.
18. Ibid., p. 342.
19. Ibid., p. 345, ¶4.
20. Pitman, *The Assassination,* p. 44.
21. Samuel Bland Arnold, *Defense and Prison Experiences of a Lincoln Conspirator* (Hattiesburg, Miss.: The Book Farm, 1943), p. 22.
22. Ibid., p. 23.
23. Ibid.
24. Ibid., p. 24.
25. Ibid.
26. DeWitt, *The Assassination of Abraham Lincoln,* p. 35.
27. Ibid., p. 263.
28. Wiechmann, *True History,* p. 428.
29. Ibid., pp. 432–33.
30. DeWitt, *The Assassination of Abraham Lincoln,* p. 25.
31. Samuel Carter, III, *The Riddle of Dr. Mudd* (New York: G. P. Putnam's Sons, 1974), p. 24.
32. Ibid., p. 22.
33. Arnold, *Defense and Prison Experiences,* p. 18.
34. William Hanchett, *The Lincoln Murder Conspiracies* (Urbana, Chicago: University of Illinois Press, 1983), p. 380.
35. DeWitt, *The Assassination of Abraham Lincoln,* pp. 6–8.

Chapter 5

1. Poore, *Conspiracy Trial,* p. 329.
2. Roy Z. Chamlee, Jr., *Lincoln's Assassins: A Complete Account of Their Capture, Trial, and Punishment* (Jefferson, N.C.: McFarland, 1990), p. 320.

3. Poore, *Conspiracy Trial,* 2:72.

4. Ibid., 1:332.

5. Ibid., 1:251–54.

6. Pitman, *The Assassination,* p. 84.

7. Ibid.

8. Ibid., p. 85.

9. Ibid.

10. James O. Hall, *John Wilkes Booth's Escape Route* (Clinton, Md.: Surratt Society, 1984), p. 4.

11. Edward Steers, Jr., and Joan L. Chaconas, *The Escape and Capture of John Wilkes Booth* (Marker Tours, 1989), p. 21.

12. Ibid., p. 23.

13. Thomas A. Jones, *J. Wilkes Booth: An Account of His Sojourn in Southern Maryland after the Assassination of Abraham Lincoln* (Chicago: Laird and Lee, 1893), p. 67.

14. George A. Townsend, "How Booth Crossed the Potomac," *Century* (Apr. 1884): 829.

15. Ibid., p. 830; Hall, *Escape Route,* p. 7; Jones, *J. Wilkes Booth,* p. 67.

16. Ibid., p. 110; Hall, *Escape Route,* p. 7.

17. Jones, *J. Wilkes Booth,* p. 36.

18. Townsend, "How Booth Crossed the Potomac," p. 831.

19. Steers and Chaconas, *Escape and Capture,* p. 27.

20. Ibid.

21. Ibid., p. 29.

22. M. B. Ruggles, "Pursuit and Death of John Wilkes Booth," *Century Illustrated* (Nov. 1889–Apr. 1890): 444.

23. Steers and Chaconas, *Escape and Capture,* p. 31.

24. DeWitt, *The Assassination of Abraham Lincoln,* p. 81.

25. Pitman, *The Assassination,* pp. 91–93.

26. DeWitt, *The Assassination of Abraham Lincoln,* p. 277.

27. Pitman, *The Assassination,* p. 90.

28. Poore, *Conspiracy Trial,* 2:70.

29. Wiechmann, *True History,* p. 418.

30. Ibid.

31. Poore, *Conspiracy Trial,* 1:322.

Chapter 6

1. Benjamin P. Thomas and Harold M. Hyman, *Stanton: The Life and Times of Lincoln's Secretary of War* (New York: Knopf, 1975), p. 151.

2. Carl Sandburg, *Abraham Lincoln* (New York: Harcourt, Brace, 1954), p. 125.

3. Hal Higdon, *The Union versus Dr. Mudd* (Chicago: Follett, 1964), p. 72.

Chapter 7

1. Richard D. Mudd, *The Mudd Family of the United States* (Ann Arbor, Mich.: Edwards Brothers, 1951), 1:14. Because no passenger records are extant, this claim cannot be verified.

2. Ibid., 2:2.
3. Ibid.
4. Ibid., 2:6.
5. Ibid., 1:522.
6. Nettie Mudd, *Life,* p. 23.

Chapter 8

1. Richard D. Mudd, *The Mudd Family,* 1:250.
2. Nettie Mudd, *Life,* p. 24.
3. Ibid., p. 25.
4. Elden C. Weckesser, *The Department of Surgery, Case Western Reserve University, 1843–1986* (CWRU, 1986), p. 3.
5. Richard D. Mudd, *Dr. Samuel Alexander Mudd and His Descendants* (Saginaw, Mich.: Richard D. Mudd, 1989), p. v.
6. The O. A. Brownson Collection, University of Notre Dame Archives.
7. *Trial of the Assassins and Conspirators at Washington, D.C., May and June 1865,* prepared by reports of special correspondents and reporters of the *Philadelphia Inquirer* (Philadelphia: T. B. Peterson, 1865), pp. 97–98.
8. Pitman, *The Assassination,* p. 386.
9. Ibid.
10. Nettie Mudd, *Life,* p. 34.
11. Ibid.
12. Ibid., p. 29.
13. Poore, *Conspiracy Trial,* 1:260.
14. Ibid., 1:286.

Chapter 9

1. Nettie Mudd, *Life,* p. 34.
2. Carter, *Riddle,* p. 154.
3. Nettie Mudd, *Life,* p. 34.
4. Pitman, *The Assassination,* pp. 18–21.
5. Chamlee, *Lincoln's Assassins,* pp. 327–34.

Chapter 11

1. Pitman, *The Assassination,* p. 17.
2. Ibid., p. 18.
3. Ibid., pp. 18–19.
4. Pitman, *The Assassination,* p. 222.
5. Arnold, *Defense and Prison Experiences,* p. 22.
6. Ibid., p. 38.
7. Pitman, *The Assassination,* p. 240.
8. Ibid., p. 333.
9. Ibid., p. 148.
10. Ibid., p. 146.
11. Ibid., p. 146.

12. Ibid., p. 144.
13. Ibid., p. 153.
14. Ibid., p. 145.
15. Ibid., p. 151.
16. Ibid., p. 222.
17. Pitman, *The Assassination*, p. 224.
18. Ibid., p. 227.
19. Ibid., p. 231.
20. Ibid., pp. 229, 230, 231.
21. Ibid., p. 308.
22. Ibid., p. 161.
23. Ibid., p. 102.
24. Ibid., p. 97.
25. Ibid., p. 110.
26. Ibid., p. 74.
27. Ibid., p. 110.
28. Ibid., p. 116.
29. John Bakeless, *Spies of the Confederacy* (New York: Lippincott, 1970), p. 122.
30. Pittman, *The Assassination*, p. 114.
31. Ibid., p. 144.
32. Ibid., p. 115b.
33. Ibid., p. 115c.
34. Ibid., pp. 100, 110.
35. Ibid., p. 115.
36. Ibid., p. 118.
37. Ibid., p. 116.
38. Ibid., p. 85.
39. Ibid., p. 85.
40. Ibid., p. 121.
41. Ibid., p. 122.
42. DeWitt, *The Assassination of Abraham Lincoln*, p. 65.
43. Pitman, *The Assassination*, p. 23.
44. Poore, *Conspiracy Trial*, 1:70.
45. Ibid., 2:258.
46. Carter, *Riddle*, p. 25.
47. Pittman, *The Assassination*, p. 171.
48. Ibid., p. 171.
49. Ibid., p. 174.
50. Ibid., p. 178.
51. Ibid., p. 170.
52. Ibid., pp. 126, 182.
53. Ibid., p. 192.
54. Ibid., pp. 71, 196.
55. Ibid., p. 206.
56. DeWitt, *The Assassination of Abraham Lincoln*, p. 123.
57. Pitman, *The Assassination*, p. 264.
58. Ibid., p. 318.
59. Ibid., p. 331.
60. Ibid., p. 351.
61. Ibid., pp. 351, 371.

62. Ibid., p. 244.
63. DeWitt, *The Assassination of Abraham Lincoln*, p. 284.
64. Ibid., p. 135.
65. Ibid., p. 284 and Pittman, *The Assassination*, p. 249.
65. Ibid., p. 284 and Ibid., p. 249.
66. Nettie Mudd, *Life*, p. 40.

Chapter 12

1. Jones, *J. Wilkes Booth*, p. 11.
2. Ibid., p. 23.
3. Ibid., p. 28.
4. General L. C. Baker, *History of the United States Secret Service* (Philadelphia: King & Baird, 1968), p. 102.
5. Pitman, *The Assassination*, p. 178; Poore, *Conspiracy Trial*, 2:268; *Trial of the Assassins*, pp. 97–98.
6. Tidwell, et al., *Come Retribution*, p. 342.
7. Jones, *J. Wilkes Booth*, p. 112.
8. Tidwell, et al., *Come Retribution*, p. 342.
9. Pitman, *The Assassination*, p. 46; Poore, *Conspiracy Trial*, 1:29.

Chapter 13

1. DeWitt, *The Assassination of Abraham Lincoln*, p. 141.
2. Baker, *Secret Service*, p. 512.
3. Ibid., p. 513.
4. Ibid., p. 513.

Chapter 14

1. Arnold, *Defense and Prison Experiences*, pp. 57–60.
2. Ibid., p. 63.
3. Ibid., p. 65.
4. Nettie Mudd, *Life*, p. 114.
5. Ibid., p. 116.
6. Ibid., p. 123.
7. Ibid., p. 135.
8. Ibid., p. 136.
9. Ibid., p. 139.

Chapter 15

1. Carter, *Riddle*, p. 60.
2. Arnold, *Defense and Prison Experiences*, p. 45.
3. DeWitt, *The Assassination of Abraham Lincoln*, p. 184.
4. Ibid., p. 186.

5. Ibid., p. 190.
6. Thomas and Hyman, *Stanton*, p. 428.
7. DeWitt, *The Assassination of Abraham Lincoln*, p. 194.
8. Arnold, *Defense and Prison Experiences*, p. 24.
9. DeWitt, *The Assassination of Abraham Lincoln*, p. 202.
10. Ibid., p. 219.
11. Carter, *Riddle*, p. 346.
12. Thomas and Hyman, *Stanton*, p. 47.

Chapter 16

1. Nettie Mudd, *Life*, p. 315.
2. Ibid., p. 271.
3. Ibid., p. 293.
4. Ibid., p. 301.
5. Ibid., p. 366.

Chapter 17

1. Harold Hirsh, et al., "Disclosures About Patients," in *Legal Medicine*, American College of Legal Medicine, p. 208.
2. Ibid., p. 9.
3. Higdon, *The Union*, p. 208.

Chapter 19

1. DeWitt, *The Assassination of Abraham Lincoln*, p. 263.
2. Thomas and Hyman, *Stanton*, p. 638.
3. Wiechmann, *True History*, p. 392.
4. Ibid.
5. Baker, *Secret Service*, p. 246.
6. Carter, *Riddle*, p. 345.

Bibliography

Arnold, Samuel Bland. *Defense and Prison Experiences of a Lincoln Conspirator.* Hattiesburg, Miss.: Book Farm, 1943.

Bakeless, John. *Spies of the Confederacy.* New York: Lippincott, 1970.

Baker, Jean H. *Mary Todd Lincoln.* New York: Norton, 1987.

Baker, L. C. *History of the United States Secret Service.* Philadelphia: King and Baird, 1868.

Benedict, Michael Les. *The Impeachment and Trial of Andrew Johnson.* New York: Norton, 1973.

Bishop, Jim. *The Day Lincoln Was Shot.* New York: Harper and Brothers, 1955.

Bowman, John S., Ivan V. Hogg, and Anthony Preson. *The Civil War Almanac.* New York: Facts on File, 1982.

The O. A. Brownson Collection. University of Notre Dame Archives.

Carter, Samuel, III. *The Riddle of Dr. Mudd.* New York: G. P. Putnam's Sons, 1974.

Castel, Albert. *The Presidency of Andrew Johnson.* Regents Press of Kansas, 1980.

Chamlee, Roy Z., Jr. *Lincoln's Assassins: A Complete Account of Their Capture, Trial and Punishment.* Jefferson, N.C.: McFarland, 1990.

Davis, Michael. *The Image of Lincoln in the South.* Knoxville: University of Tennessee Press, 1971.

DeWitt, David. *The Assassination of Abraham Lincoln and Its Expiation.* New York: Macmillan, 1909.

————. *The Judicial Murder of Mary E. Surratt.* John Murphy, 1895.

Eisenschiml, Otto. *Why Was Lincoln Murdered?* Boston: Little, Brown, 1937.

Freidel, Frank. *Our Country's Presidents.* National Geographic Society, 1963.

Hall, James O. *John Wilkes Booth's Escape Route.* Clinton, Md.: Surratt Society, 1984.

Hanchett, William. *The Lincoln Murder Conspiracies.* Chicago: University of Illinois Press, 1983.

Hayman, Leroy. *The Death of Lincoln.* New York: Scholastic Book Services, 1968.

Higdon, Hal. *The Union vs. Dr. Mudd.* Chicago: Follett, 1964.

Hirsh, Harold, et al. "Disclosures about Patients." In *Legal Medicine.* American College of Legal Medicine.

Jones, Thomas A. *J. Wilkes Booth: An Account of His Sojourn in Southern Maryland after the Assassination of Abraham Lincoln.* Chicago: Laird and Lee, 1893.

Langford, Lord. *Abraham Lincoln.* New York: G. P. Putnam's Sons, 1975.

Mudd, Nettie. *The Life of Dr. Samuel A. Mudd.* New York: Neale, 1906.

Mudd, Richard D. *Dr. Samuel Alexander Mudd and His Descendants.* 6th ed. Saginaw, Mich.: Richard D. Mudd, 1989.

_____. *The Mudd Family of the United States*. 4th ed. Ann Arbor, Mich.: Edwards, 1984.

Myers, Henry Allen. *Medieval Kingship*. Chicago: Nelson-Hall, 1934.

National Archives. Washington, D.C.

Oates, Stephen B. *With Malice Toward None: The Life of Abraham Lincoln*. New York: Harper and Row, 1977.

Pitman, Benn. *The Assassination of President Lincoln and the Trial of the Conspirators*. New York: Moore, Wilstach and Baldwin, 1865.

Poore, Ben Perley. *The Conspiracy Trial for the Murder of the President, and the Attempt to Overthrow the Government by the Assassination of Its Principal Officers*. Boston: J. E. Tilton, 1865.

Ruggles, M. B. "Pursuit and Death of John Wilkes Booth." *Century Illustrated Monthly* (Nov. 1889–Apr. 1890).

Sandburg, Carl. *Abraham Lincoln*. New York: Harcourt, Brace, 1954.

Simmons, Harry E. *A Concise Encyclopedia of the Civil War*. New York: Fairfax, 1965.

Starr, Stephen Z. *Colonel Grenfell's Wars: The Life of a Soldier of Fortune*. Baton Rouge: Louisiana State University Press, 1971.

Steers, Edward, Jr., and Joan L. Chaconas. *The Escape and Capture of John Wilkes Booth*. Marker Tours, 1989.

Surratt, John H. *The Trial in the Criminal Court of D.C.* 2 vols. Washington, D.C.: U.S. Government Printing Office, 1867.

Thomas, Benjamin P., and Harold M. Hyman. *Stanton: The Life and Times of Lincoln's Secretary of War*. New York: Knopf, 1975.

Tidwell, William A., James O. Hall, and David W. Gaddy. *Come Retribution*. London: University Press, 1988.

Townsend, Geroge A. "How Booth Crossed the Potomac." *Century* (Apr. 1884).

Trial of the Assassins and Conspirators at Washington, D.C., May and June 1865. Prepared by reports of special correspondents and reporters of the *Philadelphia Inquirer*. Philadelphia: T. B. Peterson, 1865.

Trial of the Assassins and Conspirators for the Murder of Abraham Lincoln. Philadelphia: Barclay, 1865.

Weckesser, Elden C. *The Department of Surgery, Case Western Reserve University, 1843–1986*. CWRU, 1986.

Weideman, T. *Greek and Roman Slavery*. Croom Helm, 1981.

Wiechmann, Louis J. *A True History of the Assassination of Abraham Lincoln and the Conspiracy of 1865*. New York: Knopf, 1975.

Williams, T. Harry. *Lincoln and His Generals*. New York: Grossett and Dunlap, 1952.

Index